W9-BGT-524

JUN 0 1 2000

Natural
Washington

Natural Washington

A nature-lover's guide
to parks, wildlife refuges, trails,
gardens, zoos, forests, aquariums
and arboretums within a day's
trip of the nation's capital

RICHARD L. BERMAN
DEBORAH McBRIDE

EPM Publications
An imprint of HOWELL PRESS

Library of Congress Cataloging-in-Publication Data

Berman, Richard L.
  Natural Washington : a nature-lover's guide to parks, wildlife
refuges, trails, gardens, zoos, forests, aquariums, and arboretums
within a day's trip of the nation's capital / Richard L. Berman,
Deborah McBride. — 4th Ed.
       p.   cm.
  Includes index.
  ISBN 1-889324-15-9
  1. Natural areas—Washington Region—Guidebooks. 2. Natural
areas—Maryland—Guidebooks. 3. Natural areas—Virginia—
Guidebooks. 4. Parks—Washington Region—Guidebooks. 5.
Parks—Maryland—Guidebooks. 6. Parks—Virginia—Guidebooks.
7. Washington Region—Guidebooks. 8. Maryland—Guidebooks.
9. Virginia—Guidebooks.   I. McBride, Deborah, 1952-
II. Title.
QH76.5.W18B46   1999
917.5304'4—dc21   98-38069
                                                              CIP

Copyright © 1999 Richard L. Berman and Deborah McBride
All Rights Reserved
EPM Publications is an imprint of Howell Press, Inc.,
   1713-2D Allied Lane, Charlottesville, VA 22903
   http://www.howellpress.com
Printed in the United States of America

The original edition of *Natural Washington* was written by Bill and
Phyllis Thomas and published by Henry Holt and Company, Inc. in
1980.

Cover design by Tom Huestis
Page layout by Scott Edie, E Graphics

Cover photos:
   Jefferson Memorial, courtesy National Park Service, National
      Capital Region
   Wood Ducks, courtesy U.S. Fish and Wildlife Service by Dave
      Menhe
   Lotus Blossom, Great Falls of Virginia and Boating at the Smith-
      sonian Environmental Research Center by Richard L. Berman

CONTENTS

NATURAL ATTRACTIONS IN THE DISTRICT OF COLUMBIA

NATURAL ATTRACTIONS IN MARYLAND

NATURAL ATTRACTIONS IN VIRGINIA

NATURAL ATTRACTIONS IN WEST VIRGINA

FOREWORD

We are amateur hikers and nature lovers who started visiting these parks and gardens many years ago with the 1980 edition of *Natural Washington* (originally written by Bill and Phyllis Thomas) in our knapsack. It accompanied us on many trips. Eventually, when our copy was too old and worn to use, we tried to get another copy, only to find the book was out of print. We enjoyed this book so much that we wanted to keep its tradition alive among hikers and amateur naturalists in the Washington area. The Thomases generously turned over the future of *Natural Washington* to us in 1989. Since then, we have rewritten the book three times.

In this edition, we have added several new sites and trails; we added more maps and tables where we thought they would be most useful. We have made extensive updates, updating the information on every entry and again verifying it with a local site expert. And, in keeping with the times, we have added Internet web site addresses for the many sites and organizations that now have web sites for the public. Each entry contains information about the landscape, habitats, plant and animal life in the area, a description of the trails or exhibits, and a suggestion of the best time of year to visit each location, as appropriate.

Our delight in discovering some of these little known and unexpected natural resources has created bonds of enjoyment and friendship that we will long remember. It is our hope that *Natural Washington* will guide you in discovering new wilderness areas and help you enjoy these natural areas as much as we have.

RLB and DM

INTRODUCTION

With the high degree of urbanization and the rapid pace of urban development, it is remarkable that wild places of natural beauty exist in the Washington, DC area. Yet, even amongst the federal buildings in Washington, there are natural places where you can experience a certain remoteness and find a quiet haven from the hustle of the capital city to establish a rapport with nature.

It is even more remarkable that within 50 miles of the Capitol, hundreds of American bald eagle and osprey nest along the Potomac River south of Washington and along the Patuxent River, east of the city. Tens of thousands of geese and ducks gather on their annual migration at Blackwater Refuge and other wetland wildfowl refuges surrounding the Chesapeake Bay. The Wildfowl Trust of North America is one of the best places to study a wide variety of wild waterfowl close up. Great blue herons and bitterns wade through acres of exotic waterlilies and lotuses at Kenilworth Gardens within DC's boundaries. Huntley Meadows, in suburban Virginia, attracts bird-watchers from all over the region, in all seasons. Spring brings spectacular displays of Virginia bluebells, Dutchman's-breeches, jack-in-the-pulpit, wild orchids, trillium, and trout lily at Riverbend Park, the C&O Canal Park and several other parks along the Potomac.

Within walking distance of the Lincoln Memorial is Theodore Roosevelt Island, with 88 acres of wilderness. Hiker/biker pathways lead the bicyclist northwest over 100 miles on the C&O Canal Towpath along the Potomac River, west over 30 miles toward Leesburg across Virginia meadow and forest, south about 30 miles to Mount Vernon along the Potomac past marshes thriving with wildlife, or north through Rock Creek Park's Piedmont forests with seldom a road crossing. The Billy Goat Trail in the C&O Canal National Historical Park offers a challenge to hikers and rock scramblers, with views of steep rock cliffs and river rapids. Just upstream are the roaring waterfalls of Great Falls of the Potomac.

Shenandoah National Park and the famous Skyline Drive attract hikers and car-bound naturalists from all over the east coast with its animal life, rugged mountain trails and wonderful flora in all seasons. Underground, you'll find the surreal geological experience of mineral stalactite and stalagmite formations several stories high at Luray and Skyline caverns.

Assateague Island National Seashore, is one of best wildlife watching locations in the mid-Atlantic region, with over 250 species of birds regularly observed on its dunes, meadows, marshlands and bays.

Less wild, but equally exciting for the amateur naturalist, are world-class collections in the region's gardens, arboretums, zoos and museums. The 444-acre National Arboretum has one of the foremost horticultural collections in the world but is usually overlooked by Washingtonians. The National Aquarium at Baltimore is certainly one of the foremost aquatic exhibits in the world. The Smithsonian Naturalist Center is a little-known taxonomic resource to examine biological and geological specimens, hands-on.

Probably no other area in the country is so richly endowed with natural areas—yet, generally speaking, few people are aware of the wealth of natural places around them. We have mentioned only a few of the highlights in this introduction.

In *Natural Washington,* we have attempted to provide you with information on the natural areas and wild places within 50 miles of Washington. We have included several exceptional destinations beyond the 50 mile radius that we considered "must see" sites for Washington area amateur naturalists such as Assateague Island National Seashore, Blackwater National Wildlife Refuge and the Shenandoah National Park. We hope that you will use this book to guide you to your own discovery of the beauty and inspiration of nature in this region. We believe that even long-time Washingtonians will be delighted to discover unexpected natural treasures in this region, which had hitherto escaped their notice.

To this end, we have listed each place, described what it has to offer, how to get there, and where to get additional information. We have included region maps with the major roadways to reinforce written directions. You will need a car to visit most of the places outside DC. Before you undertake an extensive trip, it is advisable to contact the sources listed to plan for your particular needs and desires.

Wherever you go, go gently. Enjoy the natural wonders of this region, but leave no signs of your passing.

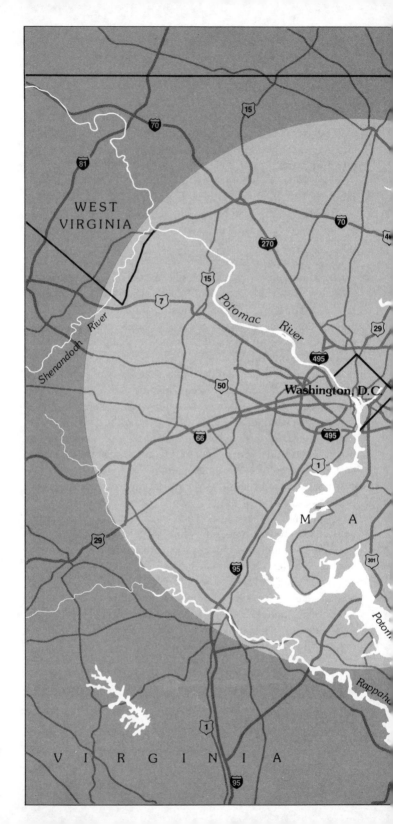

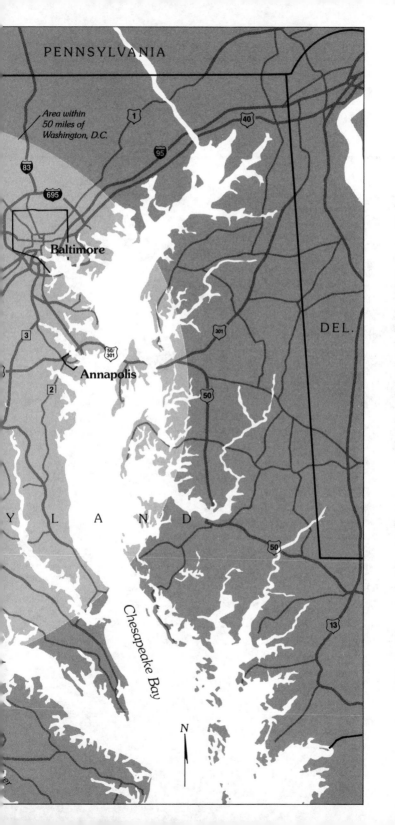

PENNSYLVANIA

Area within
50 miles of
Washington, D.C.

DEL.

Baltimore

Annapolis

M A R Y L A N D

Chesapeake Bay

N

United States Department of the Interior National Park Service Photo

NATURAL ATTRACTIONS IN
THE DISTRICT
OF COLUMBIA

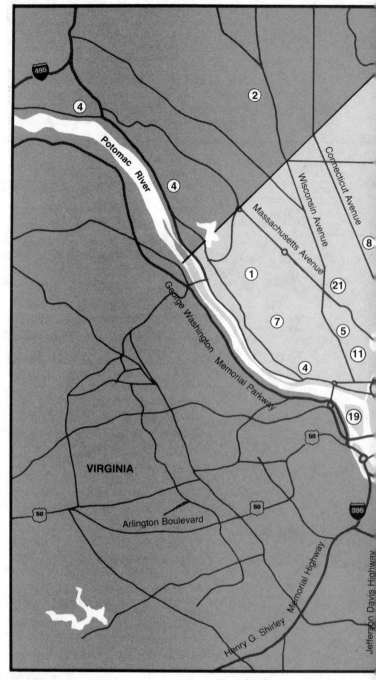

WASHINGTON, DC

1. Battery-Kemble Park
2. Capital Crescent Trail
3. Capitol Hill Trees
4. Chesapeake & Ohio Canal
   National Historical Park
5. Dumbarton Oaks and
   Dumbarton Park

6. Franciscan Monastery Garden
   and Shrine
7. Glover-Archbold Parkway
8. Hillwood Museum Gardens
9. Kenilworth Aquatic Gardens
10. Lady Bird Johnson Park and
    Lyndon Baines Johnson
    Memorial Grove

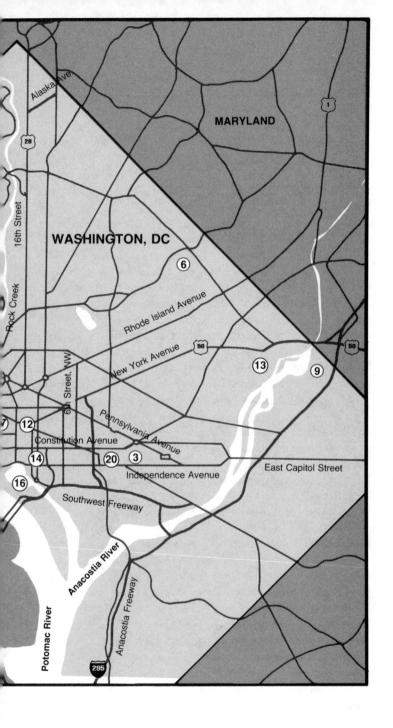

11. Montrose Park
12. National Aquarium
13. National Arboretum
14. National Museum of Natural History and the Naturalist Center
15. National Zoological Park
16. Potomac Park
17. Rawlins Park

18. Rock Creek Park
19. Theodore Roosevelt Island
20. U.S. Botanic Gardens and Conservatory
21. Washington National Cathedral Grounds

Battery-Kemble Park

Battery-Kemble is a small park—just one-eighth mile wide and approximately one mile long—but a lush and diverse deciduous woodland envelops this rocky, narrow gorge. A path twists through the shady ravine and over the small stream that splashes through the park. Tangles of Japanese honeysuckle are found throughout the park. Tree species include tulip tree, black locust, flowering dogwood, sycamore, oak, hickory, maple, beech and Virginia pine. This second-growth forest attracts a variety of birds including warblers, robins and mockingbirds. The area around the Chain Bridge entrance is an excellent place to look for veeries when they migrate, from late April to late May and late August to September. They fill the air with their ethereal song of vee-ur, vee-ur, veer, veer.

The park also preserves a part of our nation's history. A small, two-gun battery, once located on top of one of the park's highest hills, was established here early in the Civil War as part of a system of 68 forts and other structures designed to defend the capital city against enemy invasion. It is preserved as a historic site by the National Capital Region of the National Park Service. Battery-Kemble offers a brilliant array of blossoms in the spring, a green retreat in the summer, a blaze of color in the fall and downhill skiing in the winter. It is rarely crowded. The trail is an unpaved path through the woods and is susceptible to flooding. Battery-Kemble is also a favorite spot for picnicking, games, and in those years with snow—sledding and cross country skiing.

How To Get There: The park is bounded by Chain Bridge Road, MacArthur Boulevard, 49th Street and Nebraska Ave. Park along one of the side streets and join the trail as it runs beside Foxhall Road. Open daily year-round during daylight hours.

For Additional Infomation:
Superintendent, Rock Creek Park
3545 Williamsburg Lane, N.W.
Washington, DC 20008-1207
(202) 282-1063

Naturalist, Rock Creek Nature Center
5200 Glover Road, N.W.
Washington, DC 20015
(202) 426-6829

Capital Crescent Trail and Metropolitan Branch Trail

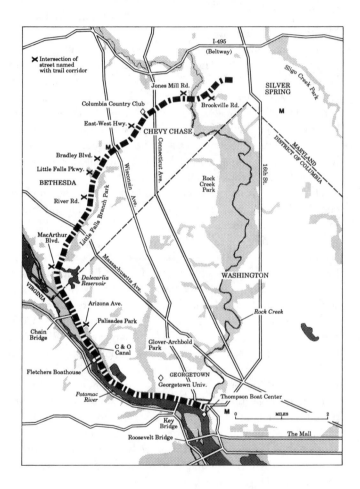

The Capital Crescent Trail (CCT) is the area's newest linear park. It is a car-free paved hiker/biker/skater greenway from K Street in Georgetown to Bethesda and Rock Creek Park (and someday to Silver Spring) on the former right-of-way of the B&O Railway Georgetown Spur. It's one of the author's favorite, relaxing bike rides.

Trains once carried coal 11 miles from the main line in Silver Spring to the coal-burning power plant in Georgetown to generate electric power for the District. Trains have not run on this spur since 1985. The CCT provides hikers and bicyclists a view of Washington and the inner Montgomery County suburbs that few have seen. One travels in a park-like setting, through woods, over three historic bridges, through a stone tunnel, over a gently graded asphalt-paved 12-foot-wide trail along the Potomac, through parks and behind the tree-lined "back yards" of DC and Montgomery County institutions and homes.

The transformation from abandoned railroad bed to paved hiker/biker trail park is nearly complete. The Georgetown to Bethesda portion is complete. The Bethesda to Silver Spring portion is now paved with a "temporary" 12-foot wide gravel hiker-biker trail to Rock Creek Park while the region's planners debate its best ultimate use, perhaps a combination of a hiker/biker trail alongside a fenced light mass transit line (bus lane, or light trolley line). The CCT is a recreational resource, wildlife habitat and a super pollution-free bike commuter conduit.

The CCT is the work of The Coalition for the Capital Crescent Trail, a volunteer group formed in 1986 (and incorporated in 1988) to make the CCT a reality. Mr. Kingdon Gould, Jr., a wealthy philanthropist, bought the option to purchase the railroad right-of-way in 1988 with his own funds to retain the land for use as a public park. Without Mr. Gould's generosity and foresight, the land might have been purchased by developers to subdivide, and the CCT could have been lost forever.

The purchase from Gould of the District portion of the CCT, funded by Congress, was concluded on November 20, 1990, with the land turned over to the National Park Service. In 1988, Montgomery County purchased the 7.4 miles of trails in the county. With the help of a large grant from PEPCO, a section of the hiker/biker trail in downtown Bethesda was completed and federal funds provided for construction of the remainder of the route to Georgetown. However, the Coalition for the Capital Crescent Trail still needs community support to ensure that the CCT is completed to Silver Spring, particularly that the trestle over Rock Creek Park is restored.

Hiking and Biking

Hikers can walk the entire length of the CCT in less than six hours. Bikers can ride from Georgetown to Bethesda and back in about 1.5 hours. The trail is gently uphill from Georgetown to Bethesda and almost level from Bethesda to Rock Creek Park. Because the trestle over Rock Creek Park has not been restored, the remaining short segment to Silver Spring is practically inac-

cessible. We recommend using the Bethesda-Georgetown section–it's paved, and more scenic. Food and drink are available
year round nearby in Georgetown, on River Road (Fresh Fields,
Seven-Eleven, etc.), and in Bethesda. In summer, there is a concession stand at Fletcher's boathouse. There is free parking at
the Little Falls road crossing. A map is available from the Coalition for the Capital Crescent Trail; send $1.00 and a stamped
self-addressed envelope to the address below.

From Georgetown to Bethesda (7 miles):

The Trail starts in Georgetown, at the end of K Street under
the Whitehurst Freeway and Key Bridge, along the Potomac
River by the Georgetown University boathouse. From there it
parallels the C&O Canal Towpath, past Fletcher's Boathouse,
crossing a bridge over the canal and Canal Road at Arizona
Avenue. It goes along Little Falls Branch Park in a short tunnel under McArthur Boulevard, on a bridge over Massachusetts
Avenue Road, and another bridge over River Road. The trail
runs behind the beautiful Kenwood neighborhood (See Kenwood
Cherry Trees in the Maryland Section), across Little Falls Parkway, over Bradley Blvd. to Bethesda Avenue in Bethesda.

From Bethesda to Georgetown:

Begin near the Bethesda Metrorail station, near Wisconsin
and East-West Highway, so you can let Metro carry you back if
you don't want to retrace your steps on the CCT. Take care of
food, water or restroom in Bethesda. From the Metro station, go
south on Wisconsin Avenue to Elm Street; the CCT passes
under Wisconsin just south of Elm. Turn right (west) on Elm
and left on Woodmont. There is a grade-level crossing at
Bethesda Avenue. From Georgetown, you can easily connect to
the Rock Creek Trail or cross the Key or Memorial bridges to
Virginia hiker/biker trails.

From Bethesda to Rock Creek Park and Trail:

With the Wisconsin Avenue tunnel completed, signs will guide
you from Bethesda Avenue towards Silver Spring. For the time
being, the trail ends at Jones Mill Road, near **Woodend** (See
description under Maryland), about 2 miles from Bethesda. You
can go up Jones Mills to Susanna Lane which connects to the
Rock Creek Trail; go further up Jones Mill to Woodend, or go
down Jones Mill to East West Highway, across Rock Creek and
connect to the Rock Creek Trail there.

No motorized vehicles are allowed on the CCT and pets must be leashed. For other connecting bike trails see the section on **Off Road Bicycle Trails**.

Metropolitan Branch Trail:

Although construction is just starting, some day the Metropolitan Branch Trial will be the CCT's twin running 7.7 miles through Northeast DC from Union Station to Silver Spring along the former CSX Railroad right of way, parallel to the Metrorail red line. The CCT and MBT combined will make a DC-Maryland "bicycle beltway". The MBT will go from Union Station to Brookland to Michigan Park to Catholic University, to Takoma Park and Silver Spring. A 1.7 mile spur from Fort Totten will connect to the **Anacostia Tributary Trail System** (See entry under Maryland). The MBT needs your support to be realized. Contact the Coalition for the Metropolitan Branch Trail c/o WABA (address below).

For Additional Information:
Coalition for the Capital Crescent Trail
P.O. Box 30703
Bethesda, MD 20824
(202) 234-4874 (recording only)

Washington Area Bicyclists Association
1511 K Street, N.W., Suite 1015
Washington, DC 20005-1401
(202) 628-2500
waba@waba.org
http://www.waba.org

Capitol Hill Trees

Whatever season you choose to visit Capitol Hill, you will be awed by the splendor and diversity of trees growing under the shadow of the Capitol dome. The approximately 200 acres that make up the Capitol grounds are planted with over 4,000 trees from four continents. Visitors from all over the world will find trees from their homelands here. Oaks, maples and elms predominate. Some unusual ones include the September elm and the hedge maple. There are also tulip poplar, white pine and silvery beech. From the South come the magnolia, bald cypress, black tupelo, sweet gum, persimmon, pecan hickory and such flowering trees as dogwood, redbud and the fringe tree. Trees from the North include the tamarack and bur oak. From the far West come four "giant" sequoias. The unusual fall-blooming cherry trees found here not only flower in the spring, but also— given the slightest touch of warm weather—blossom forth in December.

The grounds represent various regions of not only the United States but also the world. From Japan comes a star magnolia, a pine that has been trained as a bonsai, some flowering cherries and a pagoda tree. A cigar box cedar and a varnish tree represent the People's Republic of China. There are purple beeches, Christ's thorn, a jujube tree from Europe and a deodar cedar native to the Himalayas. Much of the luxuriant shrubbery around the base of the Capitol itself consists of Japanese privet and the splatter leaf acuba from Asia, as well as American holly. Ginkgoes, living fossils dating back to the Carboniferous age and native to China, are also found on Capitol Hill. Most are labeled for easy identification and many have historical importance.

Some of these trees are quite old, but none is as old as the three patriarchs that predate the Capitol itself. Two towering English elms on the east lawn and a spreading American elm (better known as the Cameron elm) next to the walk on the House of Representatives side of the Capitol are said to have been alive and growing when the blueprints for the building were drawn. The Cameron elm is so called because in 1875 Senator Simon Cameron of Pennsylvania saw workers about to uproot the tree to put in a sidewalk. He stopped them and rushed back into the Senate to deliver an impassioned speech, saving the tree for visitors to admire to this day. No evidence of such a speech saving the trees exists, but an observant visitor will notice that the walk next to the House curves around the great elm.

Until the 1940s, a beautiful American elm grew on the north side of the Capitol under which, legend has it, George Washington stood in the shade while overseeing the building of the Capitol. Another notable tree is an oak on the House side of the Capitol. After planting it in 1949, the Speaker of the House, Sam Rayburn, made daily visits there with a tape measure in hand to gauge its growth. On June 27, 1978, Senator Edward Kennedy paid this tribute to a huge English elm tree that had stood between the Capitol and the Russell Senate Office Building and fallen victim to Dutch elm disease:

"Few if any trees anywhere were better known or more loved by members of the Senate. As we walked to the Capitol from the Russell Building, we passed under its giant limb, a cantilevered miracle of nature that stretched out across the sidewalk and over the roadway. Often we would reach up to touch the limb, or give it a warm slap of recognition and appreciation for its enduring vigil. President Kennedy, when he was a Senator, liked to call it the Humility Tree, because Senators instinctively ducked or bowed their heads as they approached the limb and passed beneath it. Its loss is a real one, deeply felt. The records are dim about its origin. But those of us who enjoyed the beauty of this elm can be grateful to the ancestors who planted it long ago. For a century, it graced the grounds of the Capitol of our growing nation."

The Capitol grounds today are praised for their landscaping, but such was not always the case. During the early days, the hill was covered with scrawny scrub oak. When Frederick Law Olmsted, designer of New York's Central Park, came to Washington to lay out the landscaping for the Capitol grounds in 1874, he found the area disgusting and said so. He had the ground thoroughly drained and plowed, adding subsoil to a depth of 2 feet.

When Olmsted finished, he listed 229 varieties of trees and shrubs on the grounds. Many of them are still there today. But his list of 229 has now shrunk to 113. Occasionally trees die and have to be replaced. Today, the greatest enemy is pollution, primarily that caused by automobile emissions.

Although the variety of trees on the grounds has decreased, their numbers have increased. In a recent three-year period, more than 450 trees and 4,500 shrubs were added. The job of keeping the woody plants of the Capitol ground healthy is handled by a staff of nearly 80 people (including two landscape architects, five tree surgeons and 28 gardeners) who work under the Architect of the Capitol. The best times to visit the Capitol grounds are in the spring when the trees are in bloom and at Christmas time when a large evergreen is decorated on the west side of the Capitol.

How To Get There: The Capitol square grounds are bounded by First Street, N.E., on the east, First Street, N.W., on the west, Constitution Avenue on the north and Independence Avenue on the south. Accessible by Tourmobile. Parking can be difficult near the Capitol. On weekends, it is possible to park in front of the U.S. Botanic Garden in the spaces reserved for staff during the week. The nearest Metro stops are Capitol South on the orange or blue line and Union Station on the red line.

For Additional Information:
Office of the Architect
U.S. Capitol
Capitol Hill
Washington, DC 20515
(202) 224-6645

Dumbarton Oaks

Hidden in the midst of one of DC's most elite neighborhoods lies a world-renowned garden —Dumbarton Oaks. In the world of horticulture, Dumbarton Oaks is known for its magnificent formal gardens, which some experts consider some of the loveliest in the United States.

The estate, named for the grove of great oak trees that surrounds the mansion, was purchased by Ambassador and Mrs. Robert Woods Bliss in 1920. Both the Blisses were independently wealthy; Mrs. Bliss was heiress to the Fletcher's Castoria fortune. In 1933, after 33 years in the Foreign Service, Mr. Bliss retired. He and Mrs. Bliss returned to Dumbarton Oaks. Mildred Bliss wanted to create a garden which incorporated traditional European designs, but that would at the same time be distinctively American. The Dumbarton Oaks Gardens were designed by Beatrix Farrand, a noted landscape designer. The formal gardens, which occupy 10 acres, were completed between 1921 and 1941. As you walk through the gardens, you note the interesting use of native plants such as forsythia and cherry trees and the many varied small spaces for family living which the gardens provide.

You enter the gardens through the R Street entrance and walk up to the Orangery, a lovely old building garlanded by a single creeping fig vine that was planted before the Civil War. To the right is the Green Garden where a huge 300-year-old black oak stands. A series of four terraces is found to the east of the house. Willow, magnolia, American elm, red maple and crape myrtle are planted along the wisteria-covered garden walls. Cherry Hill, in the northeast section of the gardens, is crowned with several varieties of Japanese cherry trees and borders on Forsythia Hill with its groves of silver maples and tulip trees. The great slope of Forsythia Hill, blanketed with the shrub for which it is named, becomes a golden cascade in late

March or early April. Lover's Lane is a lovely, romantic spot to the east of the terraced gardens. Nearby is the Rose Garden, which is probably the most popular garden and was a favorite with the Blisses.

Spring is the time to visit the garden and by carefully watching the weather you can see Cherry and Forsythia Hills in bloom. Forsythia Hill is glorious in late March or early April. Cherry Hill blooms several weeks later, but it is an incredible sight, overflowing with light pink Japanese cherry trees. In the early spring you will see the wildflowers in bloom —daffodils, tulips, crocus, narcissus, violets and Virginia bluebells. In May you can catch azaleas, lilies-of-the-valley and day lilies in bloom. Later in the summer, the roses in the Rose Garden emerge. Finally in the fall, the chrysanthemums bloom. Although the spring is the best time to see this garden, you'll find a wealth of beautiful flowers virtually all year.

How To Get There: Dumbarton Oaks is located in Georgetown, in northwest Washington. The entrance to the gardens is on R Street near the intersection with 31st Street N.W., 2 blocks east of Wisconsin Avenue. On-street parking is available for up to 2 hours. There are several Metro buses that come to the vicinity of Dumbarton Oaks. The gardens are open daily April–October, 2:00–6:00 P.M. Admission is $4.00 for adults, $3.00 children and senior citizens. Season passes: $35.00 for an individual, $50.00 for a family pass. Free admission for from November 1–March 31, 2:00 P.M. –5:00 P.M. Closed on national holidays and during inclement weather.

For Additional Information:
Dumbarton Oaks
1703 32nd Street, N.W.
Washington, DC 20007
(202) 342-3200
(202) 338-8278 (Recording only)

Dumbarton Oaks Park

The ancient white oak-studded acres of Dumbarton Oaks Park perfectly complement the landscaped estate beside it, Dumbarton Oaks (described above). At Dumbarton Oaks Park there is a strong sense of wilderness and romance in spite of the fact the park consists of only 27 acres. Dumbarton is largely wooded, with several acres of meadow. Benches have been provided along the shaded trails for visitors to pause and enjoy the park. However, it is the wildflowers that are the park's special glory.

Early spring is the best time to visit. Crocus, narcissus, primrose and forsythia bloom, followed by Virginia bluebells, violets, daffodils and grape hyacinths. Wood azaleas, dogwood, forget-me-nots, lilies-of-the-valley, buttercups and wild orchids are out in May. After June, laurel, rhododendron and ferns are the principal attractions. The park remains a popular retreat throughout the year because of its cool, serene atmosphere. Birds find a sanctuary here year-round. Particularly during the migration of spring warblers, bird-watchers will find a wide variety of birds to observe. Lovers Lane at R Street, N.W. separates Montrose Park (described elsewhere) and Dumbarton Oaks Park. Lovers Lane gives access to Dumbarton Oaks Park.

How To Get There: Dumbarton Oaks Park is in Georgetown, in northwest Washington. The park is only open to foot traffic by way of Lovers Lane near 31st and R streets. The park is open year-round dawn to dusk. No entrance fee.

For Additional Information:
Superintendent , Rock Creek Park
3545 Williamsburg Lane, N.W.
Washington, DC 20008
(202) 282-1063

Franciscan Monastery Garden and Shrine

The Rev. Father Godfrey Schilling's idea, when he finished building the Franciscan Monastery in 1899, was to provide a place to train personnel for the mission activities of the Franciscan Order as well as a place in the United States for people who didn't have the time, money or health to see the shrines of the Holy Land and the catacombs of Rome. Following the Franciscan tradition, he chose a hillside to build a monastery reminiscent of the early California missions. On the 44-acre property, he built a church and monastery with a garden where he reproduced many holy shrines of the Catholic religion including the Grotto of Lourdes, the Grotto of the Nativity and the catacombs of Rome.

Thousands of tulips, daffodils, Easter lilies, flowering dogwood and cherry trees cover the springtime hillside. But it is in June that the monastery garden is in its glory—then the gardens are colored with hundreds of roses. Exotic perennials are brought out of the greenhouses during the summer: hibiscus, tiger lilies, lantanas, caladiums, palms and even banana can be seen here. The garden is known not only for the vast variety of its plants, but also for their artistic arrangement and the care lavished upon them by the friars. This garden is a welcome escape from the ordinary for visitors of all religions.

How To Get There: The monastery is located at1400 Quincy Street, N.E. From the White House take 16th Street, N.W. north to Scott Circle and turn right. Go a third of the way around the circle to Rhode Island Avenue. Head northeast along Rhode Island Avenue to 14th Street, N.E. Turn left and follow 14th Street north to its intersection with Quincy Street. The grounds are open daily from 8:30 A.M. to dusk. There is free parking. No entrance fee, but donations are accepted.

For Additional Information:
The Franciscan Monastery
1400 Quincy Street, N.E.
Washington, DC 20017-3087
(202) 526-6800 (ask for pilgrim director)

A red-bellied turtle rests among water hyacinths at a pool in front of a Washington office building.   *Bill Thomas*

Glover-Archbold Parkway

Midway between Rock Creek and the western boundary of the northwest section of Washington lies one of the least disturbed stretches of woodlands in the Washington area. Threading its way through the valley of a small stream known as Foundry Branch, Glover-Archbold is about three miles long, up to one-half-mile wide and contains some 180 acres of woodlands.

The various habitats of Glover-Archbold support a cross section of wildlife, which find food and shelter provided by the tremendous groves of trees, thick tangles of vines and shrubs and broad stretches of grassland. Glover-Archbold harbors many of the trees typical of this region. Trees found here include the tulip, oak, elm, sycamore, hickory and black walnut. An occasional wild apple tree and an aging pine offer a reminder that a part of this valley was once cultivated. A large mimosa grove bears delicate pink blossoms in early August. At yet another spot stands a tract of beechwoods.

More than 150 species of birds—including the red-shouldered hawk, barred owl and pileated woodpecker—either live here or visit during migration. And there is a diversity of wildflowers that includes buttercups, wood irises and skunk cabbage. Because the park is generally little known, it may be somewhat difficult to make your way down the narrow and sometimes very muddy trail. Its anonymity, however, contributes to its sense of wilderness and makes it appealing to many people. Once you enter the park, the only sounds you hear are the sounds of the leaves, birds, brook and numerous small animals that live in the park.

Most of this tract was given to the public in 1924 by Charles C. Glover and Anne Archbold, both of whom wished that "it might be kept in its natural state for a bird sanctuary and for the enjoyment of people." At present, no roads penetrate its length. There are a few picnic areas. A nature trail crisscrosses the stream near the water's edge for the entire length of the park.

How To Get There: Glover-Archbold Parkway reaches from the Chesapeake & Ohio Canal at its southern end to Van Ness Street at the north. Between these points, only four streets cross the width of the park—Reservoir Road, N.W., New Mexico Avenue, N.W., Massachusetts Avenue, N.W. and Cathedral Avenue, N.W. The largest undisturbed area of the park is the part extending from Reservoir Road toward New Mexico Avenue, N.W. There are no signs to direct you, so a city map would be helpful here. The most direct route is via Wisconsin Avenue north through Georgetown. You may turn left (west) off Wisconsin on Reservoir Road or proceed even farther north and turn left (west) on Cathedral Avenue to New Mexico and watch for Foundry Branch, a small stream flowing south with a nature trail near its banks. Park beside the road and join the trail where it runs alongside the stream. Open year-round dawn to dusk.

For Additional Information:
Superintendent
Rock Creek Park
3545 Williamsburg Lane, N.W.
Washington, DC 20008
(202) 282-1063

Hillwood Museum Gardens

The Hillwood Gardens reflect the taste of one woman, Marjorie Merriweather Post, heiress to the C. W. Post fortune, who owned Hillwood for over 20 years. Hillwood is 25 acres of gardens and natural areas located just 6 miles from downtown Washington. Much of the original estate became Rock Creek Park which Hillwood adjoins. The estate is a combination of lawns and formal gardens. The gardens were designed by Perry Wheeler, a noted landscape architect who helped design the Rose Garden at the White House.

There are over 3,500 trees and plants in the garden, many of which were moved during the construction of the garden. It's been said that Mrs. Post would think nothing of moving an 80-foot tree 5 feet to improve the view. From the south terrace of the mansion one can see the Washington Monument and Rock Creek Park (described elsewhere). The lawn is bordered by azaleas, laurel, rhododendrons and a number of flowering trees that lead naturally out to the woods.

A French parterre of clipped boxwoods and ivy-covered fences is at the west end of the house. Farther to the west lies the Rose Garden, at the center of which is an urn on a column. Below the column are Mrs. Post's ashes. A path lined with mountain laurel and rhododendron leads to a Japanese Garden. The Japanese Garden represents a mountainous landscape with a miniature waterfall and a small bridge.

Another path from the Rose Garden is the Friendship Walk, which was dedicated in 1957 to Mrs. Post by her friends. It leads from the Rose Garden to a terrace surrounded by clipped swags of Buckingham Palace ivy and boxwood from Mount Vernon. A plaque with the words, "Friendship outstays the hurrying flight of years and aye abides through laughter and through tears." A greenhouse displays an extensive orchid collection. Plants are sold in the greenhouse.

How To Get There: From downtown Washington, head north on Connecticut Avenue to Tilden Street, N.W. Turn right on Tilden Street, then left on Linnean Avenue, N.W. The house and garden are closed until spring of 2000 for renovations; after that time you are advised to call for current hours and fees.

For Additional Information:
Information Officer
Hillwood Museum and Gardens
4155 Linnean Avenue, N.W.
Washington, DC 20008
(202) 686-5807

Kenilworth Aquatic Gardens

Kenilworth is one of Washington's most overlooked gems. Kenilworth Aquatic Gardens is the only national park devoted entirely to water plants. Within its 12 acres of ponds is a collection of exotic waterlilies and other aquatic plants that is unsurpassed on the east coast. The park is made up of numerous small ponds surrounded by 44 acres of tidal marshes.

Kenilworth was begun by W.B. Shaw, a government clerk who had lost an arm in the Civil War. He married and bought 37 acres of land along the Anacostia from his father-in-law in the 1800s. He planted a few waterlilies from his native Maine in an ice pond near his home. Over the years Shaw collected species from all over the world, and he started a small business selling aquatic plants. His daughter, Helen Fowler, continued her father's work. In 1938. the gardens were purchased by the National Park system.

The gardens are rightly regarded as one of Washington's

botanical wonders. The ponds contain more than 100,000 water plants, including some of the most colorful waterlilies and lotuses and an abundance of native plants. Small animals living here include various frogs, toads and turtles. Bullfrogs, green, cricket, leopard and pickerel frogs thrive here as do the spade-foot, Fowler's and American toads. Musk, painted, spotted, red-bellied and snapping turtles sun themselves on the banks. Water snakes are often seen. These waters are filled with mosquito fish, gambusia, killifish, mud minnows and sunfish. Migrating waterfowl, including bald eagles, stop here. The least bittern, green heron and red-winged blackbird nest in the fringe of wild marsh. Muskrat, gray squirrel, raccoon and opossum, as well as the cottontail rabbit, reside here.

But it is the plant life—the collection of flowering aquatic plants—that makes it one of the most interesting gardens on the east coast. Many varieties were developed here during Shaw's day. Many others from around the world were imported, including the Victoria cruzziana, a tropical waterlily from the Amazon Basin with immense leaves up to 6 feet in diameter, and what is thought to have been Cleopatra's favorite flower, the Egyptian lotus. Seeds from an ancient Manchurian lake bed, which are believed to be between 350 and 575 years old, were germinated here, and their offspring grow in a special tank. More than 40 species of pond and marginal plants—some native, some exotic—are also found here. They include bamboo, umbrella plants, elephant ear, yellow-blossomed water poppy, water hyacinth, golden club, pickerel weed, arrowhead, cardinal flower, turtlehead, buttonbush, wild rice, cattail, loosestrife, water primrose and rose mallow. Native trees include willow oak, river birch, red maple, willow, elm, ash, sweet and black gums, sycamore and sweet bay magnolia.

The aquatic ponds were formed by damming the Anacostia River marsh, creating a wetland habitat of swamps and marshes. Segments of this flood plain remain unaltered today, providing an estuarine refuge for some fast-disappearing plants and creatures. Insect life is profuse, although mosquitoes are not bad except at night. Besides mosquitoes, you will see the dragonfly nymph, large scavenger diving beetle, water boatman and whirligig beetle. The only way to see the gardens is by foot on footpaths that lead around the ponds. The Park Service recommends that you plan two trips for seasonal highlights. In mid-June, some seventy varieties of hardy day-blooming waterlilies are at their peak. The lotus blossoms, often as large as basketballs rising from plants as tall as a man, are best seen in late July and early August. Then, too, some 40 varieties of day and night-blooming tropical waterlilies open. The blossoms range from white to deep purple and the perfume-filled air is intoxicating. Try to plan your trip early in the day, since many of the blooms close during the hot afternoon sun.

A park ranger conducts excellent nature walks during the summer weekends. Sometimes visitors get to taste a lotus seed, which is surprisingly tasty. Tours begin in the park's visitor's center. There are exhibits on the history of the garden, information on aquatic gardening and live animal displays. Call the park office for exact times of tours and reservations.

How To Get There: From downtown Washington, take New York Avenue east (it becomes US 50). Soon after you cross the Anacostia River, turn right (south) on Kenilworth Avenue (Anacostia Parkway—US 295). Next turn right (west) on Douglas Street to Anacostia Avenue. Turn right again to Kenilworth's parking area on the left.

From Capital Beltway (I-495) take the Baltimore-Washington Parkway (I-295) south keeping to the left (Anacostia Parkway, I-295) at the New York Avenue split. Follow signs for Kenilworth Gardens.

The **National Arboretum** (described elsewhere) lies across the river. A ferry linking the two parks is planned for sometime in the future. Open daily 7:00 A.M.–4:00 P.M. Mornings are best for viewing night-bloomers before they close and day-bloomers before they open. There are several picnic tables. Admission is free.

For Additional Information:
Superintendent
National Capital Parks—East
1900 Anacostia Drive, S.W.
Washington, DC 20020
(202) 426-6905

Lady Bird Johnson Park and Lyndon Baines Johnson Memorial Grove

Few visitors to Washington notice that the Virginia end of the Arlington Memorial Bridge rests on a 121-acre man-made island commonly known as Columbia Island. Built with dredged materials from the Potomac River in 1916, the island was designated as Lady Bird Johnson Park in 1968. Planted with clumps of trees, the island is a pleasant park area with views on the east of the Potomac and the Washington skyline. During the winter months when the leaves are off the trees, the Pentagon can be seen on the west. Although it is accessible only from Virginia, the island is geographically within the District of Columbia's borders.

Lady Bird Johnson Park was dedicated to the former first lady because of her nationwide efforts to beautify America. Dogwoods are planted here, along with oaks and maples. In the spring, one million daffodils bloom in masses both in the park and along the highway leading to the park, a lovely sight. A 15-acre grove of trees honoring the late President Lyndon B. Johnson occupies the south end of the park. Six years after the establishment of the park, President Gerald Ford and Lady Bird Johnson broke ground as the first step toward the establishment of the Lyndon Baines Johnson Memorial Grove. Several hundred white pines, flowering dogwoods, rhododendrons and azaleas were planted in 1974. In the grove is a large, rough-hewn monolith of Texas pink granite, the focal point of the memorial. More than $2 million was raised by private donations for the establishment and maintenance of the grove.

How To Get There: From East Potomac Park, take the George Mason Memorial Bridge (I-395) across the Potomac River. After crossing over the George Washington Memorial Parkway, proceed to the Boundary Drive exit. Turn right (north) and follow the signs to the visitors' parking lot. A footbridge leads from the parking lot on the Virginia shore to the park. Or you may take the George Washington Memorial Parkway, which traverses Lady Bird Johnson Park. Pull-offs are available from both lanes. The **Mount Vernon Trail** (described elsewhere) passes by the park, providing excellent hiker/biker access.

For Additional Information:
Superintendent
George Washington Memorial Parkway
Turkey Run Park
McLean, VA 22101
(703) 285-2600
http://www.nps.gov/gwmp

Montrose Park

A wooded parkland of some 16 acres, Montrose Park is bounded on the north by Rock Creek Park and to the east by Dumbarton Oaks Park. With its grassy lawns, plantings (including rose gardens and a boxwood maze), play areas and tennis courts, Montrose is more formal than either of the adjacent parks (both described elsewhere). It has a myriad of trees scattered over gently rolling hills that attract a host of sledders on snowy winter days and sunbathers during the summer. The large white oaks in the park are the few survivors of the oak forest that originally covered the area and for which Dumbarton Oaks was named. In addition, there are huge tulip trees, elm, beech, common fig and a variety of fir and pine trees in the park. Many people from the neighborhood come here to stroll, to watch the many birds that live here or to enjoy a picnic lunch.

Along the park's entire western boundary is a paved lane open only to foot traffic; it has been known as Lovers Lane since 1900 and was once a trysting place for famous lovers in local history. Montrose Park (along with Dumbarton Oaks Park) was once know as Parrot's Woods in the 18ᵀᴴ Century and was part of the Dumbarton Oaks estate, which adjoins it today. Ambassador and Mrs. Robert Woods Bliss, its former owners, deeded a portion of their estate to the U.S. government and another portion—including their home and magnificent formal gardens (described elsewhere as Dumbarton Oaks)—to Harvard University.

How To Get There: Montrose Park adjoins Rock Creek Park in Georgetown. Access to the park is via Lovers Lane, open to pedestrian traffic only; it runs off R Street, N.W., to the left, just beyond the intersection of R and 31st streets, N.W. and skirts the park's southern border. The park is open year-round dawn to dusk. No entrance fee.

For Additional Information:
Superintendent
Rock Creek Park
3545 Williamsburg Lane, N.W.
Washington, DC 20008
(202) 282-1063

National Aquarium

The oldest public aquarium in the United States, celebrating its 125th anniversary in 1998, is located in downtown Washington, DC. The National Aquarium was founded in 1873 and was operated by the U.S. Fish Commission, which became the U.S. Fish and Wildlife Service, part of the Department of the Interior in 1939. Since 1982, it has been operated by the National Aquarium Society, a non-profit organization. The Aquarium houses more than 1,700 different aquatic animals covering 260 different species, including fish, invertebrates, reptiles and amphibians in 80 different exhibits. A popular exhibit is the piranha tank. Other species on display include sharks, sea turtles and alligators. Both saltwater and freshwater species are on display here. Exhibits are changed frequently. Some of the exhibits are designed to resemble natural environments both in appearance and water conditions. Others illustrate basic biological concepts and principles. A number of unique and endangered species are also on display. The sharks are fed Monday, Wednesday and Saturday at 2:00 P.M. The piranhas are fed on Tuesday, Thursday and Sunday at 2:00 P.M. There is a Touch Tank where you can touch a horseshoe crab or have crustaceans walk over your hand.

A new, much larger, alligator exhibit will be three times the size of the previous one, with above and below water views, more tanks, and interactive displays; sorry, no touching the alligators.

How To Get There: The National Aquarium is located in the lower lobby of the U.S. Department of Commerce Building on 14th Street, N.W., between Constitution and Pennsylvania avenues, N.W. The Aquarium is open 9:00 A.M.–5:00 P.M. daily except Christmas. General admission is $2.00 for adults, $.75 for children under 10. Children under 2 years of age are free. Parking is difficult in this area, although private parking lots do operate within walking distance. The nearest Metro station is the Federal Triangle station on the blue and orange lines.

For Additional Information:
The National Aquarium
Department of Commerce Building, Room B-077
14th and Constitution Ave, N.W., Washington, DC 20230
(202) 482-2825 (recording only)
(202) 482-2826 (office)

National Arboretum

The National Arboretum is one of the foremost horticultural institutions in the world, and yet it is one of the most over-looked and under-utilized natural wonders in the capital area. On 444 acres of rolling hills on one of the highest spots in Washington, the garden encompasses more than two dozen major plant collections—among them hollies, crab apples, azaleas, magnolias, boxwoods, cherries, irises, daylilies, peonies, viburnum, rhododendrons, shade trees, ferns and wildflowers. There are flowering shrub and maples in addition to a dozen special gardens, hundreds of acres of natural forest, the National Bonsai and Penjing Collection, the Friendship Garden and National Herb Garden.

The Arboretum is concerned primarily with conducting research on trees and shrubs to develop superior forms that will grow in various climates in the United States. The Arboretum exchanges seeds and plant material with other scientific institutions throughout the world to expand genetic resources available to researchers. A herbarium containing 600,000 dried plants is also maintained for reference. While not a park in a traditional sense, many trees and shrubs are labeled for public display and arranged in botanical groupings. It's a great learning resource. It seems almost every tree, shrub and plant has a metal tag with common name, scientific name and origin on it, so you can identify them. Many landscape and plant classes take field trips to the Arboretum to see and classify plants that are difficult to find elsewhere in the region.

Established in 1927 by Congress, the National Arboretum was placed on the National Register of Historic Places in 1973. It is administered by the U.S. Department of Agriculture, Agricultural Research Service. Single genus groupings of plants, such as azaleas, boxwoods, cherries, daylilies, rhododendrons, maple, crabapples and hollies are found throughout the Arboretum grounds. One of the most extensive azalea plantings in the region is the arboretum's **Azalea Collections** with evergreen and deciduous azaleas planted along the slopes of Mount Hamilton, a small mound in the center of the Arboretum; it is spectacular in early April, with entire hillsides in pastel colors. Other significant collections include aquatic plants, the National Bonsai and Penjing Collection, the dogwood plantings of the National Women's Farm and Garden Association, the Gotelli Dwarf Conifer Collection, the National Herb Garden,

The Bonsai collection at the National Arboretum   *Bill Thomas*

the Friendship Garden featuring ornamental grasses, perennials and bulbs.

Along the **Fern Valley Trail**, you may view an unusual tree with an interesting history. The *Franklinia altamaha*, or Franklin tree, was first discovered growing wild in Georgia in 1765 by a noted American botanist, John Bartrum, who named it after his friend Ben Franklin. The botanist took one of the plants with him and nurtured it. If not for that one plant and its resulting cultivation, the Franklin tree might have been lost forever, for today it is believed to be extinct in the wild. The Fern Valley Trail is divided into three sections. The upper trail has a wooded area typical of the northeastern United States and includes hemlock, white pine and a variety of ferns and wildflowers. In the woodlands is a collection of azaleas native to eastern states. The middle section contains plants from the deciduous woodland of the Piedmont area. Chestnut, mountain laurel, tulip trees, rhododendron and May apples are found here. The lower valley has plants found in the mountains of North Carolina. These are rhododendron, azaleas, sand myrtle and blueberries. Beside the Fern Valley Trail is the **Daffodil Collection**, which provides a stunningly beautiful display each April of dozens of varieties of daffodils and narcissus, each labeled with common and scientific names; this is a "must-see".

The **National Bonsai and Penjing Museum** contains representatives of the bonsai art from China, Japan and North America, as well as the Japanese Garden. These are housed in four specially constructed pavilions adjacent to the Administration Building. Bonsai is the art of growing ornamentally shaped plants in small, shallow pots. The trees of more than 30 species found here range from 15 to over 350 years of age. Although most of the tree species would normally tower above the pavilion, with the exception of one from the Imperial Household, all stand about one to two feet in height. The Bonsai collection was started with a gift from the Japanese people of 53 master bonsai specimens and 5 viewing stones, but has been expanded by the donation of 31 trees of the **Penjing Collection** from Hong Kong and the **North American Bonsai Collection.** The student of bonsai can study the differences in the three schools of bonsai. One enters the complex through the **Japanese garden** which holds a special interest for wildflower enthusiasts, as it contains Japanese varieties of many American wildflowers such as Solomon's seal, asporea and bleeding heart under a forest of Japanese cedars. At the far end of the complex is the new **George Yamaguchi North American Garden** of over 100 species of plants, exclusively native to North America. Designed by Gordon Chappelin, this contrasts with the Japanese Garden.

Across the road from the bonsai is the **National Herb Garden**. Here is the Arboretum's collection of antique rose species, the Knot Garden in the classic design of 16th-century England and 10 specialty herb gardens including fragrance herbs, medicinal herbs, herbs for dyes, herbs with industrial uses, herbs for cooking, herbs used by early American Indians, beverage herbs and more.

Although each season has its own specialties, there are two times when a visit is particularly rewarding: in late March to early April, when the daffodils, crab apples, cherries and magnolias are in bloom and in late April and early May, when the azaleas, rhododendrons and dogwood are masses of color. Roses in the National Herb Garden bloom in June (see the National Herb Garden section). In the summer the aquatic plants, the Herb Garden, crape myrtles, New American Garden of perennials and ornamental grasses are in bloom. In early fall, the fall tree foliage displays dominate along with the brightly colored fruits and berries. Even in the winter, the holly collection and the Gotelli Collection of dwarf and slow-growing conifers make a beautiful display in the snow. The Gotelli collection is one of the most outstanding collections of this type in the world. Fir, juniper, cypress, pine, yew and spruce are some of the species on display from this collection. One must see The Arboretum

What's in Season at the Arboretum

(Boldface denotes a major attraction at that time.)

Typical Date	Display
Jan-Feb	witchhazel, conifers, holly, winter jasmine
March 2nd week	**early bulbs**, Cornelian cherry, winter-hazel, wintersweet
March 3rd week	Japanese andromeda, winter jasmine
March 4th week	**daffodils, woodland wildflowers**, pussy willows, forsythia
April 1st week	**daffodils**, crocus, early magnolias, **woodland wildflowers**, oconee bells
April 2nd week	**daffodils**, crocus, early magnolias, Korean & **early azaleas**, oconee bells
April 3rd week	daffodils, **magnolias**, flowering cherries, **azaleas**, woodland wildflowers
April 4th week	**azaleas**, magnolias, crabapples, early rhododendrons, wooland wildflowers
May 1st week	**flowering dogwoods**, late cherries, asiatic magnolias, tree peonies, lilacs, dove tree, species roses
May 2nd week	tulip trees, late azeleas, **rhododendrons**, old garden roses
May 3rd week	**mountain laurel**, Southern & sweet bay magnolias, Chinese dogwood, **iris**
May 4th week	**lilies, herbs,** fringetree, laurel, magnolia, iris
June 1st week	**annuals, waterlilies,** Linden viburnum, firethorns, rhododendrons
June 2nd week	**daylilies, golden raintree,** annuals, rosebay rhododendron,
Late Jun -July	butterfly weed, meadow & prarie flowers, annuals, **herbs**, waterlilies
July	**waterlilies**, hibiscus, crapemyrtle, daylilies, meadow wildflower, conifers, pepper
August	July items plus plumleaf azalea, cardinal flower, conifers, boxwood
Sept.	**firethorn & viburnum** in fruit, holly, osmanthus, pepper collection
Oct.	**fall foliage**, ornamental grasses
Nov.	fall foliage, **ornamental grasses**
Dec.	holly & heavenly bamboo in fruit, conifer foliage & cones, Jap. apricot

many times in all the seasons to begin to appreciate what's here; it's a joyous experience.

Lectures, classes, workshops, guided walks and films are scheduled throughout the year. The National Capital Area Federation of Garden Clubs provides volunteer guide service for group tours, but arrangements must be made well in advance. Contact the National Arboretum for more information.

Consider visiting the **Kenilworth Aquatic Gardens** (described elsewhere) which are located just across the Anacostia River, about 15 minutes by car.

Hiking and Biking

The Arboretum is extremely well suited for hiking and biking. You will see much more this way and its ten miles of hard surface roads are seldom crowded. There are places to pause by the Beech Spring Pond or Heart Pond to watch the swans, duck and geese swimming. In addition, there are many footpaths winding through the various plant groups.

How To Get There: The facility is bounded on the north by New York Avenue, N.E. (US 50) and the visitors' entrance is accessible from its eastbound lanes. From downtown Washington, take New York Avenue (US 50) east. Signs direct you to the visitors entrance about half a block past Blandensburg Road, N.E. From the north take the Baltimore Washington Parkway or take US 50 from the east to New York Avenue and watch for the U-turn sign to the Arboretum just before the Bladensburg Road light. The Arboretum grounds are open every day of the year except Christmas, 8:00 A.M.–5:00 P.M. The National Bonsai & Penjing Museum is open daily 10:00 A.M.–3:30 P.M. The gift shop is open daily 10:00 A.M.–3:00 P.M., March 1 through mid-December. A map of the facility is essential and is available at the gift shop or administration building.

For Additional Information:
Public Information Officer
U.S. National Arboretum
3501 New York Avenue, N.E.
Washington, DC 20002-1958
(202) 245-2726

National Museum of Natural History and the Naturalist Center

The Smithsonian's Museum of Natural History has been called a repository of the remarkable. It is one of the world's great treasure houses of knowledge. It is filled with amazing things such as dinosaur skeletons, living coral reefs complete with waves, an insect zoo with live insects, a 12-ton elephant, the largest blue diamond in the world, dioramas of earth millions of years ago and meteorites. But all this is just a tiny fraction of the well over 120 million specimens in the museum's inventory. Every visit to the Museum of Natural History is an educational and entertaining experience; even after dozens of visits, there is always something new and mind-expanding to be discovered here. Entire halls are devoted to animals, insects, birds, native cultures, life in the sea, prehistoric life, minerals and gems, osteology and anthropology. The exhibits open to the public are only a small part of what the Smithsonian does. Since it was founded in 1846, the Smithsonian has collected, preserved, studied and displayed specimens from the natural world and objects made by its inhabitants. James Smithson, the English scientist who bequeathed $500,000 for its creation, charged the Congress "to found at Washington, under the name of Smithsonian Institution, an establishment for the increase and diffusion of knowledge among men."

On display are some fascinating specimens. As you enter the rotunda by way of the Mall you meet one of them—a 13-foot-tall Fenykovi elephant shot in Africa in 1955 by a Hungarian engineer who donated it to the Smithsonian. When alive, it is believed to have weighed 12 tons and when dead, it took 16 months to mount. The largest tiger ever killed in India—11 feet long and weighing 857 pounds—is also on display. Other displays include the 80-foot-long *diplodocus* dinosaur skeleton, extracated from a Utah deposit, the oldest known fossil; a 92-foot-long plastic model of a blue whale, the largest animal that ever lived; and the Hope diamond, weighing 45.52 carats, the largest blue diamond in the world.

The first floor is divided into three major themes visible from the Mall entrance: Fossils: The History of Life (on your right), Human Origins and Cultures (ahead), and Diversity of Life (on your left). **The History of Life**—Early Life and Fossil Plants; Dinosaurs and Fossil Mammals; and Ancient Seas and the Ice Age is one of the museums top attractions. It traces life from its single cell beginnings through the oldest known fossils, fossil plants, early fossil animals, prehistoric sea creatures, dinosaurs, fossil mammals and the ice age. The **Dinosaur Gallery**, starring the two-story-high diplodocus dinosaur, is a favorite. **Human Origins and Cultures** documents African, Asian, American Indian and Pacific cultures and the dynamics of evolution; South American cultures are located on the second floor. The **Life in the Sea Hall** features **Ecosystems** with two living marine ecosystems complete with waves: a living **Caribbean coral reef** and a living **Maine rocky coast** marine ecosystem from shoreline to deep ocean.

The **In Search of the Giant Squid** exhibit features two of the few known specimens of the giant squid, an amazing and mysterious creature which has never been seen alive in it's natural habitat, but has been found dead or dying. Scientists believe it grows to a length of almost 60 feet and a weight of over 1000 pounds, with eyes up to 10 inches wide. Although there will be models of the full sized ones, the two preserved specimens are a mere 9 feet in length, weigh 440 pounds and would have a tentacle span of some 30 feet.

The **Janet Annenberg Hooker Hall of Geology, Gems and Mineral,** opened in 1997 on the 2nd floor, is considered one of the top earth science exhibits of the world covering 20,000 square feet. The Hope Diamond is the star of the show, followed by the jewel room with astounding gems, some the size of bricks. Then there is the Beauty of Mineral Nature Hall, with fascinating crystals and exotic minerals of all categories, very well displayed. Visitors can walk through a simulated mine to learn of commercial minerals and their extraction.

Plate Tectonics, the study of the movement of the Earth's surface is explained in the following room with excellent films on earthquakes, demonstration of plate theories, volcanoes, and earthquake detection equipment. You can even "make your own quake". The Meteor Hall features many real (and surprisingly large) meteorites—pieces of metallic asteroids that have hit the earth, with an explanation of where meteorites come from, what they are made of, and their "impact" on life on earth.

The second floor is completed with exhibits on human variation, osteology, reptiles and the insect zoo. The comparative skeletal structure (osteology) exhibit is fascinating and extensive—one can visualize the process of evolution of animal structure and form.

The **O. Orkin Insect Zoo** can be hard to find through the Bones exhibit, but is worth the search. More insects inhabit more places than any other terrestrial creatures and this exhibit demonstrates the diversity and role of insects in the ecosystem. There are amazing live exhibits of exotic (and not so exotic) insects such as the leaf insect which is virtually indistinguishable from the plant it lives on, the New Guinea walking stick, Australian stick insects, giant Madagascar cockroaches, water insects and more. A few non-insects such as the arachnid tarantula spider and giant millipedes are included. Periodically one of the zoo curators will bring out live insects—such as eight-inch-long caterpillars that daring visitors can handle.

The ground floor with the Constitution Avenue entry houses the Baird Auditorium, a favorite lecture hall with free Friday noon lectures and films, and the famous Audubon lecture series, and a large gallery space for temporary exhibits. The Natural History Museum sponsors major special exhibits here every few months. These are always fascinating, superb exhibits.

An extensive exhibit of **Birds of the DC Region**, originally shown in the first quarter of the century, is now on the ground floor near the Baird Auditorium. Preserved, but very lifelike, stuffed specimens of birds of the region from the Atlantic Ocean to the Allegheny Mountains are displayed with tags identifying their species, distribution and occurrence in the region: year-round, summer, winter, spring and fall migrants and vagrants. Any serious DC area birdwatcher will want to study this exhibit closely.

The museum is also a major facility for natural history research. In addition to its insect zoo, it contains an entomology research section consisting of more than 32,000,000 specimens. There are more than 400,000 slides in some 65,000 drawers, and a collection of more than 10 million beetles, 3 million flies and 2 million wasps and bees. The Smithsonian Museum Support Center at Silver Hill, Maryland, just outside of DC, stores many of the specimens. There are more than 12 miles of shelving in the invertebrate zoology section, filled with snails, mollusks, worms, shrimps, lobsters, crabs and jellyfish. The Smithsonian Resident Associate Program occasionally conducts tours of the Support Center.

The Samuel C. Johnson Theater featuring **3D IMAX films** will soon open to show natural history related films with stunning realism of the high-resolution image and very high fidelity sound. The **Discovery Room** on the first floor allows visitors of all ages to examine objects from the museums collection. It is recommended for ages 4 and up; children under 12 are admitted with an adult only. A new, larger Discovery Center is under construction in the West Court.

The new **Kenneth E. Behring Family Hall of Mammals** is scheduled to open in 2001; it will allow visitors to walk through animal's natural habitats to better understand how mammals interact with the environment and each other.

The Smithsonian has, or can provide information about, anything related to the field of natural history. Spend a day or two— it's worth at least that much time. No matter how many times you have been there, you will find the Museum of Natural History a wonderful place to visit again and again. A restaurant and snack bar are located in the building, as well as a large gift shop and bookstore. Free guided tours are available daily September through June at 10:30 A.M. and 1:30 P.M. (call ahead to verify times). Recorded tours for many exhibits are available for a nominal fee at the audio tour desk located in the Rotunda.

For those who live in the Washington area, the Smithsonian offers classes and lectures at all its museums on a vast number of topics both for members and non-members. A popular lecture series by experts in animal research is given each year by the Smithsonian in conjunction with the Audubon Society. It is held about once a month on Monday nights at the Natural History Museum during the school year. For information about how to become a member and a schedule of classes inquire about the **Smithsonian Resident Associate Program** at the information desk.

It should also be noted that the Smithsonian is one of the preeminent research institutions for natural history in the world. More than 500 scientists and scholars conduct research and lead expeditions on a wide range of subjects. The museum is a leader in anthropology, biodiversity, earth sciences, marine sciences, paleaobiology, and systematic and evolutionary biology.

How To Get There: Located on the north side of the Mall, between 9th and 12th streets, N.W. the museum may be entered from Madison Drive on the south or Constitution Avenue at 10th Street on the north. Parking near the mall is difficult to find, so use of public transportation is recommended. The museum is about a block away from the Metrorail Smithsonian station on the blue and orange lines or about four blocks from the Archives station on the yellow line. The museum's north entrance and all exhibits are handicapped accessible. Open every day except Christmas, 10:00 A.M.–5:30 P.M. Admission is free.

The Discovery Room is open Saturday and Sunday 10:30 A.M.–3:30 P.M. and Monday–Friday NOON–2:30 P.M. Free timed passes are always required and are distributed at the room's entrance during the day on a first come first serve basis. Tickets (available at no charge at the Discovery Room) are required for admission.

The Naturalists Center

The Naturalists Center, formerly in the Natural History Museum, has moved out to Leesburg. The Naturalists Center was created to provide a place to answer questions from the public about natural history, and provide resources for the serious amateur, collector, teacher or student who wants to study natural history in more detail than is possible to do in the main exhibits at the museum or at a local library. This miniature natural history museum has over 30,000 objects, 2,400 books and numerous scientific instruments. There are reference collections of rocks and minerals, fossils, plants, invertebrate and vertebrate animals and anthropological specimens, most of which came from the Smithsonian's own collection of specimens. The Smithsonian's Department of Mineral Sciences provided a collection of local rocks and minerals and examples of rocks that have been thin-sectioned for use with a petrographic microscope. The Department of Vertebrate Zoology section contributed hundreds of bones and skins. A representative selection of mounted and labeled local insects is available in the center. Local plants from the Blue Ridge Mountains to the Atlantic coast have been loaned from the Department of Botany. The anthropology section contains human bone materials as well as archaeological materials that allow visitors to compare materials they have found. The center contains a comprehensive library, stereo zoom microscopes, rock grinding and polishing tools. These materials are available for the public to use independently free of charge or under the supervision of one of the volunteers.

This is an excellent place to bring children over the age of 12 who show an interest in science.

How to get to The Naturalists Center:

Take the Dulles Greenway Toll Road, Route 267 to Exit 1B, turn right at Sycolin Road, and right at Miller Drive. The Center is the first building on the left. There is plenty of free parking. No admission charge. The Naturalists Center is open 10:30 A.M.–4:00 P.M., Tuesday through Saturday. Children under 10 are not admitted. Be sure to call ahead to verify hours before making a trip to the Naturalists Center; groups of six or more must call ahead before coming.

For Additional Information:
Smithsonian Institution
National Museum of Natural History
Office of Public Affairs
Washington, DC 20560
(202) 287-2020 (recording with hours, and events for all
    Smithsonian museums)
(202) 357-2700 (additional information 9:00 a.m.–5:00 p.m. only)
(202) 357-1729 (TDD for hearing impaired)
(202) 357-2804 (Naturalists Center, Room C-219)
http://www.nmnh.si.edu

The Naturalists Center
741 Miller Drive, SE
Leesburg, Virginia 20175
(800) 729-7725

To receive the free quarterly *Quest*, a mini-magazine of museum events, write with your full address to:
Quest
National Museum of Natural History
Smithsonian Museum, MRC 106
Washington, DC 20560

National Zoological Park

The National Zoological Park rates among the world's finest zoos. Probably no institution in the Washington area has changed as much since it first opened as the National Zoo. Originally it concentrated, like most zoos did at that time, on exhibiting exotic animals. The public flocked to see elephants and lions that were caught in the wild. As these animals became rarer and more difficult to find, the priority of the zoo changed from that of exhibiting animals to that of preserving and conserving entire species. In the mid-1950s it was one of the first to hire a full-time veterinarian to improve the health of the animals. In 1965, a research division was started to study the reproduction and ecology of zoo species. In 1974, a breeding and research center was established on 3,150 acres in Virginia for species threatened with extinction.

With an emphasis on conservation and preservation, animals

are beginning to be grouped in natural settings rather than as individuals. Traditional zoological displays such as the Monkey House are being replaced with walk-through environments such as the new Amazonia complex, which combines plants and a variety of animals to better explain the complexity and diversity of the earth's biosystems. Education programs have been developed for school children and families. Wildlife professionals from around the world come to the Virginia wildlife center to train in specialized aspects of wildlife management and to promote conservation . The park itself was designed by Frederick Law Olmsted, the father of American landscape architecture, who also designed Central Park in New York City. Containing 163 acres, the park is surrounded by a delightful wooded glen. Two walks, Olmsted Walk, the main path, and the very circuitous Valley Trail, slope from Connecticut Avenue to the west down to Beach Drive on the east.

The zoo's star entertainers are the **Orangutans** and their high wire commute from their home in the **Great Ape House** to the day job in the **Think Tank**. The Think Tank is a new building for educating apes and human visitors. The apes are taught symbolic language skills with touch-screen computer displays that teach them to match symbols with pictures of common objects they can identify, mostly food items. The human side shows how animals learn, and the relative brain sizes and learning capacities of different species. Don't be embarrassed to find that several other species have larger brains than ours. Some of the orangutans commute from the Ape House to the Think Tank over the large cables strung from the high towers between the buildings; the best time to see this is about 2:00 P.M.

The perennial attraction is **Hsing-Hsing the giant panda,** the survivor of a pair that was donated in 1972 by The People's Republic of China in commemoration of President Richard Nixon's historic visit there earlier that year. The beautiful blue-eyed white tiger is another popular exhibit at the zoo. The zoo also has one of the finest aviaries in the world, part of which is in a jungle-like setting where the birds fly freely all around you. Children love the prairie dog and seal exhibits as well as Monkey Island and **The Great Ape House**. The National Zoo is a leader in gorilla husbandry. Don't miss the six-gorilla family group in the rear of the Great Ape House and the orangutan family at the side of the house.

The **Reptile Discovery Center** is one of the most interesting exhibit halls, although reptiles are considered repugnant by some. It has interpretive exhibits of reptiles and amphibians in more naturalistic settings. Residents include geckos, snakes approaching a foot in diameter, crocodiles, giant komodo dragons and more. Feeding time here is especially interesting because many of the animals are hand-fed individually to be sure that the smaller ones get something to eat. This is especially important considering that some animals may eat as seldom as once a week. The diet is specialized for each species, including live giant cockroaches, whole rats or other reptile goodies. Call the information desk for feeding times. HERPlab, in the Reptile Discovery Center, has incubating reptile eggs and newborn on display.

Be sure to see the **Invertebrate Exhibit**, one of the zoo's less traditional exhibits; the entrance is somewhat hidden from view at the rear of the Reptile House. About 99 percent of the Earth's animal species are invertebrates, animals without backbones. Their morphological diversity is amazing. The stars of the exhibit are the cephalopods (literally "head feet"), including the beautiful chambered nautilus, which has a snail-like pearly shell and hovers mysteriously in mid-tank, yet can move quickly by jet propulsion to grab a shrimp in its tentacles; the unshelled cuttlefish, which can change its color instantly from sand to red to black; and a surprisingly intelligent Pacific giant octopus. Other residents include the sea cucumber (anatomically one of Earth's most bizarre animals), sea urchins (looking like living pin cushions), anemones (which look like underwater flowers), horseshoe crabs, tarantulas and much more. On the terrestrial side, there is a colony of leaf-cutter ants, giant cockroaches, and a bee colony, among others—all safely behind glass. There are numerous educational exhibits and microscopes to examine invertebrates too small to be visible to the unaided eye. You might want to check with the information desk for the exact time of the daily feeding of the octopus and other cephalopods. You exit the Invertebrate Exhibit through the wonderful **Pollinarium**, a walk-though greenhouse where numerous shimmering hummingbirds hover and dart, and butterflies fly freely around you.

The **Amazonia Pavilion** is a walk through living "life sized" Amazonian rain forest with a fish-eye view of a living Amazon River that explores the biodiversity of the Amazon rainforest. The Amazon Science Gallery puts visitors in the shoes of a biologist studying the Amazon regions recreating a field laboratory.

The new **Prairie Exhibit** will open in late 1998, with a prairie dog town, bison, other prairie animals and a walk-through live prairie plant discovery trail.

Wild animals like the zoo too. Be sure to loop in the trees near the main bird house and large bird walk for dozens of small herons who usually make their spring rookery there.

Check with the information desk to find out when the feeding and training sessions for the elephants, seals and sea lions take place. **ZOOlab**, in the Education building, offers special exhibits and activities for families.

How To Get There: The National Zoo is located in northwest Washington, its main entrance in the 3000 block of Connecticut Avenue, N.W. Other entrances are on Harvard Street, N.W., and on Beach Drive, N.W. Parking is available at an hourly rate, but the parking lots are frequently full on popular days. There is handicapped access and parking from Lots B and D. The National Zoo is a 7-minute walk from the Metrorail red line Woodley Park/Zoo station. Metrobus L2 and L4 lines stop at the zoo entrance. The zoo is also adjacent to the main Rock Creek Park hiker/biker trail and has bicycle stands, but neither bicycling nor skateboarding are allowed on zoo grounds. Strollers can be rented for $5.00 a day with a $35 deposit. For availability of strollers, call the information desk at (202) 673-4821. Most of the zoo is handicapped accessible with few exceptions, but some of the zoo paths are a bit steep. Picnic tables are available in a number of locations and there are snack stands, rest rooms and gift shops throughout the park. No pets are allowed on zoo grounds except for guide dogs.

Hours: The zoo is open every day except Christmas 8:00 A.M–8: 00 P.M. with the buildings open 9:00 A.M.–6:00 P.M. in peak season from mid-April through mid-October. The rest of the year the zoo closes at 6:00 P.M. and the buildings close at 4:30 P.M. Special exhibit hours are as follows: Amazonia 10:00 A.M.-6:00 P.M. during peak season and 10:00 A.M.-4:00 P.M. off-peak; Reptile Discovery Center 10:00 A.M.-6:00 P.M. peak and 10:00 A.M.–4:30 P.M. off-peak; Invertebrate Exhibit Wednesday, Thursday, Friday 10:00 A.M.–6:00 P.M. and weekends 9:00 A.M.–6:00 P.M. peak, closing at 4:30 P.M. off-peak; ZooLab is open only Friday 10:00 A.M.-1:00 P.M. and weekends 10:00 A.M–2:00 P.M., but closed in January and February. Hsing-Hsing, the famous giant panda is typically fed at 11:00 A.M. and 3:00 P.M. daily. The Amazonia Pavilion, Reptile Discovery Center, and Invertebrate Exhibit all have controlled access and may have lines to get in. Guided tours are given periodically; for a current schedule, call the Friends of the National Zoo at (202) 673-4955. Zoo maps are available at the Education Center near the Connecticut Street entrance. Admission is free.

It's best to arrive at the zoo before 10:00 A.M. and check at the Education Building for that day's feeding times, special events, and new zoo births. The most popular feeding time is around 10:30 A.M. Parking fills up quickly on weekends and holidays.

For Additional Information:
Public Information Specialist
National Zoological Park
Smithsonian Institution
Washington, DC 20008
(202) 673-4800 (24 hour selection of recorded information.)
(202) 673-4717
(202) 357-1300 (other information)
http://www.si.edu/natzoo/

Potomac Park

Just a century ago, the 700 acres that make up some of the most beautiful urban gardens in any city were a swamp and sewage dump. It was said during the later part of the nineteenth century that the area next to the marshland had become almost uninhabitable because of the smell, typhoid, malaria and mosquitoes that bred there. At the turn of the century the situation was such a public embarrassment that Congress created a commission to reclaim the marshland. Potomac Park is made up of two sections—East Potomac Park and West Potomac Park. West Potomac Park offers such attractions as spectacular views of the Lincoln and Jefferson memorials, Constitution Gardens, the Reflecting Pool, the Vietnam Veterans Memorial, Vietnam Women's Memorial, the Franklin Delano Roosevelt Memorial, Korean War Veterans Memorial and the Tidal Basin ringed by Washington's renowned Japanese cherry trees.

Back in 1912, during the administration of President William Howard Taft, 3,000 cherry trees representing 12 varieties were given the United States as a gift of friendship from Japan. All the trees came from Tokyo. They were planted that spring in a formal ceremony involving Mrs. Taft and Viscountess Chinada, wife of the Japanese ambassador. The two trees planted by Mrs. Taft and the Viscountess still stand side by side at the northwest side of the Tidal Basin. Today the beautiful display encircles the

Tidal Basin, framing the soft lines of the Jefferson Memorial. Approximately 1300 cherry trees line the basin, 97 percent of which are of the Yoshino variety and bear a great profusion of single white blossoms. The remaining 3 percent are mostly Akebono, which means "dawn" and are identical to the Yoshino blossoms, except for a slight tinge of pink adding a touch of color to the otherwise white landscape. These two varieties are among the earliest to bloom (more cherry trees of a later-blooming variety are planted in East Potomac Park).

Through the years, the cherry trees of Potomac Park have evoked strong feelings from Washingtonians. When the Tidal Basin site was selected for the Jefferson Memorial, it meant that several of the trees would have to be removed. Outraged admirers of the trees created a furor. The more militant of the protesters chained themselves to tree trunks while others sat in the holes where trees had already been uprooted. They were partially appeased by a promise to transplant some of those removed and to include 1,000 new plantings as part of the memorial's landscaping plan. A few years later, feelings of a different nature surfaced when the Japanese attacked Pearl Harbor on December 7, 1941. In the weeks that followed, vandals disfigured a few Tidal Basin trees. In 1952, the United States sent cuttings from the trees back to their homeland in order to restock war-devastated nurseries. In return, in 1965, Japan gave another 3,800 cherry trees to the United States; these were planted on the Washington Monument grounds and on the Mall. Today these cherry trees stand both in Washington and Tokyo as a living symbol of international friendship. In the springtime the blossoms around the Tidal Basin are breathtaking. No other display of nature in or around the capital is more highly acclaimed than the annual blossoming of these cherry trees. The event marks the beginning of spring. It is impossible to predict the exact time the cherry trees will bloom, for the date varies from year to year, depending upon weather conditions. Sometimes they bloom as early as March 20th, sometimes as late as April 17th, with an average date of April 5th. Blossoms remain on the trees for 10 to 12 days.

Also of special note in West Potomac Park are the Constitution Gardens northeast of the Lincoln Memorial, a woodland oasis of some 36 acres dedicated in May 1976. The focal point of the park is a 7-acre lake, with 2,650 feet of undulating shoreline and a maximum depth of four feet. In the center of the lake is a one-acre island, reached by a footbridge, on which you find mallard ducks and sunning turtles during the warmer months. About 18 acres of the informal gardens are covered with trees with another 10 acres left as open meadows. The rolling contours are intended to create a desirable setting for picnics and recreation. A refreshment kiosk with a terrace for tables is located at the west end of the lake. More than 5,000 trees were planted in Constitution Gardens, including scarlet oak, sweet gum, cornelian cherry, dogwood, honey locust and crab apple, as well as a variety of flowering shrubs and a myriad of flowers. Two rows of regularly spaced elms border both the Lincoln Memorial Reflecting Pool at the gardens' southern boundary and Constitution Avenue along the northern boundary. These trees have puzzled arborists for years. Thought to be a form of English elms, they appear to be a hybrid of the Dutch elm, but one of a number of hybrids resistant to the Dutch elm disease that killed off most of the Dutch elm trees in this country.

More open space to roam and relax in is provided by the expanse of East Potomac Park. Its one-way perimeter road is bordered by flowering cherry trees. The most popular variety is Kwanzan, which produces heavy clusters of deep pink double blossoms. A late-flowering tree, in the past the Kwanzan has bloomed as early as April 14 and as late as May 1. These trees have not achieved the renown of those that surround the Tidal Basin, but they are just as lovely. Wise Washingtonians who want to avoid the crowds that invade the city during the Cherry Blossom Festival come here to enjoy the profusion of blooms about two weeks later. There are also some beautiful giant weeping willows. These willows are not native to the area, and legend has it that they were propagated from cuttings taken from Napoleon's grave at St. Helena. These willow trees are complemented by the weeping cherry trees, which are the first cherry trees to bloom in the area. Hains Point, at the southern tip of East Potomac Park, is one of the more pleasant places in Washington and one where hundreds of Washingtonians visit in the summer to picnic, sun and play on the ball fields. The park is named for Peter C. Hains, the Army engineer who directed the work that made the marshland into a park. It is said that when not even a leaf stirs elsewhere in the city, there is a breeze here. Also in East Potomac Park are picnic tables, tennis courts, an 18-hole golf course, miniature golf and a swimming pool. Near the northern end of the park area is the headquarters of the U.S. Park Police, and the National Park Service Regional Headquarters.

Hiking and Bicycling

The five-mile loop around East Potomac Park offers Washington's most extensive walk directly beside the water. It follows the Potomac River and its harbor arm, the Washington Channel. A walk of a mile or so around the Tidal Basin is extremely popular, especially when the cherry trees are in bloom. Some 2,150 feet of bicycle paths and more than three miles of pedestrian pathways, including the perimeter sidewalks, traverse Constitution Gardens; all are paved and illuminated at night, but night use is not advised due to crime, except at the Jefferson and Lincoln Memorials where park rangers are present. The whole area is also a favorite spot for joggers. Bicycles are available for rent at Thompson Boat Center at Rock Creek Parkway and Virginia Ave., N.W. Phone (202) 333-9543.

How To Get There: From downtown Washington, follow 14th Street to the 14th Street Bridge. Take the Ohio Drive exit. Ohio Drive to the north leads to West Potomac Park, while to the south is East Potomac Park. The Potomac River bounds both parks on the west. Constitution Avenue forms the northern boundary of West Potomac Park, while the same park merges into the Mall on the east and meets East Potomac Park to the south. The remaining three boundaries of East Potomac Park are formed by the waters of the river and, to the east, by the waters of the Washington Channel. Free parking space is available along the roads within the park.

For Additional Information:
Public Information Officer
National Capital Region National Park Service
1100 Ohio Drive, S.W., Washington, DC 20242
(202) 619-7222 or (202) 485-9666

Rawlins Park

This small but unusually lovely park may be enjoyed at any time of the year. Named for Gen. John A. Rawlins (Chief of Staff under Gen. Ulysses S. Grant and later Grant's first secretary of war), Rawlins Park lies just north of the U.S. Department of the Interior Building in Northwest Washington. Though often overlooked by visitors, it should not be—for this narrow green rectangle is lovely. In the spring and summer, big tropical blue and rose waterlilies adorn the surface of two shallow pools in the center of the park. Rows of tulip tree magnolias at the water's edge burst forth with a mass of white with tinges of pink, saucer-like blossoms for a few days in late March or early April. The goldfish may be admired year-round.

How To Get There: Located two blocks west of the South Lawn of the White House, Rawlins Park lies between 18th and 20th streets, N.W. A divided E Street, N.W., forms both its northern and southern boundaries.

For Additional Information:
Public Information Officer
National Park Service National Capital Region
1100 Ohio Drive, S.W.
Washington, DC 20242
(202) 619-7222

Rock Creek Park

Rock Creek cuts a tumbling course through a steep, wooded and rocky ravine creating one of the nation's largest and finest city parks. Rock Creek Park in Northwest Washington offers a diversified terrain and a tremendous variety of activities, including serious nature study, horseback riding, tennis, historical sights, a planetarium, an outdoor amphitheater, a restored gristmill, a golf course, an art barn, boating and an exercise trail. The park includes nearly 2,100 acres within the District of Columbia and an additional 4,400 acres along the same stream valley in Maryland's Montgomery County, north of the District of Columbia line, known as Rock Creek Regional Park (described elsewhere). The Maryland-National Capital Park and Planning Commission administers the Maryland section while the DC portion is managed by the National Park Service.

In 1890 Rock Creek Park became the first urban natural area set aside by Congress as a park when Congress passed an act authorizing acquisition of 2,000 acres along Rock Creek Park for what it called its "pleasant valleys and deep ravines, primeval forests and open fields, its running waters, its rocks clothed with rich ferns and mosses, its repose and tranquillity,

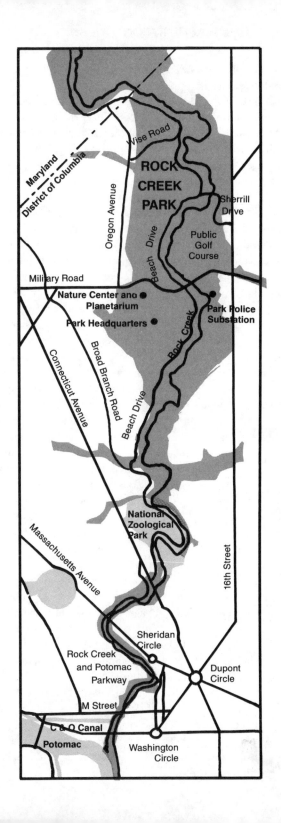

its light and shade, its ever-varying shrubbery, its beautiful and extensive views."

Great historical and political figures have walked here. John Quincy Adams, after a morning of politics, would walk in what he described as "this romantic glen, listening to the singing of a thousand birds .." Theodore Roosevelt enjoyed going out on rough cross-country walks in the park when he was president. Abraham Lincoln actually was exposed to enemy fire while witnessing a Confederate attack on Washington on July 11-12, 1864, at Fort Stevens. Parts of Rock Creek remain as wild today as they were then. Great stands of near-virgin forest adorn the hills and valleys of the park—tulip poplars, red and white oak, red ash, river birch, black cherry, papaw, American hornbeam, sycamore, dogwood, sassafras, beech, redbud, hickory and, occasionally, pine. Shrubs such as alder, spicebush, witch hazel, viburnum, mountain laurel and azalea form the understory.

Rock Creek is 30 miles long in its entirety and has many smaller tributaries, extending well beyond Rock Creek Park into Montgomery County to it's **Rock Creek Regional Park** (described under Maryland). Like virtually every other stream in the East Coast megalopolis that extends from Washington to Boston, its waters are heavily polluted, but it carves a path for itself through a most unusual area. The jumbled mass of rocks and ledges along Rock Creek represents an ancient mountain, which both time and the elements have decayed, carving the rocks until only the roots of the ancient mountains remain.

The boundary between the Coastal Plain and upland Piedmont, which forms the doorstep for the Blue Ridge Mountains to the west, runs roughly along the eastern side of Rock Creek Park. Alluvial deposits of both Coastal Plain and Piedmont are found within the park, making it an excellent area for those interested in geological formations and deposits.

From late winter through autumn, wildflowers decorate the park. They blossom most profusely during the spring months of April and May, but skunk cabbage, bloodroot and fawn lily may begin blooming as early as February and March. Virginia bluebells and golden groundsel appear in late April. On drier ridges, mountain laurel and pinxter bloom azalea are found, along with hepatica and the rare trailing arbutus.

Aquatic life along Rock Creek and its tributaries consists of over 36 species of fish. Eels, dusky salamanders and crayfish, as well as an occasional turtle and frog, inhabit the waters. Other types of wildlife living here include the gray squirrel, raccoon, flying squirrel, white-footed mouse, weasel, muskrat, fox, beaver and opossum. White-tailed deer are sometimes seen. A few nonpoisonous snakes live here.

It's also a great birding place. The white-throated sparrow, woodthrush, bluejay, pileated woodpecker, downy woodpecker, Carolina chickadee, mallard, wood duck, towhee, redstart, nuthatch, crow and cardinal are among those sharing the park's environs. Louisiana waterthrushes and veeries nest along the streams.

During earlier times, black bear, deer, American elk, wolves, wild turkey and the eastern bison roamed these woods. About the same time, the Algonquin Indians lived in villages near the Potomac and Anacostia rivers and hunted and fished. Along the shady banks of Piney Branch, in the southern section of the park, the Algonquins dug out rounded quartzite stones which they used to fashion weapons and tools. But there is virtually no evidence today of the quarries.

Later, as the white man came into this territory, gristmills and sawmills were established, utilizing the waters of Rock Creek to power the machinery. Area farmers brought grains—corn, wheat and rye—to the gristmill to be ground into meal or flour. Many of the early homes of the greater Washington area were fashioned of timbers from Rock Creek sawmills.

Remnants of later historical activity in Rock Creek Park include Fort DeRussy, one of the Washington defenses in the Civil War. Fort DeRussy stands northeast of the intersection of Oregon Avenue and Military Road, but can be reached only on foot. The small log cabin of poet Joaquin Miller is also in the park. Miller, mostly associated with California and acclaimed for his "Song of the Sierras," lived in Washington for several years. His cabin is located on Beach Drive, just north of the Military Road overpass.

A good place to learn about the natural history of the area is the **Rock Creek Nature Center** near the Military Road western entrance to the park. Featured among its exhibits are flora and fauna found in Rock Creek Park, live animals and insects and a working beehive. There are also an auditorium, planetarium (the only one in the National Park System) and nature trails, with guided nature walks and slide presentations offered regularly throughout the year. The center's hours vary, so call 202-426-6828 before visiting to be sure. No entrance fee.

Sight-Seeing

Although the park is more suitable for hiking, it can be delightful to tour by automobile. A good stop is at Pierce Mill, an old gristmill established about 1820 and now open to the public. Pause to visit the rustic log cabin of poet Joaquin Miller, have a picnic, or make short expeditions into the more remote portions of the park. You can follow a 10-mile drive through the park, where you will see the waters of Rock Creek splashing over rocks and boulders and colonies of ducks swimming and fluttering about.

You also may drive through stream fords (slow down and test your brakes after each crossing). Several scenic vistas along Rock Creek are worth parking to see; watch for them as you drive. Weekdays are best for the motorist; the park is less crowded then, except during rush hours. Much of Beach Drive is closed to automobiles on the weekends. The better parts for sight-seeing by car lie north of Military Road.

Hiking

Only day hiking is permitted in the park (there are no campsites, nor are you allowed to camp here), but this park offers some of the best hiking in greater Washington. Nearly 15 miles of hiking trails traverse many sections of the park. These trails are maintained with the assistance of the Potomac Appalachian Trail Club. A 5.2-mile long blue-blazed trail runs along the eastern side of the creek from the Maryland line to Bluff Bridge and is rated moderately easy. Along the western ridge of the park runs the green-blazed trail that is 4.3 miles long and strenuous. Tan-blazed trails connect the two. Maps are available from the Nature Center and the Visitor Information Center, located off Beach Drive just south of Military Road, or from the park headquarters near the Nature Center on Glover Road.

Hikers who might want to search for one of the original historical boundary markers in the northwest corner of the park can follow a footpath leading about 100 yards from the trail through the woodland to where it is located. A park ranger could mark the location of the boundary marker for you on a map. The boundary is not of the park but is a survey marker between the District of Columbia and the state of Maryland. During warm weather months, take insect repellent and wear comfortable shoes for traversing all kinds of trails. In some places it can be muddy, slippery or even wet. The trails go up and down grades and cross the creek via several bridges. Riders may use the bridle paths.

Jogging

An exercise course is located in the woods along Rock Creek, just south of the National Zoological Park. Along its 1.5-mile oval route are 18 calisthenics stations, each with a sign illustrating how to do the prescribed exercise. The path starts near the intersection of Cathedral Avenue and Rock Creek Parkway, N.W. (also known as Shoreham Hill).

Bicycling and Horseback Riding

The paved bike route begins along the western boundary of the nature center's grounds, southeast of the intersection of Glover and Military roads, N.W. It is 8.4 miles long and the southern part is particularly easy, while the northern part is moderately difficult. You may park your car at the nature center. The bike path is well marked on free Park Service maps of Rock Creek Park. You should obtain one before setting out, or ask about the route at the nature center or park headquarters. On weekends and adjoining holidays 7:00 A.M.–7:00 P.M. sections of Beach Drive are open to bicycles and closed to motor vehicles. No bicycles are available for rent in the park, but they can be rented elsewhere in the Washington area. Check the Yellow Pages of the phone directory for a bike rental agency.

About 11 miles of wide, graveled bridle paths traverse a varied park landscape. Rock Creek Horse Center, near the Nature Center on Glover, offers rental horses and riding instruction. Riding through Rock Creek Park after the leaves have changed color in the fall, in a spring shower or just after a snowstorm is an experience well worth the effort. Call ahead for reservations.

Picnicking

About 30 picnic groves with tables are scattered throughout the park. You should bring your own fuel. At several groves, small shelters are provided and some of these can be reserved in advance. Fires are permitted only in designated picnic areas.

How To Get There: Numerous roads crisscross Rock Creek Park. Travel north on 16th Street, N.W. (picked up just north of Lafayette Square in downtown Washington) and turn left (west) on either Park Road, N.W., or farther north, on Military Road, N.W. Both roads cut through the park and intersect Beach Drive. Beach Drive passes all the way through Rock Creek Park in a generally north-south direction, following the twisting path of Rock Creek. Several side roads lead off Beach Drive into various parts of the park. To reach the Nature Center or the Visitor Information Center, go to Military Road and follow the signs.

For Additional Information:
Superintendent, Rock Creek Park
3545 Williamsburg Lane, N.W.
Washington, DC 20008
(202) 282-1063

Naturalist, Rock Creek Nature Center
5200 Glover Road, N.W.
Washington, DC 20015
(202) 426-6829

Superintendent, Rock Creek Regional Park
Maryland-National Capital Park and Planning Commission
8787 Georgia Avenue
Silver Spring, MD 20907
(301) 948-5053

Rock Creek Park Horse Center
(202) 362-0117

Thompson Boat House-Bike Rentals and Boats
(202) 333-9543

Theodore Roosevelt Island

Roosevelt Island is perhaps the most dramatic example of wilderness within the metropolitan area. In few other places can you immerse yourself in a natural setting so deeply—and within ten minutes' drive of downtown Washington. Cloaked in deep forests of sycamore, oak, hickory, elm, dogwood, maple and ash, the island is composed of several ecological systems. Parts of it are marsh, swamp, upland wood and rocky shore. Because of this variety, it provides an interesting ecological study of the various types of plant growth and geological formations.

One-half mile long and one-fourth mile wide, the island is separated from the shoreline of the District of Columbia by the main stream of the Potomac; along the Virginia side runs a portion of the Potomac that is locally called Little River. The island was purchased in 1931 by the Theodore Roosevelt Memorial Association and presented a year later as a gift to the American people. It was not until 1960, however, that Congress approved funds for a permanent memorial and the monument was dedicated in 1967. The sculptor, Paul Manship, formed the 23-foot statue of President Roosevelt in a characteristically vigorous pose, and Eric Gugler designed a complex consisting of granite shafts, moat and terrace. Flanking the statue on the oval terrace are four granite tablets suitably inscribed with Roosevelt's philosophy on nature, manhood, youth and the state. During the summer months, two decorative fountains shoot spouts of water 20 feet into the air. There are no picnic areas in the park, but many people bring their lunches and eat on the terrace of the monument.

The surrounding water and the marshland attract a wide diversity of wildlife to this 88-acre island. This wild refuge is a haven for wood thrush, rabbit, groundhog, chipmunk, squirrel, beaver, red-tailed hawk, great owl, turtle, frog and opossum. Cattails, arrow-arum and pickerelweed in the marsh areas provide habitat for the marsh wren, red-winged blackbird and kingfisher. Willow, ash and maple trees root on the mudflats, creating the swamp environment favored by the raccoon searching for crayfish. Red and gray fox are sometimes seen here, particularly in the upland portions of the island. Occasionally, deer are seen on the island, but none are thought to make this a permanent habitat. Wood duck visit and nest there too and there are some pileated woodpeckers. Of special interest is the swamp trail, a boardwalk trail at the southern end of the island. This goes by a rare tidal freshwater marsh, shaded by cypress trees. You will also see yellow flag and crimson wildflowers nearby.

Roosevelt Island and Little Island—a smaller island located off the downstream tip of Roosevelt Island—are administered by the National Park Service, which provides brochures free of charge in a dispenser box at the bulletin board on the island. The brochures give some of the history and the natural history of the island. During the summer months, National Park Service rangers conduct group hikes.

Hiking

You can hike the 2.5 miles of nature trails that circumvent the island's various ecosystems. Public restrooms are located near the lower end of the island on the outer rim trail. During the summer, take insect repellent, since the mosquitoes can make you miserable. The trails are well marked, but the portions leading through the marsh and swamp can be treacherous and slippery during wet weather. Drinking water is available on the island during the summer months; at other times, carry your own. Pets must be on a leash. Bicycles are not permitted on the islands, but the parking lot here is an excellent starting point for a bicycle trip down the Virginia side of the Potomac on the Mount Vernon Trail or northwest toward Leesburg on the W&OD Trail which meet here.

Canoeing

You can canoe around the entire area of both Little Island and Roosevelt Island. Remember, the waters here are affected by the tides and will fluctuate. There are no canoe rentals nearby, so bring your own.

How To Get There: Take the George Washington Memorial Parkway exit north from the Theodore Roosevelt Bridge, which crosses the southern tip of the island. Access to the parking lot is from only the northbound lane of the parkway. A footbridge leads to the island from the parking lot on the Virginia shore of the Potomac. The **Mount Vernon Trail** and **Potomac Heritage Trail** (described elsewhere under Virginia) now connect to the Roosevelt Island bridge. This dedicated paved hiker/biker path connects to a pedestrian bridge to the west and goes south to Mount Vernon. The island can also be reached by canoe or small boat. Little Island can not be reached except by canoe or small boat. Open daily, 8:00 A.M. until dark.

For Additional Information:
Superintendent, George Washington Memorial Parkway
Turkey Run Park
McLean, VA 22101
(703) 285-2600
http://www.nps.gov/gwmp

U.S. Botanic Garden

Visitors to Capitol Hill will enjoy a change of pace at the U.S. Botanic Garden, just south of the Capitol's Reflecting Pool. It includes a conservatory, outdoor gardens and greenhouse facilities about six miles away. Through its classes, displays, special exhibits and flower shows, the U.S. Botanic Garden delivers dramatic lessons about the importance of plants to humankind and the environment.

The 65-year-old Conservatory is currently closed for major renovation until late in the year 2000 and all public programs have been discontinued until then. The plans include a new entrance from Independence Avenue, new exhibits, and improved amenities. Exhibits in the west half of the building will focus on the importance of plants to people. Themes within the glass houses will emphasize plant conservation and endangered species, plant discoveries, orchids and tropical medicinal plants. Case exhibits will explore how plants have influenced the development of civilization, the therapeutic value of plants, and how plants are represented in the arts. Exhibits in the east half of the Conservatory will focus on ecology and evolutionary biology of plants. Glass house themes will include representation of primitive plants in a reconstructed Jurassic landscape, an oasis and plants of the desert. The former Palm House will be recreated as a jungle. The former Subtropical House will become an expanded exhibit of economic plants focusing attention on how the diversity of plants supports the vast majority of our food, fiber, cosmetic, and industrial products.

The **National Garden**, constructed on three acres west of the Conservatory will open at the same time. This outdoor display will feature the First Ladies Water Garden, a formal Rose Garden, and a Showcase Garden of native plants of the mid-Atlantic region with the spectrum of habitats from bog to stream to pond to woodland. Next door will be the **Senator John Heinz Environmental Learning Center** where visitors can hear lectures, and participate in workshops and demonstrations.

Another worthwhile attraction is **Bartholdi Park**, across Independence Avenue from the Conservatory. The large Bartholdi fountain designed by Frederic Auguste Bartholdi, designer of the Statue of Liberty, is the focal point. A variety of herbs, perennials, annuals, and shrubs combine their colors and fragrances in the area that has become a favorite for daytime strolls and musings at lunch.

The original Conservatory's glass structure was modeled after London's Crystal Palace, and its masonry facade is modeled after Versailles. In the summer, the 29,000 square feet of glass is white-washed to protect the plants from the intense sun; the building looks like a translucent castle. The Conservatory's first forerunner was a greenhouse built in 1842 to house the plants brought back from the South Seas by Captain Charles Wilkes. The current facility is about 60 years old.

How To Get There: The Botanic Garden is located at First Street and Maryland Avenue, S.W., below the west side of the

The large fountain across Independence Avenue from the Conservatory was sculpted by Frederic August Bartholdi, designer of the Statue of Liberty.
Architect of the Capitol

Capitol. It is accessible via public transportation, The Federal Center SW Metrorail Station is three blocks from the Garden. Metrobus stops at Independence and First Street, S.W. The Garden is open year-round daily, 9:00 A.M.–5:00 P.M. The Conservatory is closed until late in the year 2000 for a major renovation, and all programs suspended until then.

For Additional Information:
Public Programs Coordinator, U.S. Botanic Garden
245 First Street, S.W., Washington, DC 20024
(202) 225-8333 (Public Programs Office) (202) 225-7099 (recording)

Washington National Cathedral Grounds

The spacious 57 acres surrounding the Washington National Cathedral are called the Close. The Bishop's Garden, including the Hortulus or "little garden" of ninth century herbs, the shadow house, two perennial borders and a rose garden, and the Olmsted Woods are part of the Close. Frederick Law Olmsted, Jr. was Cathedral landscape architect from 1907, when the cornerstone was laid, to 1928.

Florence Brown Bratenahl, wife of the Cathedral's Dean, continued Olmsted's work after his departure in 1928. Earlier, in 1916, she founded All Hallows Guild "to provide for the care and beautification of the gardens and grounds of Washington National Cathedral," a mission the Guild continues today with fundraising and oversight of all landscape design and replanting.

The gardens are designed to reflect the Gothic style of a 14th-century cathedral. You enter through a replica of the original 12th-century Norman arch onto a stone path lined with boxwood. Some of the original boxwood in the Bishop's Garden is from George Washington's Hayfield Manor and Ellerslie Plantation in Virginia. The path leads through a 12th-century Norman carriage arch and court to the Bishop's lawn, part of the Gardens. From the lawn, paths lead to the Shadow House, built with stones from President Grover Cleveland's summer home, the Hortulus, and other "rooms" of the Gothic gardens.

Within the upper perennial garden lies a Wayside Cross inscribed with the sacred monogram for Jesus and dating from early Christian pilgrimages in France. The cross once reminded medieval Christians of their faith and helped direct pilgrims along the roads.

Southwest of the Wayside Cross is an Old English sundial sitting atop a 13th-century Gothic capital discovered in monastery ruins near Rheims Cathedral in France. Leaving the garden through the east gate you come to the 51 Pilgrim Steps leading up to the Cathedral or down to the statue of George Washington by the sculptor Herbert Hazeltine. Florence Bratenahl designed the steps in 1930.

A path behind the statue of George Washington leads through the Olmsted Woods, all that remains of the oak and beech forest which originally covered the Close when Washington first suggested a "great church for national purposes in the capital city." All Hallows Guild has begun a five year restoration process costing more than $500,000 to bring the Woods back to its original state. The path crosses a Japanese bridge and winds around the hill through the Woods.

Near the little sanctuary of the St. Albans School for Boys is an unusual tree brought from Glastonbury, England. Known as the Glastonbury Thorn, it possesses an interesting legend. According to this legend, the tree blooms only when royalty visits the Cathedral.

One of the oldest buildings on the Close is the small, octagonal Herb Cottage on the Cathedral's south side, near the entrance to the Bishop's Garden. The cottage is a gift shop run by the All Hallows Guild, but originally was the Cathedral baptistry. Renovated in 1997, the Herb Cottage is filled with scented oils, jams, jellies, specialty teas, card, dried herbs, ceramic dishes, flowerpots, and seasonal goods.

At the east end of the Cathedral is the Greenhouse where you can find a wide array of herbs, houseplants and in season perennial and annual plants, hanging baskets and outdoor pots.

How To Get There: From Georgetown in Northwest Washington, head north on Wisconsin Avenue to its intersection with Massachusetts Avenue. The entrance to the Cathedral is on Wisconsin just north of this intersection. The Cathedral is located on Mount Saint Alban, 400 feet above sea level, one of the highest points in the District of Columbia. The gardens are open daily, dawn to dusk.

For Additional Information:
Washington National Cathedral
Massachusetts and Wisconsin Avenue, N.W.
Washington, DC 20016
(202) 537-6200
http://www.cathedral.org/cathedral

The C&O Canal Towpath offers hiking, bicycling, and horseback riding for more than a hundred miles from Washington. *United States Department of the Interior National Park Service Photo*

United States Department of the Interior National Park Service Photo

NATURAL ATTRACTIONS IN
MARYLAND

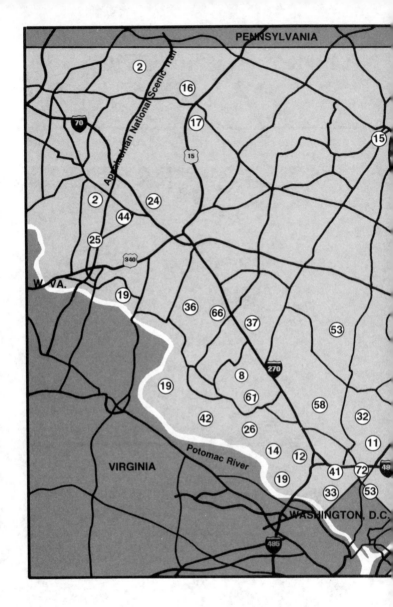

MARYLAND – NORTH

Note: Attractions not listed below appear on the following Maryland map.

1. Anacostia Tributary Trail System
2. Appalachian National Scenic Trail
4. Baltimore and Annapolis Trail Park
5. Baltimore Zoo
6. Battle Creek Cypress Swamp
7. Behnke Nurseries
8. Black Hill Regional Park
11. Brookside Gardens, Brookside Nature Center and Wheaton Regional Park
12. Cabin John Regional Park, Cabin John Trail, and Locust Grove Nature Center

15. Carroll County Farm Museum
16. Catoctin Mountain Park and Cunningham Falls State Park
17. Catoctin Wildlife Preserve and Zoo
19. Chesapeake & Ohio Canal National Historical Park
20. Cylburn Arboretum
22. Eastern Neck National Wildlife Refuge
24. Gambrill State Park
25. Gathland State Park
26. Great Falls and The Billy Goat Trail
27. Greenbelt Park
28. Gunpowder Falls State Park
29. Gwynnbrook Wildlife Management Area
31. Hugg-Thomas Wildlife Management Area

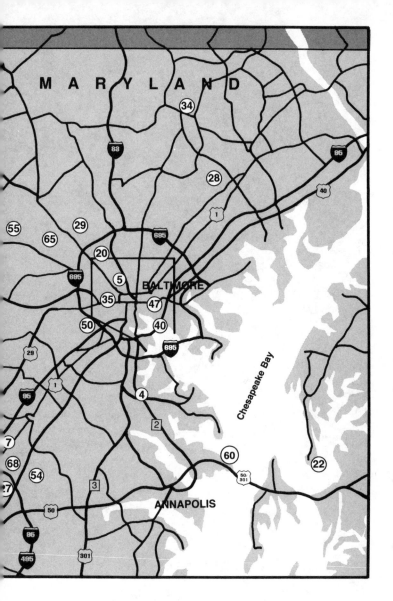

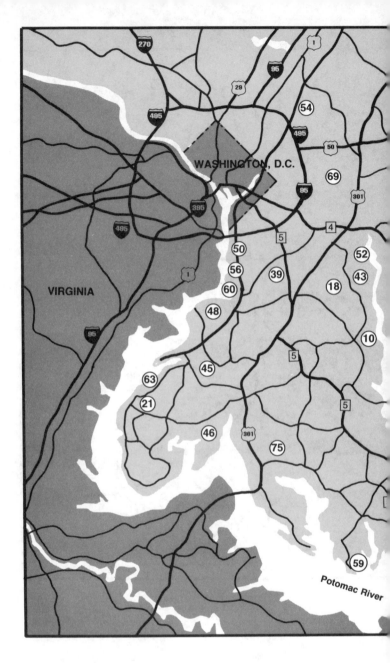

MARYLAND – SOUTH

3. Assateague Island National Seashore
   and Chincoteague National Wildlife
   Refuge
6. Battle Creek Cypress Swamp
9. Blackwater National Wildlife Refuge
10. Bowen Wildlife Management Area
   and Aquasco Farm
13. Calvert Cliffs State Park
14. Calvert Marine Museum
18. Cedarville State Forest

21. Doncaster State Forest
22. Eastern Neck National Wildlife Refuge
23. Flag Ponds Nature Park
30. Helen Avalynne Tawes Garden
38. London Town
39. Louise F. Cosca Regional Park and
   Clearwater Nature Center Herb Garden
43. Merkle Wildlife Sanctuary and Visitor
   Center
45. Myrtle Grove Wildlife Management
   Area
46. Nanjemoy Marsh Sanctuary

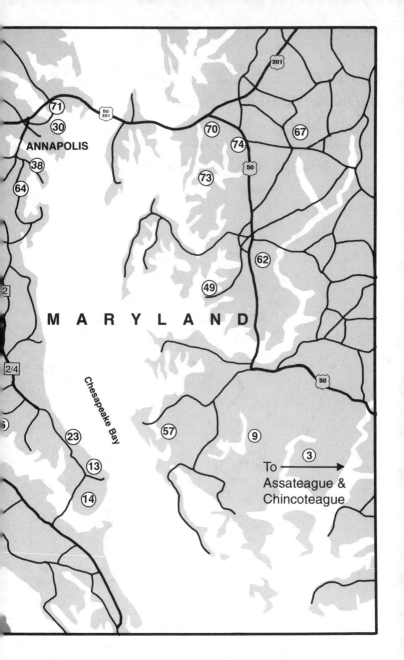

Anacostia Tributary Trail System
including Northwest Branch, Northeast Branch and Indian Creek Parks

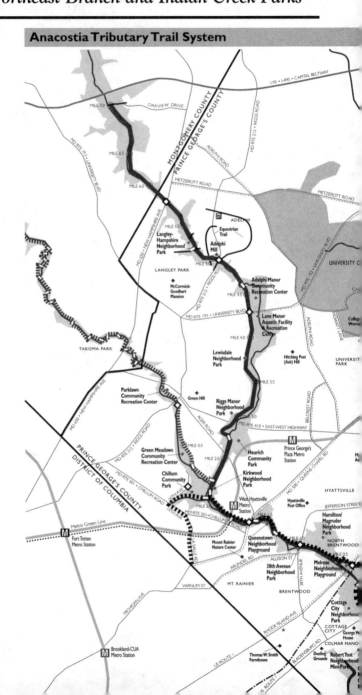

The new Anacostia Tributary Trail System is a network of over 17 miles of interconnected hiker/biker trails through stream valley parks in Prince Georges County in the vicinity of College Park, plus more than 12 additional miles along Sligo Creek in Montgomery County. The Maryland National Capital

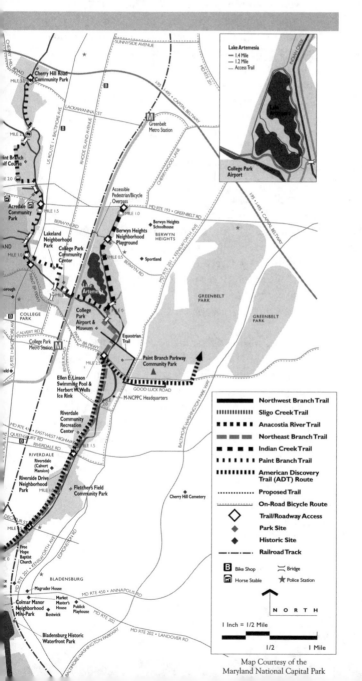

Map Courtesy of the
Maryland National Capital Park

Park and Planning Commission upgraded and connected trails through the Northwest Branch, the Northeast Branch, Indian Creek, Paint Branch and Sligo Creek, all tributaries of the Anacostia River.

The Anacostia River, tributaries and nearby areas have been greatly improved over the past decade. These trails offer a chance to get some exercise, see some wildlife and could even be used by some to commute. Most of the trails run through wooded areas alongside the streams; the woods are typically red maple, red and white oak, beech and hickory, with typical suburban woodland fauna.

The trails are wide asphalt paved paths that are well suited to bicycling and reasonably barrier free for handicapped access.

Fishermen catch perch, catfish and bass in the streams.

Hiking, Biking, and Horseback Riding

These are excellent trails for distance biking or hiking in an urban park setting. The map shows the major trails. It is recommended that you call or write the MNCPPC (see below) for a more detailed free map, if you plan to ride the trail system much. Beyond the map, the Sligo Creek trail goes through Takoma Park to Wheaton and Wheaton Regional Park. Someday there will be a link from the Northwest Branch Trail to the Metropolitan Branch Trail (see Capital Crescent Trail under DC).

How To Get There: Take the Washington Beltway to Kenilworth Avenue, Route 201 south (Greenbelt). Turn right (west) at Greenbelt Road to access the Greenbelt Road State Parkway, which joins the park's hiker/biker trail at the northern end of the park. Turn right on Decatur Street and then left on Alt. US 1 to reach the trail system hub. Or turn right off almost any side street from Kenilworth Avenue to intersect the park. Maps of the park are available in the MNCPPC at 6600 Kenilworth Avenue (about 2.2 miles south of Greenbelt Road) during business hours.

For Additional Information:
Public Information Officer or Trail Co-ordinator
The Maryland-National Capital Park and Planning Commission
Prince George's County
6600 Kenilworth Avenue,
Riverdale, MD 20737
(301) 699-2407
(301) 699-2544 (TTY)
http://www.mncppc.org

Appalachian National Scenic Trail

The Appalachian Trail has been called "a gift of nature Americans give themselves" because it was built and is maintained primarily by volunteers. The movement began in 1921 when Benton MacKaye, a regional planner and Harvard-trained forester conceived the idea of linking existing trails and building new ones along the ridges of the Appalachian Mountains.

APPALACHIAN TRAIL
MARYLAND

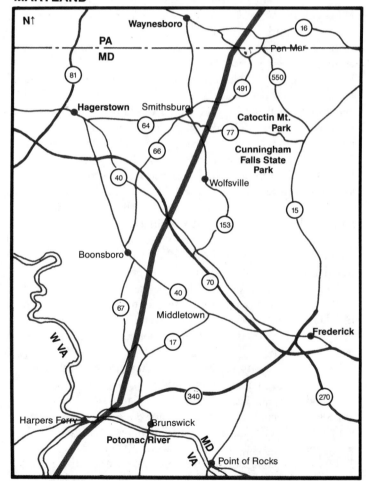

The Appalachian Trail Conference was formed in 1925 to coordinate these efforts. Completed 12 years later by volunteers from the local trail clubs and crews from the Civilian Conservation Corps, the trail crosses 14 states, 8 national forests, 6 other units of the National Park System, about 60 state parks and scores of community parks.

In 1968, Congress designated the trail the first "national scenic trail" and authorized money to purchase land around the trail. Extending for more than 2,160 miles from Springer Mountain, Georgia, to Mount Katahdin in central Maine, it is one of the longest continuously marked trails in the world. A short portion of it passes within the 50-mile radius we have included in this book. That portion is worth mentioning, however, for it might encourage you to continue hiking along other portions of the trail. The part discussed here extends from just south of Harpers Ferry, West Virginia, to the area near Pen Mar in western Maryland (described elsewhere).

In 1986, the AT was rerouted to pass through, instead of around, Harpers Ferry. The AT now crosses the Shenandoah River on the US 340 bridge (westbound) from Loudoun Heights, which overlooks Harpers Ferry from the south. The AT goes though the historic district of Harpers Ferry, passing the firehouse where John Brown made his final stand during his famous 1859 raid. The AT crosses the Potomac River on the Goodloe Byron Memorial Footbridge on the same bridge as the Norfolk & Western and the B&O railroads. On the Maryland side of the bridge is a spiral staircase down to the Chesapeake & Ohio Canal towpath. The AT follows the towpath to the right for 2.5 miles downriver toward Washington.

However, to the left (upriver) is the very scenic "Needles" section of the Potomac and the trailhead for the trail to historic Maryland Heights, which overlooks Harpers Ferry.

The AT crosses under US 340 and, leaving the canal behind at Weverton, climbs Weverton Heights to the top of a ridge. Excellent views of the Potomac River's gorges and Harpers Ferry may be enjoyed from lookout points found at intervals along the trail here.

From atop Weverton Heights, the trail proceeds north along South Mountain, passing through three Maryland state parks—Gathland (described elsewhere), Washington Monument and Greenbrier—before leaving the Old Line State at Pen Mar. There is a total of 39 miles of this famed trail in Maryland, with five shelters along this stretch. Every year about 300 persons (of about 1,500 who try) complete the "thru-hike" of the entire trail in one five-to-six month time period, but this requires a great deal of stamina. For those interested in doing this, the Potomac Appalachian Trail Club and the Appalachian Trail Conference offer maps and guide books as well as advice and information. Thanks to the more than 4,000 volunteers who maintain it every year, the trail is kept in excellent condition and provides an outstanding hiking experience for millions of visitors each year.

How To Get There: For access from Harpers Ferry, see the **Harpers Ferry** entry under West Virginia. For access to other areas of the Appalachian Trail in Maryland refer to the detailed maps available from the Potomac Appalachian Trail Club or Appalachian Trail Conference (below).

For Additional Information: Please refer to the Appalachian National Scenic Trail entries under Virginia and West Virginia; also refer to Harpers Ferry under West Virginia, Shenandoah National Park and Sky Meadows Park under Virginia.

PATC Headquarters and Bookstore
Monday–Thursday 7:00 A.M.–9:00 P.M.
Thursdays and Fridays NOON–2:00 P.M.
118 Park Street, SE, Vienna, VA 22180-0469
(703) 242-0315 (Store or General Information Tape)
(703) 242-0965 (Outings Tape)
(703) 242-0693 Headquarters main number
(703) 242-0968 Fax
http://patc.simplenet.com/

Appalachian Trail Conference
Information Center & Bookstore open 9:00 A.M.—5:00 P.M. Monday through Friday; Saturday and Sunday 9:00 A.M.–4:00 P.M. mid-May through October
Washington & Jackson streets
P.O. Box 807,   Harpers Ferry, WV 25425
(304) 535-6331
info@atconf.org
http://www.atconf.org/

Appalachian National Scenic Trail
National Park Service Project Office
c/o Harpers Ferry Center
P.O. Box 50,
Harpers Ferry, WV 25425-0050
(304)-535-6278
http://www.nps.gov/aptr/

Assateague Island National Seashore and Chincoteague National Wildlife Refuge

Assateague and Chincoteague are must-see sites for amateur naturalists in the Capital area, even though they are far outside of our usual 50-mile limit. Assateague Island National Seashore includes the National Park, the Maryland State Park and the Chincoteague National Wildlife Refuge. It is one of only 10 national seashores in the U.S. and one of our national treasures. Assateague Island is a barrier island on the Atlantic; its exact shape and size change as the winds and currents add sand here and remove it there over the years. White sandy beaches merge into grassland dunes. Behind that, grassy dunes transition into myrtle brush, then loblolly pine, then scattered hardwoods on higher ground. Lowlands become salt meadows, marshes or bays.

The dominant mammals on the island are the famous "wild ponies of Chincoteague," feral horses, descendants of domesticated animals which have been wild for many decades; they are

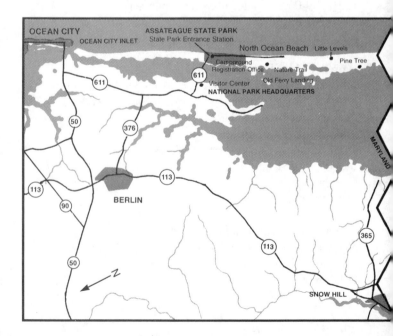

frequently seen at dawn and dusk, especially along the drive on the Maryland end. The Sika elk (*cervus nippon*), natives of Japan, were released here in the 1920s. They are about half the size of domestic deer and abundant on the island; you can usually see them poking out from the scrub forests beside the road, especially on the drive to Chincoteague refuge. Delmarva Peninsula fox squirrel, an endangered species about twice the size of the common gray squirrel, breeds in the woods here.

Other animals found on the island include several species of turtles, a number of snakes, especially the hognose and rat snakes (none poisonous) and frogs. Many types of crustaceans inhabit the waters and shoreline. The most conspicuous is the horseshoe crab, dark brown and helmet-shaped, which comes ashore, usually in May, to lay its eggs.

The Chincoteague refuge is a bird watcher's paradise, especially in the fall migration. With its freshwater and marshes, it is one of the best bird watching locales in our area. Herons, egrets, ibis, snow geese, grebes, sanderlings, sandpipers, gulls, turns, dunlins, dowicthers, warblers, redstarts, swallows, vireos red-winged blackbirds and yellowthroat are all abundant in at least one season. About 100 other species are common in at least one season. The Visitors Center has a bird list and recent sightings.

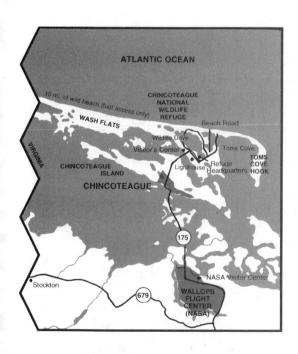

Hiking

Be sure to hike the Wildlife Loop at Chincoteague, especially early in the morning. The Loop is reserved for hikers and bikers until 3:00 P.M. but vehicles are permitted from 3:00 P.M. until dusk. The Wildlife drive is one of the best places to view wildlife, especially migrating songbirds; take many stops. There are several other marked nature trails in the Maryland section too. Of course, walk on the beach—12 miles of Chincoteague Wildlife Refuge beach is "wild" and accessible by foot only.

Camping

There are several backcountry backpack and canoe campsites. All require a $5.00 permit and the closest is 4 miles from parking. Each site has a picnic table and a chemical toilet, but no drinking water or shelter. Bring plenty of water and wear sunscreen and insect repellent.

There are two year-round campgrounds at the Maryland end with toilets, water and cold showers. There are sites for vehicle and tent campers. Call for more details and reservations: (301)641-1441 for the national park; (301) 641-2120 for the state park. There is no camping on Chincoteague National Wildlife Refuge.

Precautions

Don't feed anything to the wildlife. Leave pets at home. Cover your flesh and wear sunscreen in the daytime—the beach sun is intense and there is little shelter.

Beware of ticks and mosquitoes; both are numerous except in cold weather. The deer and ponies carry immense numbers of ticks wherever they go, including the Northern deer tick, known to carry Lyme disease. To avoid ticks, avoid grass, brush and shrubs, where ticks wait to pounce on the next mammal to pass by. If you go off the paved path, wear insect repellent and long sleeves tucked in; even then, check yourself carefully for ticks.

Where to Stay

There are numerous small motels in the city of Chincoteague, just minutes by car, or a modest walk or bike ride from the refuge. Rates are very seasonal, and rooms fill up in the summer. Rooms are usually cheap and plentiful except during the summer months, but book ahead to be sure. In Maryland, Ocean City is about 10 miles from the national park headquarters.

Boating and Fishing

Canoes and low-powered boats can be rented in the city of Chincoteague or Ocean City for use on the bay side. Ask about local conditions before heading out. It is illegal to land in some places.

How To Get There: For Assateague, take US 50 east from Washington across the Chesapeake Bay Bridge through Easton, Cambridge and Salisbury. Turn right (south) on MD 611 a few miles before Ocean City and follow the signs for Assateague State Park and Assateague National Seashore.

To reach Chincoteague, take US 50 east to Salisbury. From there take US 13 south through Pokomoke City to SR 175 to the city of Chincoteague; follow the signs to the refuge and Assateague Island. Drive slowly on the island. The entrance fee is $5.00 per car, but Golden Eagle cards are honored. The Wildlife Refuge is open May through September, 5:00 A.M.–10:00 P.M.; October and April, 6:00 A.M.–8:00 P.M.; November through March, 6:00 A.M.–6:00 P.M. Pets are totally prohibited; even on a leash they can disturb wildlife.

For Additional Information:
Superintendent
Assateague Island National Seashore
7206 National Seashore Lane
Berlin, MD 21811
(410) 641-1441 or 641-3030
http://www.nps.gov

Superintendent
Assateague State Park
7303 Stephen Decatur Highway
Berlin, MD 21811
(410) 641-2120

Refuge Manager
Chincoteague National Wildlife Refuge
P.O. Box 62
Chincoteague, VA 23336
(757) 336-6122

Baltimore and Annapolis Trail Park

The B&A Trail Park officially opened in October 1990; it follows the former B&A Railroad right of way, replacing the rails with a ten-foot-wide paved hiker/biker path. The path has gentle inclines, so is accessible by wheelchair and baby stroller. Over 13 miles of gently sloping trail through open space and wooded areas make up the B&A Trail. Starting at Dorsey Road and ending at US Route 50, the B&A Trail parallels Route 2 and passes through woods, urban and suburban sections. Dotted with rest areas providing benches, picnic tables and bicycle racks, the trail is designed to give cyclists a clearly marked and safe path from Baltimore to Annapolis. Split-rail fences protect riders from highways and ravines. Although there are no restrooms or water fountains, the trail passes several malls and riders are welcome to use the facilities.

Park rangers patrol the entire trail on a daily basis. Restrooms are found at Earleigh Heights Ranger Station; water fountains are at Oak Street, Jones Station Road, Chestnut Street, Earleigh Heights and Riggs Road. Park patrons are welcome at several malls and numerous fast food places near the park.

A major addition to the "rails to trails" system is expected in the not too distant future. The Washington Baltimore & Annapolis Electric Railroad Company tracks which run from Baltimore to DC through Anne Arundel and Prince George's counties were abandoned in 1935, but the right of way still exists. Local governments are acquiring rights to the former rail-

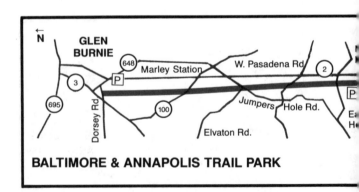

BALTIMORE & ANNAPOLIS TRAIL PARK

road right-of-way and funding to convert it to a hiker/biker trail, like the existing B&A Trail. Hopefully, there will be a **WB&A** Trail park soon; maybe we'll even be able to "commute" by bike to DC or Baltimore from PG and Anne Arundel suburbs.

How To Get There: From Washington, take Route 50 east toward Annapolis to Maryland Route 2. Take Route 2 north 3 miles, turn left on Jones Station Road. Park in the MTA Park & Ride lot (free) and cross the street to the Anne Arundel Historical Society in a white brick building. The B&A Trail runs behind the Historical Society. Ask inside for information.

There are a number of places to park along the trail. In Glen Burnie, the trail passes two major malls and a free indoor parking garage. In Pasadena there is another mall where park visitors are welcome to park. A newly constructed commuter lot is available in Severna Park. In addition, two lots specifically for park visitors have been built. The first is located at Earleigh Heights Road adjacent to the ranger station, and the second lot is on Route 450 at the southern end of the trail. Since the park is closed at night, park rangers lock these lots at dusk.

For More Information:
Baltimore and Annapolis Trail Park
P.O. Box 1007
Severna Park, MD 21146
(410) 222-6244

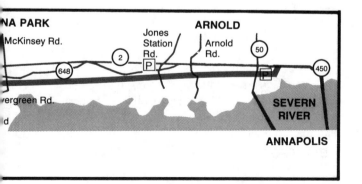

Baltimore Zoo

Chartered in 1876, the Baltimore Zoo is the third oldest in the United States and home to over 2,250 birds, mammals and reptiles. Set amid 180 acres of beautifully landscaped hills and valleys, the zoo has more than 251 species including 16 listed by the U.S. Fish and Wildlife Service as threatened or endangered. The new Children's Zoo has been called the finest in the world. It has 100 different species and 6 different habitats—the Farmyard, Marsh Aviary, Tree, River, Cave and Meadow exhibits. The zoo is designed to encourage children to imitate animals in order to learn about them. For example, in the River area children crawl through a beaver lodge and view the otters underwater. In the Farmyard, children can pet a lamb, visit a chicken coop and milk a cow. Pony rides, a Zoo Choo train and a carousel are favorites. Special demonstrations are held at the Children's Zoo most weekends. Over 125 species of reptiles, including iguanas, crocodiles and giant snakes can be found in the Reptile House. A world-famous Crane Conservation Center contains nine rare species of cranes. The zoo has the highest success rate for breeding lion-tailed macaques and specializes in in-vitro fertilization of endangered species. Its black-footed penguin colony is the most productive in the world and has received numerous awards. The penguins are fed at 3:00 P.M. daily. At 2:30 P.M. the elephants demonstrate their routines at the elephant house. Parking is free, and picnic facilities are provided. Maryland school groups are admitted free by prior arrangement.

How To Get There: From downtown Baltimore, take Martin Luther King Boulevard, north. Turn left on McCulloh Street to Druid Hill Park. Follow signs for the Baltimore Zoo. From Exit 23 of the Baltimore Beltway (I-695), take Jones Falls Expressway (I-83) south to the Druid Park Lake Drive exit (Exit 7). Turn west and follow the zoo signs. Parking is free. Open daily, 10:00 A.M.–4:00 P.M. with extended hours in the summer. The Reptile House is closed on Mondays. Admission is $8.50, seniors and children ages 2 to 11 pay $5.00; children under 2 can enter free. On the first Saturday of every month, all children are admitted free before noon.

For Additional Information:
Director
Baltimore Zoo
Druid Hill Park
Baltimore, MD 21217
(410) 396-7102

Battle Creek Cypress Swamp

Battle Creek Cypress Swamp in Calvert County, southeast of Washington is one of the most enchanting places in the area. This swamp began over 10,000 years ago after the last glacier retreated and the climate got warmer. It contains one of the northern-most stands of bald cypress trees in the United States. It sits between the Patuxent River and the Chesapeake Bay, a location that creates a warm microclimate suitable for bald cypress to thrive. Cypress are adapted to a wet environment in a number of ways. The base of the trees is wider relative to their height to support the tree in the wet soil. Characteristic "cypress knees," or roots, protrude from the soil around the trees. Scientists are not sure what purpose they serve, but some believe they give added support to the trees in the mud or that they take in oxygen for the plant, which it can't get from the swamp muck. Bald cypress wood is soft and thick with resin that protects the tree from insects and water rot. Cypress trees can live to be over 1,000 years, but the oldest specimen in this swamp is estimated to be 450 years old. It cannot be seen from the boardwalk.

While the 100-acre swamp is owned and preserved primarily by the Nature Conservancy for a wildlife sanctuary, the local government of Calvert County has constructed a quarter-mile boardwalk that gives visitors the opportunity to enter the swamp and experience the peaceful solitude of this place. Ferns, lady's-slippers, cardinal flowers, lizard's tail and gigantic vines of poison ivy line the boardwalk. It is a sanctuary for all kinds of wildlife—the drumming of the pileated woodpecker echoes through the forest, waves of warblers pass through each spring, and the raccoon, opossum and mink leave their footprints in the mud here.

Numerous reptiles live in the swamp, too, including eight different species of salamanders and mud, painted and spotted turtles. In 1965 the swamp was designated a National Natural

Landmark by the National Park Service. A nature center with exhibits and a helpful staff is located on the road leading to the boardwalk. Although the entire boardwalk can be covered in 15 minutes, it is well worth the time to stop and look carefully at the 100-foot leafy canopy and the 4-foot-wide trees. The best times to visit are in the spring or early summer and in the fall and winter months.

How To Get There: From the Capital Beltway (I-495), take MD 4 east and south through Prince Frederick. About one mile out of Prince Frederick, at Sixes Road (MD 506), turn right (west) and continue for 2 miles to Grays Road. Take a left on Grays Road. One-half mile on the right is the center. The sanctuary is open April through September 10:00 A.M.–5:00 P.M., Tuesday through Saturday, and Sunday 1:00–5:00 P.M. From October through March, it closes at 4:30 P.M.; closed Mondays, Thanksgiving, Christmas, and New Year's Day. No admission charge.

For Additional Information:
Battle Creek Cypress Swamp Sanctuary
c/o Calvert County Courthouse
Prince Frederick, MD 20678
(410) 535-5327

The Nature Conservancy
Maryland Field Office
2 Wisconsin Circle, Suite 600
Chevy Chase, MD 20815-7065
(301) 656-8673

Behnke Nurseries

Millions of plants, including over 170 varieties of trees, 1,500 varieties of houseplants, 350 varieties of annuals, 200 varieties of roses and 1,500 varieties of perennials (the largest collection on the east coast) fill this 12-acre nursery. The staff of up to 200 employees including dozens of horticulturists is knowledgeable and able to answer most gardening questions. One of the finest nurseries on the east coast, Behnke's has been open since 1930 when Albert Behnke started the business in Beltsville. He arrived at the age of 26 in the United States from Germany where his family owned a nursery. He began investigating the gardening and greenhouse business in the United States and soon opened his own nursery.

The nursery is very spacious with over 200,000 feet of greenhouse and a large area outside. Seasonal favorites include the poinsettia display from November to December, and Easter lilies in the spring. Pansies are another specialization for Behnke's. Houseplants including cacti, orchids, bonsai and terrarium plants are emphasized, especially African violets.

Winter and spring weekends feature free lectures at which local and national experts provide garden advice on a wide range of topics. Late spring and summer feature an excellent collection of lily pond plants and supplies.

Whether you are an expert horticulturist, a beginner gardener or just someone who loves the sight of plants you will want to visit Behnke's.

How To Get There: Take the Washington Beltway to the Route 1 Beltsville Exit, North. Behnke's is several miles up Route 1, on the left.

For Additional Information:
The Behnke Nurseries Company
11300 Baltimore Avenue (Route 1)
Beltsville, MD 20705
(301) 937-1100

Black Hill Regional Park

Black Hill Regional Park is one of the newest parks in Montgomery County. Its 1,854 acres are centered around the 505-acre Little Seneca Lake, a lake created by the Maryland-National Capital Park and Planning Commission and the Washington-Suburban Sanitary Commission for the dual purpose of providing recreation and drinking water to the area.

Black Hill has both a developed and a natural area. The developed part, around the lake, has 10 shelters for picnics (with grills and tables), volleyball courts, horseshoe pits, playgrounds, boat rentals, boat launch (only battery-powered motors allowed), water fountains and restrooms. Shelters can be reserved for a fee by calling the Park permit office. The lake has largemouth bass, smallmouth bass, catfish, panfish and forage fish. Fishing is allowed with the appropriate Maryland fishing license; special "trophy largemouth bass regulations" are in effect. A visitor center has many interesting displays of flora, fauna and the natural history of the area. The natural side has large areas of wetlands, mature forests, new growth forests and meadows for wildlife.

Hiking and Bicycling

Several nature trails are available, with access from Lake Ridge Drive and MD 121. A map is available at the visitor center. The trails cover a variety of habitats: second growth hardwood forests, transitional forest area, meadows and wetlands.

Bicyclists can ride on the paved hiker/biker trails along the lakeside. Mountain bikes are permitted on unpaved trails. Please stay on the trails at all times.

How To Get There: Take I-270 north past Gaithersburg to the Clarksburg Exit, MD 121 and go southwest on MD 121 to West Old Baltimore Road; turn left. Turn right on Lake Ridge Drive (marked by a sign for Black Hill Regional Park). The visitor center, lake and most facilities are on a loop drive at the end of Lake Ridge Drive. Parking is allowed in designated areas only, not on the road shoulders.

If you continue on MD 121 past West Old Baltimore Road, you can reach another part of the park. A nature trail starts at MD 121 about midway between Old Baltimore and Little Seneca Lake. Here parking is allowed only on the road shoulders, not on the privately owned streets in the adjacent developments. The hours are 6:00 A.M. to sunset March through October and 7:00 A.M. to sunset November through February.

For More Information:
Park Office, Black Hill Regional Park
20930 Lake Ridge Drive
Boyds, MD 20841
(301) 972-9396
(301) 495-2525 (reservations)
(301) 495-2480 (for picnic shelter reservation information)
Office hours: 7:00 A.M.–3:15 P.M. Monday through Friday
http://www.mncppc.org

Blackwater National Wildlife Refuge

Although Blackwater National Wildlife Refuge is just a shade beyond the 50-mile limit we have established for areas included in this book, we feel it is so outstanding that it should be mentioned anyway. Blackwater is made up of marshland, forest and field. Located 12 miles south of Cambridge on Maryland's Eastern Shore, it was established in 1933 as a migratory waterfowl refuge for birds using the Atlantic Flyway. Containing over 23,000 acres, Blackwater is a major wintering place for Canada geese. Some geese merely stop over, then fly south to areas in the Carolinas and Georgia. But during the peak migration period—October and November—nearly 35,000-40,000 Canada geese and more than 15,000-28,000 ducks may be seen.

Blackwater contains three endangered species: the bald eagle, Delmarva fox squirrel and the peregrine falcon. Blackwater is the foremost breeding center for bald eagles in the bay so sightings of eagles are common. Look toward the top of the loblolly pines on the other side of the marsh from the boardwalk and you may see one of the six or seven pairs that have been seen in the park. Eagles often perch on dead trees at the edge of the marsh looking for food. They eat fish, birds and small mammals that they kill by strangling them or puncturing their organs with their talons. The population of eagles seems to be increasing now that their habitat is becoming more protected, laws against poaching are being enforced and the pesticide DDT, which was adversely affecting their ability to reproduce, has been banned.

Among other types of birds found here are the whistling swan, great blue heron, egrets and woodpeckers, towhees, great-horned owls and brown-headed nuthatches. About twenty different types of ducks are found, including mallard, black, blue-winged teal, green-winged teal, shoveler, American widgeon and wood duck. Snow and blue geese also come this way. The best time to watch waterfowl is mid-October to mid-March during the thaws. Some birds remain through the summer, raising their hatchlings there, while others arrive in the spring searching for food. White-tailed deer, raccoon, opossum, otter, red fox, skunk, muskrat and nutria live here; so do the exotic Sika deer from Japan. The Wildlife Interpretive Center provides exhibits and an auditorium for special programs. Free refuge maps are available, and a staff naturalist is on hand to tell you the best areas for viewing wildlife on the day of your visit. There is a 5-mile wildlife drive past fresh water impoundments, fields (providing crops for migratory wildfowl and other wildlife) and woodlands managed to provide habitat for the endangered Delmarva Peninsula fox squirrel. An observation tower allows visitors to look out over the marshland at the junction of the Big and Little Blackwater rivers.

Sight-Seeing

The 6.5 mile scenic wildlife drive through the refuge has frequent stopping areas where you are most likely to see wildlife. Drive it slowly and stop frequently; you are virtually guaranteed success in your wildlife-watching. Bicyclists can travel the same drive. During the peak migration season, in October and November, you may also see wildlife on nearby Egypt, Bucktown, and Maple Dam roads, which extend north from the refuge toward Cambridge. They are good roads for leisurely driving.

Hiking

Several woodland walking trails, ideal for bird-watching and nature study, are provided along the wildlife drive and at the picnic area. However, no extensive hiking trails are available. The marsh-edge trail is a 0.3 mile trail that loops through a marsh. The woods trail is a 0.5 mile trail through a hardwood forest. If you wish, you may hike the entire wildlife drive; just be alert for traffic.

How To Get There: From Washington, take US 50 east, across the Chesapeake Bay Bridge, and south to Cambridge. Just east of Cambridge, off US 50 pick up MD 16 south and west to MD 335. A turn to the left onto MD 335 will lead you directly to the refuge, about 4 miles down the road. The refuge is open daily from dawn to dusk, except for the Wildlife Interpretive Center, which is open 8:00 A. M.–4:00 P.M.; weekends 9:00 A.M.–5:00 P.M. Entrance fees are $3.00 per car including motorbikes; $1.00 for pedestrians and bicyclists. The "Duck Stamp" can be used in lieu of the fee for daily entry, as can the BNWR, Golden Access, Golden Eagle and Golden Age Passports.

For Additional Information:
Refuge Manager
Blackwater National Wildlife Refuge
2145 Key Wallace Drive
Cambridge, MD 21613
(410) 228-2677
http://www.gorp.com/gorp/resource/us_nwr

Bowen Wildlife Management Area and Aquasco Farm

The Bowen Wildlife Management Area and the Aquasco Farm adjoin the shores of the Patuxent River in the southern part of Prince George's County. Bowen, under the jurisdiction of the Maryland Department of Natural Resources, is one of the most untouched areas of the Old Line State. Consisting of 310 acres, it is primarily a brackish tidal marsh. Hoards of wild ducks and geese pause here during the autumn and early winter months. During the summer it also supports trillions of mosquitoes. Numerous songbirds are found here too year-round. Many wading birds, such as the great blue heron and egret, use the area during the warm weather months. Although not generally open to the public, you may obtain permission to visit by contacting the Cheltenham Work Center. This area is open to public waterfowl hunting and birdwatching through a permit system. Contact the Cheltenham Work Center for permit information.

Aquasco Farm may be toured by groups only (usually 15 or more in number), although exceptions for smaller numbers are sometimes made. It is a working farm, but there are also stretches of marshland with thriving wildlife. Land is leased to local farmers who raise primarily soybeans and corn, as well as some tobacco. Six miles of wood-edged trails are maintained with volunteer help from the Girl Scouts. The Maryland-National Capital Park and Planning Commission administers this farm.

How To Get There: From Washington, take MD 5 south to MD 381. Turn left (to the southeast) and continue through Poplar Hill to Aquasco Farm Road. A left (east) turn here will lead you to both Bowen and Aquasco Farm. No entrance fee.

For Additional Information:
District Manager
Maryland Department of Natural Resources–Wildlife Division
Myrtle Grove Work Center
(301) 743-5161

Maryland Department of Natural Resources
Wildlife Service
Tawes State Office Building
Annapolis, MD 21401
(410) 260-3195
(800) 825-PARK
http://www.dnr.state.md.us/publiclands

Brookside Gardens, Brookside Nature Center and Wheaton Regional Park

Just 6 miles north of the District of Columbia is Wheaton Regional Park administered by the Maryland-National Capital Park and Planning Commission. Established in 1960, it includes 496 acres of woodland intersected by small brooks. While it is relatively small, it does include some nice natural areas where you can hike, picnic, study wildflowers, look for wildlife or bird-watch. The Nature Center alone is worth a visit. So are the **Brookside Gardens**, featuring 50 acres of outstanding floral displays. In the conservatory, a small stream meanders among lush green tropical trees and plants and masses of colorful annuals and perennials. Banana, coffee and cacao trees grow there. The Boston fern is probably the largest in the world. For the serious gardener there is a fine reference library with over 3,000 volumes on horticulture and gardening. Included in the outdoor areas are an azalea walk, a rose garden with dozens of rose varieties, a trial garden for the testing and evaluation of plants and a fragrance garden featuring plants selected primarily for their taste, texture or aroma. Water plants are featured in the aquatic garden's series of ponds. A Japanese teahouse and garden, on an island in a pond complex, serve as the focal point for the Gude collection of nature tree and plant specimens. The winter garden offers off-season interest.

Educational lectures, tours, trips and workshops are offered March through June and September through December by prior arrangement.

The **Brookside Nature Center** provides naturalist-led environmental education programs. Nature Center exhibits interpret local natural history though live reptile, amphibian and fish displays, the hands-on children's discovery room, insect and mammal displays, and information on current and seasonal environmental issues. The pioneer homestead, wildlife viewing areas, self-guided trail, wheelchair accessible interpretive boardwalk, and native landscape gardens add to the uniqueness of Brookside Nature Center. The self-guided nature trail is one of several that wind through the rolling, heavily wooded parklands. Be sure to spend some time observing the wildlife at the nearby protected nature pond. There's always something interesting, such as a group of the extraordinarily beautiful wood ducks, which frequent the pond; wildlife seems to flock to where it's most welcome. Brookside Nature Center is open Tuesday-Saturday from 9:00 A.M. –5:00 P.M., and Sunday 1:00 A.M.–5:00 P.M.

Wheaton Regional Park also offers play areas, a miniature scenic railroad, horseback and bicycling trails, and, in season, ice-skating. A five-acre lake is stocked with fish but boating and swimming are prohibited.

Hiking, Bicycling, Horseback Riding

Hiking is limited here because of the size of the facility, but you can plan to walk about 4 miles. A bridle path encircles the camping area, and there are two loop bicycling trails. Both horses and bikes may be rented in the park. Children will enjoy the pony rides. Horseback riding lessons are offered for beginners and advanced riders. An indoor arena and 1.6 miles of horse trails are available. Call the Riding Stable for information at (301) 622-3311.

Picnicking

An excellent shaded picnic area with tables and grills is provided at Wheaton Regional Park.

Viewing Gardens

The Brookside Gardens grounds and conservatory are open year-round. Typical flowering dates are as follows:

Gardens	
March–April	bulbs, cherries, crab apples
May	azaleas, rhododendrons, dogwoods, wisteria, vibernums, buckeye, magnolia
June	perennials, herbs, roses
July–September	annuals, perennials, water plants
September–October	chrysanthemums, ornamental grasses, fall foliage, cabbage & kale
Winter	attractive berries, whitchhazel, bark of paperbark maple, yellow and red twig dogwood, white canes of brambles, cream and apricot bark of birch trees

Conservatory Displays	
February–March	bulbs, geraniums, daisies
April	fuchsias, Easter lilies, forced bulbs
May–October	caladiums, impatiens, tropicals
November	Japanese chrysanthemums
December–January	poinsettias, holiday decorations

How To Get To Wheaton Regional Park: From the Capital Beltway (I-495), take MD 97 (Georgia Avenue) north. Turn right (east) onto Shorefield Road, which leads directly to the park. The Park and most facilities are open year-round. Nominal admission fee charged.

How To Get To Brookside Gardens and Brookside Nature Center: Take Georgia Avenue north to Randolph Road, turn right. Look for Glenallan Avenue on your right; turn right and drive approximately .5 mile to the entrance to Brookside Gardens; the entrance to the Nature Center is about 100 yards further. The conservatories are open 10:00 A.M.–5:00 P.M. daily. The grounds are open sunrise to sunset daily. No admission charge. The gardens are partially accessible by wheelchair. Pets, food and drinks are not permitted.

For Additional Information:
Park Manager
Wheaton Regional Park
2000 Shorefield Road
Wheaton, MD 20902
(301) 946-7033
http://www.mncppc.org

Director
Brookside Gardens
1800 Glenallen Avenue
Wheaton, MD 20902
(301) 949-8230

Naturalist
Brookside Nature Center
1400 Glenallen Avenue
Wheaton, MD 20902
(301) 946-9071

Cabin John Regional Park, Cabin John Trail and Locust Grove Nature Center

On Cabin John Creek, one of Montgomery County's major watersheds, is Cabin John Regional Park. This 525-acre park of rolling wooded hills is open year-round. While the park is mainly used for recreation, it does have some good natural qualities. There are multitudes of wildflowers, particularly during the spring and early summer, and a variety of trees including oaks, hickories, sassafras, sycamore, walnut and some pine. The pileated woodpecker, barred owl, raccoon, skunk, opossum, woodchuck, cottontail rabbit and gray squirrel live here, as well as the poisonous copperhead snake. You can hike, picnic or bird-watch. Evening musical concerts are conducted during midsummer free of charge. There are indoor tennis courts, the Locust Grove Nature Center, an ice rink, a miniature train, play grounds, outdoor tennis courts, handball courts and a snack bar.

The Locust Grove Nature Center provides a wide variety of year-round nature events and programs for visitors of all ages. Through exhibits and naturalist-led program you can learn to appreciate our rich cultural and natural history.

Hiking the Cabin John Trail

The Cabin John Trail is a blue-blazed trail maintained by the Potomac Appalachian Trail Club that runs nine miles along the

Cabin John Creek. It is an outstanding hiking trail with an opportunity to see a great variety of wildlife, including deer, a large number of songbirds and a variety of plant species. The trail is almost entirely through mature woods, with the exception of four road crossings and a 0.5-mile section on River Road. With the exception of the last half mile, the trail is easy walking with no steep sections. The north end of the trail is at the end of Goya Drive (Take I-270 to Montrose Exit, west, turn left on Seven Locks Road, then take the first left on Goya Drive). The south end of the trail is by the parking lot at a small developed park by the Clara Barton School on MacArthur Blvd. (Take the Capital Beltway to River Road, north, turn left at the light onto Seven Locks Road, at the end of Seven Locks, turn left on MacArthur Blvd. The park is 0.5 mile on the left, just before the one-lane bridge.) An excellent topographical map of the Cabin John Trail and Potomac Gorge is available for a few dollars at the nature center and at the park manager office.

Camping and Picnicking

A nine-acre area accommodates up to 1,200 picnickers. No ground fires are permitted; grills are provided at some sites. Shelters are available on a first-come basis or you may reserve a shelter. Picnic areas, restrooms and drinking fountains operate only from April through October. Play area restrooms are open year-round. A limited number of tent sites are available only to residents of Montgomery and Prince George's counties. Each secluded site has a charcoal grill, a picnic table and drinking water. No showers. All vehicles must be left in the designated parking lot. Camping is by special permit only.

How To Get There: The Locust Grove Nature Center is on 7777 Democracy Blvd., about 0.25 mile west of Montgomery Mall. Take the Democracy west exit from I-270 and go about 0.25 mile past the mall; the nature center is on the right. From the Capital Beltway (I-495), take Old Georgetown Road north about 2 miles to Tuckerman Lane, turn left (west), and proceed about 1.5 miles. Park entrance (to the playground, train station, picnic areas and trail) is on the left. Other main access points are from Democracy Boulevard and Westlake Drive. Open year-round, sunrise until sunset.

For Additional Information:
Park Manager
Cabin John Regional Park
7400 Tuckerman Lane
Rockville, MD 20852

Locust Grove Nature Center
7777 Democracy Blvd.
Bethesda, MD 20817
(301) 299-1990 (Locust Grove Nature Center)
(301) 495-2525 (Park Permit Office)
http://www.mncppc.org

Calvert Cliffs State Park

The Calvert Cliffs border the western side of Chesapeake Bay in Calvert County; these are Miocene age formations studied by scientists and students along the entire Atlantic coast. Some 30 miles long and up to 120 feet high, they expose a continuous section of clays rich in marine fossils. These fossils provide a detailed picture of what life in the sea was like over 12 to 17 million years ago. Besides a multitude of shellfish, the fauna of the epoch included angelfish, sharks, turtles, crocodiles, whales, dolphins, gannets and shearwaters.

The cliffs are as impressive today as they were when Capt. John Smith came upon them in his exploration of the bay in 1608. He named them Rickard's Cliffs. They were formed over 15 million years ago when a wide, shallow sea covered all of southern Maryland. As marine creatures died, they fell to the bottom of the sea where they were covered and preserved in many layers of sediment. Standing on the beach and looking north you can see the layers, each of which represent the varying conditions that existed when the layer was created. When the great ice sheets of the glacier period receded, there was a period of uplift in mid-America, causing the sea to fall to its present level and exposing the bottom of this shallow sea.

More than 600 species of fossils have been taken from the cliffs and identified. Most abundant are the teeth of various species of sharks, along with shells of the mollusk family—oysters, clams and crabs. The large number of whale and porpoise seems to indicate that this area may have been a breeding ground for these animals. Many of the bones also show signs of

shark attacks and the large number of shark teeth found in the area supports the theory that many immature mammals were present in this area when the cliffs were formed. You may also spot osprey, great blue heron or even eagles in this park. The white-tailed deer, raccoon, opossum and skunk inhabit the area, along with rabbit and squirrel. Calvert Cliffs is also a good park for spring wildflowers, including yellow lady's-slipper, skunk cabbage and false hellebore. There is also interesting wildlife around the several swampy areas in the park. The 1,600 acres of dense woodlands and shady shoreline remain virtually untouched and are rarely crowded. A naturalist conducts guided nature walks, fossil talks and other interpretive activities from May through August. During the remaining months of the year, arrangements for such services may be made through the park superintendent.

Hiking

Nearly 13 miles of marked hiking trails are open to the public. The 2-mile walk to the cliffs takes approximately 45 minutes and passes through a beautiful climax forest of beech, oak and pine trees. Bicycles are restricted to the service road. Some trails may be closed in the hunting season. A trail map is available.

Fossil Hunting

Visitors may hunt for fossils on the open beach but not on the cliffs. No digging or climbing is allowed on the cliffs because of erosion problems. You are permitted to keep the specimens that you find.

Fishing

Fishing from the beach in Chesapeake Bay is permitted, but there is no vehicle access. Spot, croaker and bluefish are commonly caught in the bay here. A one-acre fishing pond contains largemouth bass, catfish and bluegill. A fishing license is required for those 16 years of age and older.

Picnicking and Camping

A few picnic tables and grills are available, and there is a

Calvert Cliffs are often referred to as Scientists Cliffs because of their rich fossil beds. *Bill Thomas* pavilion available for the use of large groups (this should be reserved in advance; a small fee is charged). No family camping is allowed, but there is a youth group camp, for which reservations must be made 30 days in advance.

How To Get There: From the Capital Beltway (I-495), take MD 4 east and south through Prince Frederick. About 16 miles south of Prince Frederick, watch for the park entrance on the left. The park is open from sunrise to sunset, but the beach closes at 5:30 P.M. No pets are allowed in the park. All Maryland State parks are "Trash Free".

For Additional Information:
Point Lookout State Park
P.O. Box 48
Scotland, MD 20687
(301) 872-5688

Department of Natural Resources
Maryland Forest, and Park Service
Tawes State Office Building
Annapolis, MD 21401
(410) 260-8186
http://www.dnr.state.md.us/publiclands

Calvert Marine Museum

The Calvert Marine Museum is located in Solomons, Maryland, near the confluence of the Patuxent River and the Chesapeake Bay. The museum is ideally situated for the study of three inter-related topics: paleontology, estuarine biology and maritime history. The nearby Calvert Cliffs have provided the museum with a paleontological collection of the Miocene Epoch second only to the Smithsonian Institution's. The Chesapeake Bay is North America's largest tidal estuary, where fresh and salt water mix. Estuaries are particularly important biologically because they are among the world's most productive plant and animal breeding grounds.

Solomons Island was also the site of an active commercial fishing fleet and boat building center. Exhibits in the J.C. Lore & Sons Oyster House trace techniques of oystering, eeling, clamming, fishing and crabbing from colonial days to the present. Along one end of the building is a fully equipped oyster-shucking room. The museum's small craft collection contains the world's second largest collection of Chesapeake Bay boats including multi-log canoes, a double-ended crab skiff, a Potomac River dory, a clam dredge work boat and many more.

The museum's principal exhibition building consists of separate halls for the museum's three themes. A 16-tank estuarium traces the natural history of the Patuxent River from its mouth to fresh water areas with live specimens shown in appropriate habitats. Special features include an indoor touch tank and an outdoor pool exhibit for live river otters, adjacent to both salt water and fresh water marshes. A paleontology hall features the 12-20 million-year-old fossils of the nearby Calvert Cliffs: whales, sharks, mollusks and sea birds. A full-scale reconstruction of the jaws of a 38-foot-long fossil great white shark highlights the exhibit. A discovery room gives children hands-on contact with local animal life. In the museum's changing exhibits gallery, marine art and photography are on display.

On the museum grounds be sure to visit the woodcarver's shop, where models, figureheads and other nautical carvings are made and exhibited. At the waterfront, the Drum Point Lighthouse, constructed in 1883 to mark the entrance to the Patuxent River, has been restored and moved to the museum grounds. The museum also offers public education programs throughout the year, including field trips, lectures, movies, classes and demonstrations. Programs for school groups may be arranged in advance by contacting the museum. It is possible to cruise the Patuxent River on the *Wm. B. Tennison*, an historic bugeye built in 1899. Cruises depart from the Museum Dock between May 1 and October 31, Wednesday through Sunday, at 2:00 P.M. for a one-hour cruise, weather permitting. Fares are $5.00 for adults and $2.00 for children 5–12 years of age. Children under 5 ride free. The museum is maintained by the citizens of Calvert County.

How To Get There: From the Pennsylvania Avenue/Upper Marlboro exit of the Capital Beltway (I-95/495), take MD 4 east and south to its junction with MD 2 and continue south to Solomons. If you come by boat, the museum is located in the west shore of Back Creek, just off Solomons Harbor, 2 nautical miles from the Chesapeake Bay. Limited museum docking facilities are free to visitors, but no overnighting is permitted. The museum is open year-round 10:00 A.M.–5:00 P.M., daily. Admission to the exhibit, lighthouse and oysterhouse is $5.00 for adults, $2.00 for children (5-12) and $4.00 for seniors (over 55) and free for children under 5.

For Additional Information:
Director
Calvert Marine Museum
P.O. Box 97
Solomons, MD 20688-0097
(410) 326-2042

Carroll County Farm Museum

The museum depicts the lifestyles of an 1800s farm family, offering an opportunity to observe a self-sufficient way of life that disappeared with the advent of mechanization during the 19th century. The museum buildings are surrounded by 140 acres of rolling field, with huge old shade trees, a pond, nature trails and fields where farm animals graze. The farm brings to mind an earlier era when life was less complex and people were more self-sufficient. Prior to becoming a museum, the farm was known as the Almshouse or poorhouse where people who could not support themselves came to live. The Almshouse was a working farm from 1850 until 1965 when Carroll County established the museum. Cows, pigs and sheep, chickens and geese live here now. Guests may see demonstrations of skills such as quilting, blacksmithing, apple butter making, tinsmithing, spinning and broom making.

How To Get There: From Exit 19 of the Baltimore Beltway (I-695), take Route 795 north to the end, follow the sign to Route 140 west to Westminster. Turn left onto Center Street. The Farm Museum is on the right. Open early May to the end of October on weekends NOON– 5:00 P.M. and Tuesday through Friday 10:00 A.M.–4:00 P.M. during July and August. Admission is $3.00 for adults, $2.00 for children 12 to 18 and adults over 60. Children under 6 are admitted free. Tour groups of 20 or more, $2.00 per person.

For Additional Information:
Carroll County Farm Museum
500 South Center Street
Westminster, MD 21157-5615
(410) 876-2667 or (410) 848-7775

Catoctin Mountain Park and Cunningham Falls State Park

Although Catoctin Mountain Park and Cunningham Falls State Park are a bit beyond the 50-mile radius of Washington, DC, established for this book, we feel they should be included because they have so much to offer. This is a place of great scenic beauty, and it has a remoteness difficult to find elsewhere near DC. Verdant green mountains highlight the area of some 10,500 acres of beautiful scenery and exhibits. There are great places for camping, hiking, horseback riding and bird-watching. Much of the land has a sense of complete wilderness. The National Park Service and the Maryland State Forest and Park Service have permitted this area to develop into an eastern hardwood climax forest. When you walk the trails, you will find stately chestnut oak, hickory, black birch and a few other tree types. In the old fields of the mountain valleys are black locust, wild cherry, sassafras and yellow poplar trees; in moist areas, beech, red oak, hemlock, ash and white oak trees are found. Wildlife includes the ruffed grouse, white-tailed deer, raccoon, woodchuck, chipmunk, red and gray fox, and barred owl.

Here, too, is a good study site for geologists, for this area is covered by what is known as the Catoctin greenstone, a remnant of a lava flow that occurred some 600 million years ago. It may be seen as a distinctive green rock along Hog Rock Nature Trail. Catoctin is also known as the location of **Camp David**, the presidential retreat (closed to the public, of course). **Cunningham Falls State Park**, just south of Catoctin, was a part of Catoctin until it was deeded to the state of Maryland in 1954 by the National Park Service. The centerpieces of this park are the spectacular Cunningham Falls where the waters of the Big Hunting Creek cascade down a 220-foot gorge with 78 feet of vertical drop, and a 3,500-acre wildlands (Maryland's version of national wilderness areas). The Falls is accessible by a 0.5 mile trail from the lake area or a 1.1 mile trail from Catoctin Mountain Park Visitor Center.

It is an excellent bird-watching area. Birds to be on the lookout for include ruby-throated hummingbirds, great blue herons, kingfishers, eastern screech owls, scarlet tanagers, wild turkeys, turkey vultures and various species of woodpeckers. It offers nature walks, hiking, picnicking and camping; there is a man-made lake that has facilities for swimming, fishing and boating.

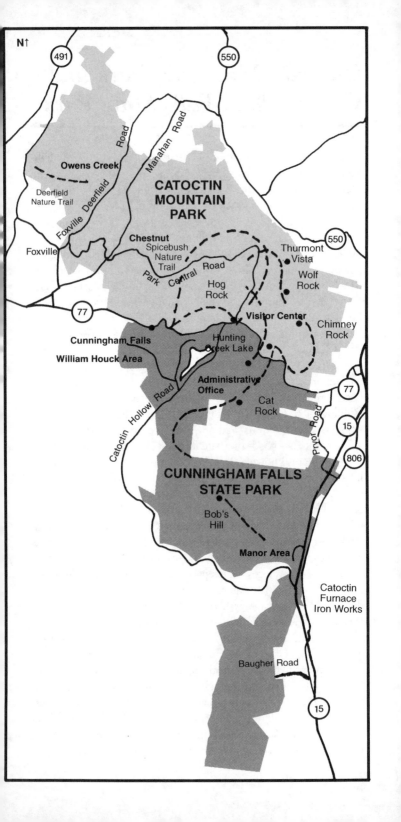

Hiking Trails

Round-trip Distance	Time	Name; Blaze	Description	Remarks
3miles	2 hrs.	Cat Rock	strenuous	good views
3 miles	6hrs.	Bob's Hill	strenuous	nice overlook
2.2 miles	2 hrs.	Chimney Rock	strenuous	good rock formations
0.3 miles	0.5 hr.	Cunningham Falls	easy; handicapped accessible	handicapped parking only
1.5miles	1 hr.	Cunningham Falls– lower trail; red	easy to moderate	goes to falls
1.5 miles	1.25 hr.	Cunningham Falls– cliff; yellow	strenuous	rough terrain
1 mile	3/4 hr.	Thurmount Vista	moderate	good view of town
1.8 miles	1.75 hrs.	Wolf Rock	strenuous	scenic view
4 miles	2 hrs.	Old Misery Trail	strenous	good views
27 miles	?	Catoctin Trail	strenous	Contact PATC

Interpretive Trails

0.6 miles	1/2 hr.	Blue Blazes	easy	story of whiskey making
0.4 miles	1/2 hrs.	Brown's Farm	easy	ecology of region
0.5 miles	1/2 hr.	Charcoal	easy	story of char coal making
0.5 miles	3/4 hr.	Catoctin Furnace	easy	ironmaking & natural history
2.8 miles	2 hrs.	Cunningham Falls	moderate	goes to falls
1.3 miles	1 hr.	Deerfield	moderate	look for deer
1 mile	3/4 hr.	Hog Rock	easy	goes to falls

Sight-Seeing

A number of roads lead through and around the parks, giving you ample opportunity to explore from your automobile. Park Central, the main park road in Catoctin, begins at the visitor center, off MD 77, and winds through the park for 4.5 miles to its junction with Foxville-Deerfield Road. Catoctin Hollow Road, in Cunningham Falls State Park, features a panoramic view of Hunting Creek Lake from a scenic overlook.

Hiking

The two parks offer a trail system totaling nearly 50 miles of well-marked trails that are most interesting, varying in length from 0.3 to 9.4 miles. Some lead to outstanding vistas and natural features. Parking areas are provided at trailheads. To visit Cunningham Falls, park at the William Houck Area near the lake and walk the 3/4-mile trail. The Cat Rock Trail (9 miles long), Wolf Rock (1.8 miles) and Chimney Rock (2.2 miles) hikes are the most difficult hikes in the parks but have beautiful overlooks of the mountains. Self-guiding trails include: Hog Rock, Browns Farm Environmental Study Area, Cunningham Falls and Blue Blazes Whiskey Still. Charcoal, Spicebush and the Catoctin Furnace Historical trails have interpretive signs along the trail. Deerfield Nature Trail is 1.3 miles long and is a particularly good place to look for white-tailed deer. Deer especially like this area because they enjoy the tender young beech leaves and beechnuts growing on the abandoned farmland around this trail. Evenings or early mornings are the best time to look for the white flash of tail as a deer bounds away. Hog Rock Nature Trail is a one-mile loop path that follows numbered stakes that identify the most common trees in the park. Charcoal Trail features trailside signs that explain the charcoaling process that flourished here in the 1800s. Blue Blazes Whiskey Trail starts at the visitor center and is one of the shortest in the park. These are generally easy trails to hike, and they get fairly heavy use during the summer season and on weekends year-round. You may also use these trails for cross-country skiing or snow-shoeing. A portion of the famed Appalachian Trail (described elsewhere) passes near Catoctin's western boundary.

Camping

Catoctin Mountain Park's primitive tent camping area is available only for youth groups and only on a reservation basis, but no camping is permitted along the trails. The Owens Creek Campground in Catoctin is open for family and individual camping from mid-April through the third Sunday of November. It features restrooms, tables and fireplaces, but there is a seven-day limit for any one visit, or a limit of 14 days per season. Misty Mount Camp offers cabin rentals between April 15 and October 31; call (301) 271-3140 for reservations. Groups may rent Greentop or Round Meadows camps. Two campgrounds in Cunningham Falls are limited to an occupancy of 14 consecutive days. Maximum trailer length in both parks is 22 feet at CMP and varies at CFSP. Both campgrounds have restrooms, hot water and showers. Some sites have electricity and cabins are available. Reservations are accepted and advised.

How To Get There: From Washington, take I-270 northwest through Frederick to US 15. Continue north on US 15 to Thurmont, then take MD 77 west about a mile to Catoctin's main entrance. The state park may also be entered from this route, as well as via a park road off US 15, approximately 15 miles north of Frederick. Both parks are open year-round. Fees are charged for some park services and access to some areas; call for details, as these change. Many of the trails can be accessed outside the fee area. Pets are prohibited in most areas.

For Additional Information:
Superintendent
Catoctin Mountain Park
National Park Service
6602 Foxville Road
Thurmont, MD 21788-1598
(301) 663-9388
http://www.nps.gov

Park Manager
Cunningham Falls State Park
14039 Catoctin Hollow Road
Thurmont, MD 21788
(301) 271-7574 (info & camping reservations)
http://www.dnr.state.md.us/publiclands

Catoctin Wildlife Preserve and Zoo

At Thurmont, near the presidential retreat, Camp David, is the Catoctin Wildlife Preserve and Zoo (formerly the Catoctin Mountain Zoo). The zoo is located on Route 15, opposite the entrance to Cunningham Falls State Park - Manor Area (described elsewhere). Though a few miles beyond the 50-mile radius from Washington DC, established for this book, it lies in an area of outstanding scenic beauty. A visit here can easily be combined with a trip to the Cunningham Falls State Park or Catoctin Mountain National Park. The zoo is an intimate 26 acres so visitors are able to get closer to the animals than they would in a larger zoo. It displays a number of creatures not normally found in other zoos, several of them endangered species. Among the wildlife to be seen on the wooded, 25-acre grounds of the zoo are a 500-pound Aldabra tortoise named Tank who likes to have visitors rub his head; Sachmo, a Vietnamese pot-bellied pig who often runs free in the Touch & Learn area and expects to be petted by visitors; a 14-foot Albino Burmese Python, which is a member of the world's largest non-poisonous snake family that constricts its prey to kill it. A huge 1/2-ton brown bear named Griz, mountain lions, several species of monkeys (some on exhibit islands), rare Golden Bengal tigers, wolves, Sicilian donkeys, alligators and much more live in the zoo. Over 300 animals of 125 different species can be seen here. Special educational demonstrations, using live animals, are held in the summertime at the stage area. There is a two-acre affection section where children can pet several dozen unusual domestic animals and feed a small herd of European Fallow deer.

New exhibits include walk-through, free flight aviaries, Lorikeet feeding stations, alligator feeding and lemur encounters.

How To Get There: From the Capital Beltway (I-495), take I-270 northwest through Frederick to US 15. Continue north on US 15. The zoo is located on US 15, 2 miles south of Thurmont. Open daily April 1 through October 31, 9:00 A.M–5:00 P.M. From May 1 though Labor Day the zoo is open 9:00 A.M.–6:00 P.M. daily. March and November the zoo is open daily 10:00 A.M.–4:00 P.M. weekends only, weather permitting. Admission is $8.00 for adults, $5.25 for children (2-12) and free for children under 2.

For Additional Information:
Catoctin Wildlife Preserve and Zoo
Route 15
Thurmont, MD 21788
(301) 271-3180 (recording)
(301) 271-4922 (office)
http://www.fwp.net/CWPZoo

Cedarville State Forest

In Maryland's tidewater country is the remarkable Cedarville State Forest. Heavily forested with evergreens and deciduous trees—mostly Virginia pine, oak, poplar, sweet and sour gums, sycamore and willow—Cedarville encompasses nearly 4,000 acres. The headwaters of **Zekiah Swamp** (see separate listing), the largest freshwater swamp in the state, are found here. A small pond and a number of streams and creeks feed the swamp and create a marsh environment where ladies'-tresses, sundews and other bog plants grow. The most unusual plant is the carnivorous pitcher plant. The pitcher plant attracts insects with its nectar garlands and then uses downward pointed bristles to trap them. Visitors are permitted to fish in the swamp in the summer and to ice skate on its frozen surface in the winter.

Located about 25 miles southeast of Washington, Cedarville provides a place of escape for those who want to get away from the pressure of civilization. It is interesting year-round. In fact, winters are traditionally so mild that the Piscataway Indians used it as a winter camping ground. Legend says there is an Indian burial ground here, but to date it has not been discovered. Rabbit, gray squirrels, fox, opossum, raccoon, mink and white-tailed deer live here. Many different birds take advantage of the food here as they migrate. Warblers, vireos, pileated and red-bellied woodpeckers, red-shouldered hawks and barred owls are seen here. Marked trails for horseback riding and hiking extend through the forest. There are also self-guided nature trails, orienteering courses, a compass course, forestry management demonstration areas, tree plantations and a charcoal kiln. Picnicking, youth group camping, fishing and bird-watching are other activities enjoyed here.

Hiking and Horseback Riding

More than 20 miles of hiking and horseback riding trails are located in the forest. All are well marked and can be used during all seasons.

Hiking Trails

Distance	Time	Name	Description	Remarks
2.5 miles	1.5 hrs.	Plantation	moderate	circles pond
3 miles	2 hrs.	Holly	moderate	follows the marsh
3 miles	2 hrs.	Bird watchers'	moderate	popular with bird-watchers
2 miles	1.5 hrs.	Swamp Trail	moderate	enters swamp
3.5 miles	2.5 hrs.	Heritage Trail	strenuous	past charcoal kiln

Fishing

A 4-acre fishing pond is stocked with bluegill, largemouth bass and catfish. Fishing is also permitted in Zekiah Swamp. A state fishing license is required for persons 16 and older.

Hunting

There are 1,400 acres open for hunting during the established hunting season. Squirrel and deer are the primary game found here.

How To Get There: From Washington, take the Capital Beltway (I-495) to MD 5, then head south to MD 5 and US 301 to the Cedarville exit. The forest is located three miles east of this exit. A right turn on Cedarville Road will take you right into the forest. Open year-round. No entrance fee. Due to state budget problems, Cedarville State Forest has limited facilities available.

For Additional Information:
Forest Manager
Cedarville State Forest
11704 Fenno Road
Upper Marlboro, MD 20772
(301) 888-1410

Maryland Department of Natural Resources
Forest and Park Service
Tawes Office Building
Annapolis, MD 21401
(410) 260-8186
(800) 825-PARK
http://www.dnr.state.md.us/publiclands

Chesapeake & Ohio Canal National Historical Park

When you walk along the Chesapeake & Ohio Canal you are walking in the footsteps of some famous Americans. Both Supreme Court Justice William O. Douglas and President

Theodore Roosevelt are known to have visited the canal regularly during their time in office. One can almost imagine these men walking alongside the canal, meditating upon the great issues of their day. Douglas spent much time hiking along the towpath. During the summer of 1977, President Jimmy Carter dedicated the C&O Canal National Historical Park in his honor. The abandoned canal extends 184.5 miles from the mountains to the tidewater and parallels the eastern shore of the Potomac River from Cumberland, Maryland to Georgetown in Washington, DC. George Washington envisioned the canal as a way of transporting the raw materials from the west to the capital. It was to extend to the headwaters of the Ohio River but never reached its mark. The creation of the Baltimore & Ohio Railroad at about the same time took most of the freight and passengers and reduced the importance of the canal. But the waterway did serve a purpose, and during the 1870s it carried as many as 540 boats daily. A typical boat carried from 110 to 120 tons of cargo, including grain, lumber, stone, whiskey and, most important, coal from the west to the east.

The canal boats were towed by mules and moved at a steady pace of about two to four miles an hour. Entering the locks required great skill and accidents often occurred. Children drove the mules and were paid four cents a day. Boats were often handed down from father to son in part because most operators carried their families with them. Children brought up on the boats did not attend school so that many were illiterate. Wives helped steer the boats and often continued operating the boats after their husbands were deceased, although they were registered in their husbands name because women were not allowed to register boats in their own names. The boats kept moving down the canal for as many hours as the family could stand, often up to 18 hours a day. Some were operated continuously. Seventy-four lift locks raised the elevation from near sea level to 605 feet at Cumberland. By 1930, however, the canal had become totally obsolete and useless. Many years after it was abandoned parts of it were restored. The best-preserved section today extends 22 miles from Georgetown in the District of Columbia to Seneca, Maryland, but you can travel the entire distance via the towpath. In many sections, it is a quiet, serene place where you can hear your own footsteps.

In addition to being a historical park, the canal functions as a sanctuary for wildlife attracted to a deciduous flood plain environment. A large number of songbirds, waterfowl and woodpeckers are attracted to this habitat. The concentration of birds along the canal is extraordinary. Elsewhere, no more

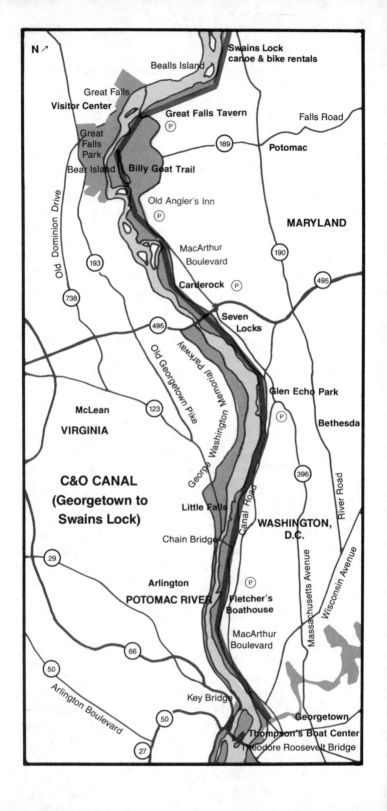

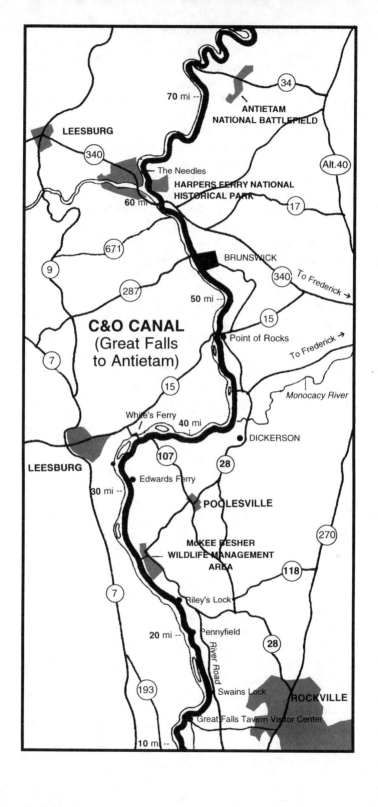

then four or five breeding birds per acre are generally found, but here the density is 14 or 15 per acre. Fox, squirrel, raccoon, white-tailed deer, cottontail rabbit, muskrat, beaver and snakes also live along the canal.

The waterway is nearly always shrouded from civilization by a cloak of woods—giant sycamore, willows, beech, oak, red maple, yellow poplar, sassafras and cottonwood. In spring, the canal towpath becomes a study in wildflowers, framed in carpets of larkspur, dandelion, violets, daisies, wild rose, buttercups, spring beauty, jack-in-the-pulpit, wild ginger, green dragon, wild phlox, Virginia bluebells, wild columbine and wild pinks. A dozen different types of mushrooms thrive along the route, including the delectable morel. At places, in the right season, you will find wild persimmons, pawpaws and raspberries. The Carderock area is a favorite rock climbing area—it is a good place to view wildflowers and is not as heavily used as Great Falls. The **Great Falls** area of the C&O Canal (see the entry under Great Falls) enjoys more intensive use than any other portion and has more variety to offer. Located about 10 miles northwest of the Washington city limits, it is the site of several abandoned gold mines as well as an excellent place for hiking, rock climbing, bicycling and canoeing. The Great Falls Tavern, which houses an exhibit on the history of the canal, was an inn when the canal was being used as a major waterway west.

Hiking and Bicycling

The C&O Canal towpath is one of the most popular walking and bicycling places in the Washington area. The stretch between Great Falls Tavern and Old Anglers Inn is particularly nice. The path is 12-feet wide, almost level, and covered with gravel or packed earth almost all of its length. There are also numerous side trails between the towpath and river that are interesting to walk. Most of the towpath from Georgetown to Harpers Ferry can be easily traveled by bicycle, wheelchair or baby stroller, with little problem (except possibly mud or temporary washouts). Two notable exceptions to this are the rocky area about midway between Old Anglers Inn and Great Falls Tavern Visitors Center, where even bicycles must be carried (or bounced over the rocks) about 30 yards; farther north at Riley's Lock where the towpath crosses Seneca Creek, the bridge braces crossing the bridge force bicyclists to carry their bikes (conceivably, a very determined person could push a wheelchair or stroller across the over 20 six-inch ramped bumps). The towpath is heavily used below Great Falls Tavern, especially on weekends, so both hikers and bikers should keep to the right and be mindful of other users. (See the Appendix for additional information on bicycling.) Dogs are permitted, but should be keep closely tethered to the owner. Visitors should keep out of the river itself or any of its branches; the currents in this area are very deceptive and every year a number of persons drown. Most of the park is closed to visitors after dark, with the exception of overnight campers at approved sites (all north of Great Falls).

The Billy Goat Trail which runs between the towpath and the Potomac just downriver of Great Falls is one of the favorite hiking trails in the DC area (see the description under Great Falls).

The Capital Crescent Trail now connects with the towpath near Fletcher's boathouse (see the entry on the CCT under DC).

Camping

Serious hikers and bikers can travel the 184 miles from Georgetown to Cumberland, Maryland. There are hiker-biker overnight campsites, with toilets (out-houses) and water about every five miles between Riley's Lock (Seneca Creek) and Cumberland. There is no drive-in or multiday camping downriver from Harpers Ferry.

Canoeing

Canoes can be rented at Fletcher's Boathouse (202-244-0461) along Canal Road in the District and Swain's Lock (301-299-9006) off River Road north of Falls Road. Canoes should be used only on designated stretches of the canal, not on the river. Canoes can be rented at Thompson's Boat Center near the Watergate (202-333-9543) for use on the relatively safe part of the Potomac downriver of Key Bridge.

Picnicking

There are numerous picnic areas with picnic tables along the entire length of the C&O, including facilities adjacent to almost every parking area. Simple fare is available, in season at Fletcher's Boathouse, Great Falls Tavern and Swains Lock. Food is available near the park in Georgetown, Glen Echo, Old Anglers Inn, Riley's Lock, White's Ferry, Harpers Ferry and other points.

How To Get There: There are numerous entry points to the C&O Towpath. (See map.) In Georgetown, access to the towpath is by foot from 29th through 33rd Street between M and K; paths or stairs from most of the bridges lead to the towpath. There are many entryways along Canal Road north of Georgetown, along the Clara Barton Parkway and MacArthur Boulevard west of Cabin John, and from side roads off River Road north of Falls Road. Great Falls Tavern Visitor Center is at the west end of MacArthur and Falls Road. As of 1998, $4.00 per car admission is charged for entrance to the Great Falls Tavern parking lot, with a reduced charge for biker and pedestrians who pass through the main entrance; the annual Golden Eagle Pass is accepted. At publication time, parking was free elsewhere.

For Additional Information:
National Park Service
C&O Canal National Historical Park
P.O. Box 4
Sharpsburg, MD 21782
(301) 739-4200
http://www.nps.gov/choh

Cylburn Arboretum

In Baltimore, Cylburn Arboretum is a wildflower preserve, garden center and bird sanctuary. Located on 176 acres in the center of Baltimore, the area was established in 1954 by a group of citizens who wished to preserve the unique beauty of the former estate of Mrs. Bruce Cotton. Built in 1863, it was designed by George Frederick, the architect of Baltimore's city hall. The city purchased the property in 1942. The mansion, until 1954, was used by the Department of Public Welfare to house children from broken homes.

Since 1954, however, it has become the city's horticultural center with trails, gardens and a nature museum. The City of Baltimore Bureau of Parks maintains an extensive planting of trees and shrubs. Collections of magnolias, Japanese maples and Maryland oaks are planted on the grounds. Gardens include a perennial garden, an herb garden, a collection of tree peonies and a heritage rose garden, a shade garden, a vegetable garden, three small city garden displays, and a Garden of the Senses. This special garden has been designed to accommodate the physically handicapped. The paths are wide enough for wheelchairs and the flowers are labeled with Braille signs. A wildflower trail with many labeled flowering and non-flowering plants is especially helpful to those interested in studying plants, while a woodland trail, through an area almost in a virginal state, is of more interest to hikers.

Activities include tours, workshops, lectures and demonstrations of environmental topics. A naturalist and volunteers lead the tours. The arboretum is open year-round. No picnicking, ball playing or collecting of any kind is allowed. In 1972 the mansion and arboretum were entered into the National Register of Historic Places.

Hiking

Eleven nature trails wind through the arboretum. Guided nature hikes are scheduled periodically and are announced in Baltimore newspapers. But you are also welcome to hike the trails yourself. A trail map is available. Flyers are sent to members of the Cylburn Organization outlining upcoming activities, such as open houses & festivals.

How To Get There: From Exit 23 of the Baltimore Beltway (I-695), take I-83 (Jones Falls Expressway) south to Northern Parkway and turn right (west). Turn left on Cylburn Avenue, then left on Greenspring Avenue. The arboretum is located on the east side of Greenspring Avenue, between Northern Parkway and Cold Spring Lane in Baltimore. The entrance is at 4915 Greenspring Avenue. Trails are open 6:00 A.M.–9:00 P.M. daily; the mansion is open 8:00 A.M–3:30 P.M. Monday through Friday. No entrance fee.

For Additional Information:
Cylburn Arboretum
4915 Greenspring Avenue
Baltimore, MD 21209-4698
(410) 367-2217

Doncaster State Forest

Much of the land covered in this book is abandoned farmland in its third or fourth regrowth. Doncaster State Forest is an example of once cultivated land that is reverting back to forest. Its 1,447 acres of pine, poplar and oak demonstrate a process called succession, in which a natural progression of vegetation regenerates soil, flora and fauna. Fields, pine forests and forest edges are excellent places for many animals to live. Among the many species of game that have returned here to live are the white-tailed deer, raccoon, quail, rabbit, fox squirrel and opossum. Hunting is allowed with appropriate permits.

Hiking and Horseback Riding

Two developed hiking-nature trails, each following a circuit of two miles, are marked with blue blazes. One trail leads off a small picnic area located just east of the main entrance road for about three-quarters of a mile. The beginning of each trail is well marked by a large tree with a blue band around its trunk. There are several miles of fire roads that hikers may use; it is best to check your proposed route with a ranger first, however, since the trails have many intersections. There is also a well-used bridle trail. Forest rangers ask that you check with them for information on trail conditions, which vary considerably with season and weather.

Picnicking

The only picnic area in the forest has four tables in a lovely shaded and scenic area.

How To Get There: From the Capital Beltway (I-495), take MD 5 south to its intersection with US 301. Continue south on 301 to its junction with MD 6, and turn right; proceed west for 13 miles. The forest's main entrance road will be on your right. Some fire-access roads within the forest are impassable, and even dangerous in places, so private vehicles should stay on the main road.

For Additional Information:
Doncaster Demonstration Forest
Route 1, Box 425
Indian Head, MD 20640
(301) 934-2282

Eastern Neck National Wildlife Refuge

An excellent place to view waterfowl migration is at Eastern Neck National Wildlife Refuge just north of the Chesapeake Bay Bridge on Maryland's Eastern Shore. Eastern Neck is one of the over 500 National Wildlife Refuges administered by the U.S. Fish and Wildlife Service. The refuge system is managed specifically for the protection of wildlife habitat. Established in 1962, Eastern Neck contains 2,285 acres and is a major wintering area for migratory and wintering waterfowl. Over 243 species of birds have been sighted on the island. The refuge also contains two endangered/threatened species, the Delmarva fox squirrel and the southern bald eagle. Strategically located at the confluence of the Chester River and the bay, this refuge occupies one of the most interesting of the Chesapeake islands. It offers marshes, coves, ponds and abundant vegetation for thousands of wintering waterfowl. Both diving and puddle ducks can be found on the refuge and the refuge is a major staging area where thousands of tundra swan congregate around the island during the late fall and winter.

Most waterfowl begin arriving by early October with the numbers reaching a peak in November. Canada geese, swans, widgeon, mallard, black duck, canvasback and scaup are the principal waterfowl using the refuge. Sea ducks—old squaw and white-winged scoter—also thrive. Migrating waterfowl vacate the area by early to mid-April while numerous wading and shore birds including herons, egrets, rails, sandpipers, killdeer and many other species arrive and can be observed through fall. Upland game birds, including turkey, quail and mourning dove, as well as a wide variety of other bird life, are found here. Both bald eagle and osprey nest here. Other wildlife includes white-tailed deer, red fox, cottontail rabbit, raccoon, woodchuck, muskrat, skunk and opossum. There is an observation platform for viewing the waterfowl and other bird life. Eastern Neck is one of the few remaining areas where the Delmarva fox squirrel can be found. This large, light gray squirrel can be found in hedgerows bordering the roads on the island.

Hiking

Six miles of roads and three wildlife trails and a handicapped accessible boardwalk trail and observation tower are open to public traffic most of the year for those who wish to observe the refuge on foot. All areas delineated by "Closed Area" signs are strictly off limits to the public.

Sight-Seeing and Boating

You many drive around parts of the refuge. The Ingleside Recreation Area, operated by the Kent County Department of Parks and Recreation under a cooperative agreement, on the northwest side of the refuge has facilities for picnicking, crabbing and car-top boat launching from May 1 to October 1. Boat launching facilities are also available at Bogle's Wharf on the east side of the island. This county operated facility offers trailered boat launching requiring a Kent County permit.

Excellent fishing is available from the bridge that spans Eastern Neck Narrows at the entrance to the refuge.

How To Get There: From Washington, take US 50 east through Annapolis and across the Chesapeake Bay Bridge to MD 301 north. Then head north on MD 213 to Chestertown. Turn left (west) on MD 219 and right on MD 20; proceed to Rock Hall and then take MD 445 left (south) across the bridge to the refuge. Open daily all year during daylight hours; refuge office hours are 7:30 A.M–4:00 P.M., Monday through Friday. No entrance fee.

For Additional Information:
Refuge Manager
Eastern Neck National Wildlife Refuge
1730 Eastern Neck Road
Rock Hall, MD 21661
(410) 639-7056
http://www.fws.gov

Flag Ponds Nature Park

Flag Ponds Nature Park is one of the newest parks in Calvert County. Its 450 acres are located just north of Calvert Cliffs Nuclear Power Station and Calvert Cliffs State Park on the Chesapeake Bay. Like Calvert Cliffs Park, Flag Ponds is rich in fossils at ground level; unlike Calvert Cliffs, Flag Ponds has no exposed cliffs. Nature has been enlarging this park for nearly the last 1,000 years by washing sand from other areas of the bay onto these shores. You can see remnants of a fisherman's shanty, with pier and fishnets, formerly on the shore, now separated by hundreds of yards of new land, which has already become reforested. Some of the most interesting wildlife is to be seen in Duncan's and Todd's ponds, which were created when these former saltwater inlets were cut off from the bay by the influx of sand. A fishing pier is available for public fishing (flounder and bluefish are caught here), as well as a beach for beachcombing.

Trails and boardwalks lead to an observation blind and platform. Deer, raccoon, muskrat, otter, wild turkey, fox and tiger beetles are found in the park. Kingfishers, pileated woodpecker, warblers and a wide variety of waterfowl are part of the diverse bird life here. Late November through March is the best time to see migrating waterfowl. Flora ranges from hardwood forests to the blue flag iris, for which the park is named. Open daily Memorial Day through Labor Day 9:00 A.M.–6:00 P.M. (8:00 P.M. weekends); weekends only, 9:00 A.M.–6:00 P.M. the rest of the year. A visitor's center features exhibits of fossils and local wildlife, plus restrooms and drinking fountains.

How To Get There: From the Washington Beltway, take Route 4 southwest into Calvert County. About 10 miles south of Prince Frederick, you will see signs for Flag Ponds; turn left into the park. (If you pass Calvert Cliffs Nuclear Power Station, you've missed the entrance.) Nominal Fee.

For Additional Information:
Flag Ponds Nature Park
Calvert County Natural Resources Division
Calvert County Courthouse
175 Main Street
Prince Frederick, MD 20678-9998
(410) 535-5327 or 586-1477

Gambrill State Park

The Gambrill State Park on Catoctin Mountain was established when conservationists from Frederick County purchased the land and donated it to the city of Frederick to be used as a municipal mountain park. In 1934 the city turned it over to the state for use as a state park. The park is named for James H. Gambrill, Jr., a private citizen whom a plaque at the park identifies as being "the first to call attention to the beauties of this spot and its availability for its use by the public." Consisting of 1,139 forest-draped acres, it lies along the 1,600-foot summit of High Knob, midway between the Mason-Dixon line and the Potomac River. On a clear day, it offers views of the surrounding area, including the rugged tree-shrouded mountains of the Frederick City Municipal Forests, Crampton's Gap, a Civil War landmark, Gathland State Park (described elsewhere), and the Middletown and Monocacy valleys, dotted with farms and pasture land. To the west is the battle-scarred South Mountain where many Civil War skirmishes took place.

One of the best times to visit is in the spring when the park is alive with the blossoms of the many flowering trees and shrubs; the dogwood and mountain laurel are particularly beautiful then. The fall foliage peak, with its explosion of color, is another good time to explore the countryside. One of the more interesting aspects of the park is that it contains a full set of buildings constructed during the 1930s by the Civilian Conservation Corps. The CCC built three stone overlooks, a small log nature center, three log picnic shelters, the tea house and the manager's residence. The buildings are typical of architecture built by the CCC and are listed on the inventory of state historic sites. The CCC was particularly important in western Maryland where large tracts of forest were developed to provide jobs and training for residents during the Great Depression.

Hiking

There are 15 miles of marked wooded trails through areas covered with wildflowers, ferns, trees and shrubs and a large variety of birds and other wildlife. Guided nature hikes are offered during the summer season. All the trails begin at the parking lot on the east side of the Gambrill State Park Road. The Lost Chestnut nature trail (1 mile) is an interesting, easy hike; self-guided leaflets help explain many of the interesting features along the way. The Red Trail (1.1 miles) is another fairly easy hike. The Green Trail (2.0 miles) is a steep hike that is said to give hikers a taste of what crossing the Appalachian Mountains was like. The Black Trail (3.3 miles) is moderately easy and is designed to give interesting views of the Frederick Valley and the Middletown Valley. The Yellow Trail (4.6 miles) is the longest of the trails, but it is only moderately difficult. The Catoctin Trail (26.5 miles) cuts across the park for three miles and continues north to the Cunningham Falls State Park and the Catoctin Mountain National Park (described elsewhere).

Camping

Thirty-five family units are located on the upper portion of the Rock Run area. There is a modern wash house with showers, laundry tubs and hot water.

Fishing

A small pond, located in the Rock Run area, may be used for bank fishing. It is stocked with largemouth bass, channel catfish and bluegill. A state fishing license is required for persons 16 and older.

Picnicking

Tables, fireplaces, shelters, modern restrooms and playgrounds are provided at both the Rock Run and High Knob areas. A lodge-type shelter with a stone fireplace and a kitchen is available on a rental basis for outings 9:00 A.M.–9:00 P.M. April through October at High Knob. It can accommodate 50 people.

How To Get There: From the Capital Beltway (I-495), take I-270 northwest for 33 miles to Frederick. Take US Route 15 north and get off at the second exit ramp (US Route 40 west). Follow US 40 northwest about 5 miles to Gambrill Park Road, turn right and follow for approximately one mile to the park entrance. No entrance fee. Due to state budget problems, Gambrill State Park is tentatively scheduled to be closed; call before visiting to confirm availability.

For Additional Information:
Park Manager
Cunningham Falls/Gambrill State Park
14039 Catoctin Hollow Rd.
Thurmont, MD 21788
(301) 271-7574

Maryland Department of Natural Resources
Forest and Park Service
Tawes Office Building
Annapolis, MD 21401
(410) 974-3771 (business hours)   (410) 461-0053 (other hours)
http://www.dnr.state.md.us/publiclands

Gathland State Park

The 2,000-mile-long Appalachian National Scenic Trail (described elsewhere) leads directly through Gathland State Park. Sitting astride the South Mountain ridge near Burkittsville at Crampton's Gap, this 135-acre park offers excellent views of the Pleasant and Middletown valleys and surrounding pastoral countryside. Much of the park is forest and rolling meadow.

The park is noted for the War Correspondents Memorial Arch and other structures that made up the estate of George A. Townsend, one of the youngest war correspondents of the Civil War. He used the pen name Gath, from which the park gets its name. Townsend purchased the site in 1884 because of its proximity to Antietam and other areas of interest to Civil War historians, and because of its natural beauty.

The site is also one of the three gaps fought over during the Battle of South Mountain. This battle, fought on September 14, 1862, three days before the battle of Antietam, is considered by many as the turning point of Lee's first invasion of the North. Over 6,000 men fell during this day-long battle.

Hiking

One-half mile of the Appalachian Trail passes through the park, offering excellent hiking in or out of the park.

Picnicking

Picnic areas with tables, fireplaces, a play field, water and sanitary facilities are available.

How To Get There: From the Capital Beltway (I-495), take I-270 northwest to Frederick. Pick up I-70 west to Exit 50, and take Alt. 40 west to MD 17. Turn left (south) and follow the signs to the park. It is located one mile west of Burkittsville, off MD 17, and one mile east of Gapland, off MD 67. No entrance fee. Gathland State Park may have restricted access; call before visiting to confirm availability.

For Additional Information:
Park Superintendent
c/o South Mountain State Park
21843 National Pike
Boonsboro, MD 21713-9535
301-791-4767

Maryland Department of Natural Resources
Fores and Park Service
Tawes Office Building
Annapolis, MD 21401
(410) 974-3771 (business hours)
(410) 461-0053 (other hours)
http://www.dnr.state.md.us/publiclands

Great Falls and the Billy Goat Trail

The Great Falls of the Potomac River, located about 10 miles north of Washington, is the most spectacular natural sight in the Washington area and the Billy Goat Trail along the Potomac just downstream from the Great Falls is one of the area's favorite short hikes. Both upstream and downstream, the river appears docile, its flow barely discernible, but it is very treacherous. At Great Falls, the river becomes a raging torrent a quarter-mile wide and in places 50 feet deep. At full spring flood, 134,000 cubic feet of water tumble over Great Falls each second. Here, the Potomac drops a total of 76 feet—not in one abrupt fall, but in several that look like a series of rapids. From the Virginia side, the single largest fall is visible, but from the Olmsted Island overlook on the Maryland side the sheer power of the Potomac is displayed as vast volumes of water crash around boulders through the steep rapids. The appearance of the falls changes with the water level, but is never short of majestic.

The Great Falls overlook on the Maryland side had been inaccessible until the recent completion of the Olmsted Island bridge & walkway. The original bridge and observation area had been washed away by high water during a hurricane; keep that in mind as you walk over it. The new bridge has quickly remov-able railings and a thin vertical cross-section. In the event of another flood, the railings would be removed to minimize the force of the water on the bridge and hopefully keep it. During the years of isolation from the mainland and mainland predators and herbivores, the Olmsted Island flora and fauna developed in a unique way; species thrived there that could not compete on the mainland. For this reason, visitors are confined to the boardwalks.

Olmsted Island and the Great Falls overlook can be accessed from either the Great Falls Tavern parking area or from Old Angler's Inn. From Great Falls Tavern, it is about 0.25 mile downriver on the C&O towpath to the bridge. From Old Anglers Inn, it's about a mile. The bridge and boardwalk are handicapped accessible. However, no pets, bicycles, smoking, or eating are allowed on or beyond the bridge. It is illegal (punish-able by a stiff fine) to stray from the boardwalk.

The view from the bridge over the rushing waters of the side channel is a favorite. The boardwalk continues with bridges across two other side channels to the overlook, about 100 feet over the normal level of the Potomac, just downstream from the falls—the perfect viewpoint. But keep in mind that all of this can be underwater in the river during very high water. The boardwalk is one of the most picturesque walks around.

The Great Falls Tavern, which houses an exhibit on the his-tory of the canal and a book shop, was an inn when the canal was being used as a major waterway west.

Hiking the Billy Goat Trail

Perhaps the favorite trail near Washington (and certainly one of the authors' favorites) is the Billy Goat Trail. The trail is in three sections and runs mostly along the high stony cliffs overlooking the Potomac on the Maryland side. The trail requires travel over large boulders, along a narrow ledge and traversing some steep ravines. Therefore, it is not recommended for those in poor physical shape, those unsure of their footing, children or pets, although one sees all of the above every weekend. Hiking boots are recommended. There is excellent terrain for rock scrambling along the rocks beside the trail.

The head of the Billy Goat Trail is marked by a large sign on the left of the towpath, less than 0.5 miles west (up-river) of the Old Anglers Inn. The trail ends less than 0.5 miles east (down-river) of the Great Falls Tavern, also marked by a large sign. This section of the trail itself is 1.9 miles long, one way, marked with blue blazes and runs mostly along the Potomac River, parallel to the towpath. There are numerous (unmarked) short-circuits back to the towpath, so shorter hikes can be done.

Inexperienced hikers would be well advised to start from the Great Falls Tavern end, which features some wonderful views of Potomac River Rapids and the cliffs along the Virginia side and backtrack if they become uncomfortable with the increasing difficulty of the trail. The entire circuit trip from Old Anglers Inn (or Great Falls Tavern) over the Billy Goat Trail and back to the starting point is 4.0 miles (allow two to three hours). The trail features rich vistas with interesting flora and fauna. There are potholes along the path filled with various life forms, including beautiful waterlily ponds. The side trails are loaded with jack-in-the-pulpit and other wildflowers in the spring. This trail is highly recommended.

There are also a number of short trails through the woods between the towpath and the Potomac and in the area between Great Falls and Old Anglers Inn between the towpath and MacArthur Blvd. There is a refreshment stand near Great Falls Tavern and a restaurant at the Old Anglers Inn. Parking is available at both sites.

The Potomac Appalachian Trail Club (See Hiking Clubs) publishes an excellent topographical map of the Potomac Gorge Area including the Billy Goat Trail and trails on both sides of the Potomac from the American Legion Bridge to west (upstream) of the Great Falls, including the Great Falls area of the C&O Canal NHP, and Cabin John Park in Maryland, plus Great Falls and Riverbend parks in Virginia. The map is available at the Locust Grove Nature Center, and the PATC for a few dollars.

How To Get There: From DC, take the Clara Barton Parkway north to the end. Turn left on MacArthur Blvd., pass the historic

Old Anglers Inn and follow it to the end, where you will see signs for Great Falls Tavern. Proceed straight ahead about a mile down a steep winding road to the ranger station and parking lot.

From the Washington Beltway (I-495), on the Maryland side of the American Legion Bridge over the Potomac north of Washington, take the Carderock exit (Exit 15) onto the Clara Barton Parkway north and proceed as above.

The admission fee is $4.00 per car. U.S. Golden Eagle or Golden Age passes are accepted. On good weather weekends, lines can form at the fee station, but rarely does the large parking lot fill up. Handicapped accessibility is fair. Restrooms are available near the Great Falls Tavern; port-a-johns are available near the Old Anglers Inn access.

To avoid the fee and the line, try parking (off the road) in the very limited area across from Old Anglers Inn (don't park at the Inn) and walk up the C&O towpath about a mile. This part of the towpath is one of the few not passable by wheeled vehicles and frequently blocked by water.

For Additional Information:
National Park Service
Great Falls Tavern
11710 MacArthur Blvd.
Potomac, MD 20854
(301) 299-3613
http://www.nps.gov/choh

Greenbelt Park

Just 12 miles from downtown Washington is Greenbelt Park, a study in land reclamation, administered by the National Capital Region of the National Park Service. It exemplifies the history of much of the land in this area. The 18th century saw most of the land in the Piedmont logged or farmed by European colonists. If a farm became depleted, it was abandoned and the settlers moved on. Little was known about soil conservation, and farmers expected to move after the soil was exhausted. This movement only stopped when there were no more western lands to be settled. Later immigrants recut the Piedmont forests and several cycles of pioneers probably settled on most of the land before the 19th century. Overall, more than 90 percent of the land in the Piedmont has been farmed at some time, the only exceptions being steep slopes, ravines and marshes. During the 20th century, farms continued to be abandoned as economic forces made the flatter, less divided western lands more profitable to farm. A survey of plants taken in 1980 showed that only 45 percent of all farm land was being actively farmed in Maryland and only 35 percent in Virginia. Greenbelt Park is an example of natural reforestation following abrupt abandonment. The succession in the Piedmont follows a pattern beginning with crabgrass, then moving into horseweed the first year, asters the second year, broomsedge the third year, pine trees the fourth to fiftieth years, hardwoods the fiftieth to ninetieth years and finally, climax to hardwoods after ninety years.

Greenbelt was farmed for approximately 150 years and was abandoned around the turn of the century. Today it is a second-growth mixed pine-hardwood forest containing Virginia, white, pitch, shortleaf pine, maple oak, and sweetgum trees. There is a good understory of dogwood, laurel and wild azalea. Deer, raccoon, squirrel and red fox live here. With 1,100 acres of woodland and streams laced with hiking trails, Greenbelt Park provides a solitary atmosphere all its own. In spring, the wildflowers splash a burst of color upon the landscape; in winter, the quiet solitude of snow among the pines makes for a peaceful, serene setting. If possible, it is best to visit here at any time other than during the summer months because it is heavily crowded then with local people and also out-of-towners.

Hiking, Bicycling, and Horseback Riding

Some 12 miles of trails, all well marked, offer contact with outstanding natural features throughout the park. A 6-mile horse trail circles the park's western half; however there are no stables in the park, you must bring your own horse. Guided walks are conducted seasonally; check with the park headquarters for a schedule. Bicycles are allowed but are restricted to paved roads. Three nature trails introduce visitors to the park's natural history. The Azalea Trail (1.2 miles) loops past the picnic areas and the north branch of Still Creek where wildlife is often seen. Blueberry Trail (1.2 miles) is a relatively easy hike through a variety of habitats including former farmland, mature forest and a wooded wetland. It is used as an environmental study area during the school year. The Dogwood Trail (1.4 miles) is designed to illustrate human activity on the land and early plant use by settlers. A pamphlet for self-guiding walks is available at the park headquarters.

Camping

A 174-site family campground is open year-round. Facilities are available for tents, recreation vehicles and trailers up to 30 feet long. Fireplaces, tables and restrooms are provided. No hookups. From Memorial Day to Labor Day, camping is limited to a stay of no more than seven days; a 14-day total is allowed during the remainder of the year. Campsites are available on a first-come, first-serve basis; reservations are accepted only for non-profit groups of 40 or fewer. The camping fee is $13.00. Reservations are made through the NPS national line at (800) 365-2267.

Picnicking

Holly, Sweetgum and Laurel picnic areas offer comfort stations, picnic tables and fireplaces. No ground fires; only charcoal burning is permitted in grills for preparing food.

How To Get There: From Exit 23 of the Capital Beltway (I-495,95) take Kenilworth Avenue (MD 201) south. Take Greenbelt Road (MD193) left (east). Follow signs to the entrance on the right.

For Additional Information:
Manager
Greenbelt Park
6565 Greenbelt Road
Greenbelt, MD 20770
(301) 344-3948

Gunpowder Falls State Park

Just eight miles from Chesapeake Bay, the Big and Little Gunpowder rivers join to form a scenic valley. Here lies 18,000 acres of marsh and deciduous forest called Gunpowder Falls State Park. Two tales explain the origin of the valley's name. According to legend, settlers here gave gunpowder to the Indians, who misunderstood its purpose. They planted it hoping to produce crops, and the river flowing past the fields was named after this incident. Another more plausible story is that a man named

Winter had a mill on the stream prior to the Revolutionary War, where he made gunpowder by grinding the coals of burnt willow branches. Although its origin is questionable, the river's name has remained the same since 1658.

This park is the state's largest. It includes woodlands, flood plains, high plateaus, marshes and swamp shrub lands. A freshwater marsh has formed at the mouth of the Gunpowder River. Although inaccessible by foot, it is well worth joining one of the guided canoe trips and other nature programs in the area, which allow visitors to explore the area with a Park Ranger. Giant cattails, wild rice and various smartweeds support a large bird population. Owls, sparrows, least bitterns, Virginia rails, whippoorwills, bald eagles, whistling swans, green and blue herons and bobolinks are frequent visitors to the park. The marsh is a breeding ground for fish and acts as a filter preventing pollutants and sediment from getting into the bay. Along the edge of the marsh is a deciduous flood plain where ash, sycamores, willow and a variety of swamp shrubs provide wildlife with shelter during the winter. The best time to canoe in this area is in the early morning when deer, raccoon and muskrat come down to the river's edge to feed.

Although the area looks similar to the way it was when early settlers came into the region, in fact, it has changed substantially. As the land around the marsh was cleared for farming, sediment flowing into the area increased, causing the existing marsh to become covered in silt and eventually vegetation. At the same time marshland was created further out into the bay. This process has been reduced but new marshland is still being created, although at a slower rate. The Hammerman area, located near the Chesapeake Bay, contains the marsh, while the Hereford area, 35 miles to the north, has rugged, steep slopes and a river that rushes down rock ledges. Between the two river valleys is an area known as the Central area which is comprised of undeveloped areas with trails. An historic village, Jerusalem, located just outside of Kingsville, is in the process of being restored. The park is of particular interest to bird-watchers, hikers and amateur geologists, but will appeal to all nature lovers in general.

Hiking

More than 100 miles of hiking trails extend through the park. The woods abound with a great variety of trees, as well as many wildflowers and ferns. Because of the varied topography of the area, there is something to suit almost everyone. The Sweet Air Area features wooded area, river bottoms and high plateaus. Three main trails run through this area. The Big Rock Trail (2.6

miles) crosses the Little Gunpowder River. The Sweet Air Trail (2.4 miles) also crosses the river and runs from the Big Rock and back to the trailhead parking area. The Park Loop Trail (2 miles) leaves and returns from the trailhead parking lot. A much longer trail follows the former Northern Central Railroad line. This trail is 21 miles long and runs from Ashland to the Maryland state line. Trails follow the Big and Little Gunpowder Falls rivers throughout the central area. For trail maps and advice on planning your hike, contact park headquarters.

Camping

Camping facilities are provided for youth groups. Two locations are available. Arrangements should be made in advance with park headquarters. Family camping is provided on Hart-Miller Island, 6 miles south of the Hammerman Area in the Chesapeake Bay; it is accessible only by private boat. A nominal primitive camping fee is charged from Memorial Day to Labor Day.

Boating and Swimming

The Maryland Department of Natural Resources operates the entire park including a marina with launching ramps and docks near the Hammerman area; rental boats are available. The Hammerman area has a 1,500-foot swimming beach under life-guard supervision.

Fishing

Sections of the Big Gunpowder and Little Gunpowder Falls are designated trout fishing areas. Call park headquarters for the exact locations. A Maryland fishing license is required for those 16 and older, and a trout stamp is required for those interested in fishing for trout. The tidal waters start near Route 40 (Pulaski Highway) and include the Hammerman area. A sport-fishing license is required for fishing in the tidal waters. The Hammerman area is inhabited by perch, pickerel, largemouth bass and catfish. A striped bass moratorium was in effect until the fall of 1990. The allowable catch is still limited. From late summer through early fall, blue crab are abundant near the Hammerman area.

Picnicking

More than 200 tables, many in the shade, await you in the

Hammerman area of the park. Some have adjacent picnic grills.

How To Get There: From the Baltimore Beltway (I-695), take US 40 (Exit 35) to get to the Hammerman area. Head northeast to Ebenezer Road and turn right to the small town of Chase. Grace's Quarter Road out of Chase leads to the entrance of the Hammerman area of the park. Open year-round. Nominal entrance fee.

For Additional Information:
Park Manager , Gunpowder Falls State Park
2813 Jerusalem Road
P.O. Box 480
Kingsville, MD 21057
(410) 592-2897
http://www.dnr.state.md.us/publiclands

Gwynnbrook Wildlife Management Area

Gwynnbrook Wildlife Management Area, made up of some 74 acres in Baltimore County, is maintained primarily as a wildlife sanctuary. It is the oldest wildlife management area in the state, purchased in 1917 as a game farm. It houses a work center, equipment barns and workshop. There is a pond stocked each spring for public fishing. Bird-watchers and hikers interested in nature study are particularly welcome. A self-guided Wild Acres nature trail has been created with funds from the Chesapeake Bay and Endangered Species Fund to demonstrate how homeowners can provide food, cover and water for wildlife in their backyards. This is an ideal place to explore a placid natural setting and see such wildlife as fox, squirrel, rabbit and white-tailed deer. The managing agency is the Maryland State Forest and Park Service.

How To Get There: From I-695 (Baltimore Beltway) take I-795 (Northwest Expressway) to Owings Mills Blvd. Turn right and proceed 2 miles to Gwynnbrook Avenue. Turn right and go a few hundred feet to the parking lot on the left. The grounds are open dawn to dusk everyday, but the Wild Acres Trail is closed to the public on Wednesdays. No entrance fee.

For Additional Information:
Area Land Manager , Gwynnbrook District Office
3740 Gwynnbrook Avenue
Owings Mills, MD 21117
(410) 356-9272
http://www.dnr.state.md.us/publiclands

Helen Avalynne Tawes Garden

The Tawes garden is a six-acre, barrier-free botanical garden at the Tawes State Office Building featuring a diverse series of native plantings representing various regions of the State—an Eastern Shore peninsula, a Western Maryland mountainscape and a streamside community. In addition there are pleasant ponds, cultivated plantings and a separate "hands-on" garden where visitors are encouraged to touch, taste and smell the foliage.

The garden is open daily from dawn to dusk. A self-guiding booklet is available. The lobby of the Tawes State Office Building is open weekdays 8:00 A.M.–5:00 P.M. and provides direct access to the garden. A cafeteria is open to the public weekdays, except for state holidays, 7:30 A.M.–3:00 P.M. The building lobby contains a small gift shop, open 9-3 and various educational exhibits.

How To Get There: From Washington, take Route 50 east to Annapolis; exit at Rowe Blvd.; follow Rowe Blvd. to Taylor Avenue (second traffic light), turn right. During the work week, park on the right side of Taylor Avenue in the stadium lot ($3.00 fee). On weekdays after 3:30 and weekends park on the left side of Taylor Avenue in the DNR lot. Non-working hours garden access is via a path off the right side of the front walk.

For Additional Information:
Helen Avalynne Tawes Garden
Department of Natural Resources
Tawes State Office Building, E-3
Annapolis, MD 21401
(410) 260-8189
http://www.dnr.state.md.us/publiclands

Hugg-Thomas Wildlife Management Area

The Hugg-Thomas Wildlife Management Area, under the jurisdiction of the Maryland State Forest and Park Service, is home to white-tailed deer, rabbit and squirrel. It encompasses 276 acres in Howard County, the gift of William S. Thomas in cooperation with the Maggie V. Hugg Memorial Fund, Inc. Bird-watchers and other nature enthusiasts are particularly welcome at this area year-round. However the area is popular with hunters so, during hunting seasons, the general public should visit here on Sundays when hunting is prohibited. There is a self-guided nature trail that begins at the parking lot. No restrooms available.

How To Get There: From the Baltimore Beltway (I-695) Exit 16, take I-70 west. At MD 32 (Exit 78), turn north to Sykesville. Turn left (northeast) to the wildlife area. The parking lot is on the right. Forsythe Road runs through the heart of Hugg-Thomas. The grounds are open dawn to dusk everyday.

For Additional Information:
Area Land Manager
Hugg-Thomas Wildlife Management Area
3740 Gwynnbrook Avenue
Owings Mills, MD 21117
(410) 356-9272
http://www.dnr.state.md.us/publiclands

Kensington Orchids

Orchids (family Orchidaceae) belong to the largest family of flowering plants, containing over 25,000 species of plants, most of them epiphytes or airplants. Orchids thrive in places as frosty as Alaska and as steamy as the Amazon Basin. From the thimble-sized Mystacidium Caffrum to the 20-foot-tall Renanthera Storei, orchids come in a vast variety of sizes and shapes. Some orchid blossoms are as small as a mosquito, others as large as a dinner plate. These and many other facts about orchids can be learned at Kensington Orchids, the largest orchid nursery on the East Coast. Even if you only want to breathe in the sweet, heavy scent of orchid blooms and see their remarkable flowers, you will want to visit the greenhouses of Kensington Orchids. They have over 100,000 plants in more than eight greenhouses.

In addition to a variety of marketable flowers, Kensington also devotes space to botanic orchids found nowhere else in the Washington area. The Royal Horticultural Society maintains a list of the parentage of notable orchids; one plant in this list in the Kensington greenhouses goes back to a 1913 hybrid. Although beginners can buy a plant for around $10.00, some of the plants here can cost up to $2,000. Information and beginners kits are sold here and are hard to resist when you see the beautiful flowers in bloom. The orchid center began when the late Dr. Edgar McPeak, a radiologist in Washington, turned the gift of a single blooming plant into a collection. The first greenhouse was built in 1946, and the orchid center opened for business in 1947. In 1964 Merritt Huntington took over the operation of the greenhouse. Visitors today will see a fascinating cross section of the world of tropical orchids.

How To Get There: From the Capital Beltway (I-495), take MD 185 north to Plyers Mill Road (it runs east and west between Connecticut Avenue in Kensington and Georgia Avenue in Wheaton). Turn right (east) and look for the Kensington Orchids sign. Visitors are welcome 7 days a week 8:00 A.M.–NOON and 1:00 P.M–5:00 P.M. No entrance fee.

For Additional Information
Kensington Orchids Associates
3301 Plyers Mill Road
Kensington, MD 20795
(301) 933-0036

Kenwood Cherry Trees

The famed cherry blossoms in Washington's Potomac Park (described elsewhere) fully deserve the reputation they have achieved through the years. So famous have they become, however, that the streets clog with traffic around the Tidal Basin when the trees are in bloom. Hotels and motels bulge, prices skyrocket, parking places—never easy to find—are virtually nonexistent. To enjoy the beauty without the hassle, cross the District of Columbia/Montgomery County line to Kenwood. Here since 1928 hundreds of Yoshino cherry trees have been grown from cuttings of their better-known relatives around the Tidal Basin and grafted onto native wild cherries. Today they are the pride of this small community, spreading an exotic canopy of pink and white blossoms over the town. Even many Washingtonians, who over the years have become discriminating connoisseurs of cherry trees, find the Kenwood display so outstanding that they make an annual pilgrimage to view the spectacle. The trees may bloom anywhere from mid-March through the month of April, keeping their showy flowers for about ten days. Typically they lag the DC trees by one or two weeks due to the higher elevation.

How To Get There: From the Capital Beltway (I-495), head southeast on River Road, which runs through part of Kenwood. For a good tour, just after passing the Kenwood Country Club on the left, turn left on Brookside Avenue, then left on Highland Avenue. At the end, turn right on Chamberlain Road to the end, right on Kennedy Road, right on Parkway, left on Brookside and back to River Road.

From downtown Washington take Wisconsin Avenue north to River Road. Follow River Road to the 5500 block and turn right on Dorset Avenue. You may explore Kenwood via Highland Drive and the many side streets leading off it. Kenwood lies south of Bethesda and west of Chevy Chase.

By Bicycle: The **Capital Crescent Trail** passes the Kenwood neighborhood at Dorset Avenue. Going south from Bethesda, Dorset is the first grade-level street crossing south of Little Falls Parkway; turn right (east) on Dorset to Highland and proceed as above. Going north from Georgetown, Dorset is the first street after the River Road bridge; turn left onto Dorset at the stop sign on the path. Refer to the Capital Crescent Trail in the DC chapter.

For Additional Information:
Bethesda-Chevy Chase Chamber of Commerce
7910 Woodmont Avenue, Suite 1204
Bethesda, MD 20814
(301) 652-4900

Information Officer, Tourism Division
Economic Development Office of Montgomery County
101 Monroe Street, Rockville, MD 20850
(301) 217-2345

Ladew Topiary Gardens

Though a bit beyond the 50-mile limit, we're sure you'll think the drive was well worth it. Outside the gates of Ladew, you are in Maryland hunt country, with huge estates of great wealth. When you pass through the gate, you go "through the looking glass" into a horticultural wonderland. One of your first visions is of a two-story-high topiary chicken on a nest. Turn your head to see a life-size hunter jumping his steed over a hurdle, following the hunt hounds that are chasing a fox.

Horticultural experts and garden lovers alike recognize the Ladew Topiary Gardens, just north of Towson, as one of the great topiary gardens of the world. Covering some 22 acres, the gardens range from exquisite formal design to absolute whimsy. Flowers are in bloom throughout the growing season, but the stately topiary hedges, (totaling a third of a mile in length, some up to 14 feet tall) and the topiary sculptures are the special glory. These include life-size lyre birds, a Buddha, sea horses and terraces framed by sculptured hedges of yew and hemlock. Around the central pool are 15 individual flower gardens reflecting the artistry of Harvey Smith Ladew, who conceived and created the topiary and flower gardens here over 50 years ago. In 1971, Mr. Ladew was awarded the Distinguished Service Medal of the Garden Club of America for his "great interest in developing and maintaining the most outstanding topiary garden in America without professional help." There is a small carriage museum, a gift shop and a cafe. The cafe is located in the former stable house with indoor and outdoor seating, and is usually open during garden hours. The cafe is serves beer, wine, and light lunch in a very pleasant setting.

In addition, you should tour Mr. Ladew's house built over three centuries, now resembling an English country house, furnished with the original English antiques, paintings and hunting paraphernalia. Its oval library with secret doors is considered one of the 100 most beautiful rooms in America.

How To Get There: Take Exit 27B from the Baltimore Beltway (I-695) and drive north on MD 146 about 14 miles to the garden (signs on the right). Open from mid-April through October 31 10:00 A.M.–4:00 P.M., Monday through Friday, and 10:30 A.M.–5:00 P.M., Saturday and Sunday. Admission to the gardens is $6.00 for adults, $5.00 for students and senior citizens, and $1.00 for children under 12. Admission to the house and gardens is $8.00 for adults, $7.00 for students and senior citizens and $2.00 for children under 12.

For Additional Information:
Ladew Topiary Gardens
3535 Jarrettsville Pike
Monkton, MD 21111
(410) 557-9466

Leakin and Gwynns Falls Parks

Two of the finest natural parks in the city of Baltimore—Leakin and Gwynns Falls—are located adjacent to each other in the southwestern portion of the city. Woods and meadows abound, and there is a great variety of birds, wildflowers and trees, including Leakin Park's 250-year-old tulip poplar. The parks together are composed of 1,216 acres of excellent mixed-mesophytic forest with upland areas of oak, hickory, beech and birch and the river-bottom hardwood forest of maple, ash and box elder. Such mixed forests are rare. Quite a number of the trees here are more than a century old, and several have a life span of over two centuries. The forest has been a part of Baltimore since about 1730. Many of the white oaks that once occupied the parks no longer exist. They apparently were used for shipbuilding and cooperage 100 years ago. The grounds of Leakin Park were acquired with money left to the city by J. Wilson Leakin, a lawyer and philanthropist whose grandfather, Major Sheppard Leakin, was a veteran of the War of 1812 and the tenth mayor of the city. Besides its heavily forested hills, Leakin Park is filled with spectacular deep gorges and rapidly running streams. During the winter months, Leakin Park is a popular skiing and sleigh-riding area.

Hiking

There are many short circuitous hikes in Leakin Park. The park contains undeveloped natural areas with a variety of birds, wildflowers and wildlife to view. Gwynns Falls offers an easy, level walk of 1.5 miles in length. Trail guides are available for circuit hikes in both parks.

The Gwynns Falls Greenways Trail project is to begin construction this fall. The Greenway Trail will begin in Leakin Park and will be both a biking and hiking trail. Eventually it will connect to Baltimore's Inner Harbor area.

Picnicking

Shaded picnic tables and grills are scattered throughout the parklands. No ground fires are permitted. Group areas are available for rent in the Crimea Area of Leakin Park.

Outdoor Education Programs

The Carrie Murray Outdoor Education Campus, located in Leakin Park, offers year-round activities, camps and outdoor activities to groups, families and individuals. Weekend workshops and nature walks are offered in the spring and fall. The facility is open Monday through Friday, 8:30 A.M.–4:30 P.M. and during special events. A newsletter and schedule of classes can be received by calling (410) 396-0808.

The campus building will undergo new construction within the next year, adding a large classroom. The Carrie Murray Outdoor Education Campus will also have a new entrance off Windsor Mill Road and a large parking area near the building. The Campus will be open weekends beginning in the fall of 1998. Summer day camp is also available.

How To Get There: From the Baltimore Beltway (I-695), take Exit 17 east onto Security Boulevard. Follow Security to Forest Park Avenue, and turn left (north) and proceed to Windsor Mill Road. A turn to the right (east) will bring you first to the northern boundary of Leakin Park and next to the northern boundary of Gwynns Falls. Look for signs directing you into the picnic areas and outdoor education areas. The Windsor Mill Road approach to the park, along a tree-lined drive, is a romantic fantasy of park splendor. For another pleasant drive, continue east on Windsor Mill, which becomes Gwynns Falls Parkway, extending to Druid Hill Park. The route is very picturesque.

For Additional Information:
Department of Recreation and Parks
City of Baltimore
Carrie Murray Outdoor Education Campus
1901 Ridgetop Road
Baltimore, MD 21207
(410) 396-0808

Lilypons Water Gardens

Not far from the Potomac River, just north of the Mont-gomery/Frederick County line, along the banks of the Monoca-cy River, is a most unusual farm called Lilypons. Its fields are 500 rectangular pools of water. Its crops are water lilies, other orna-mental aquatic plants and fish. Founded by George Leicester Thomas in 1917, the 300-acre farm has been operated for almost four generations by the Thomas family. As with many unique gardens such as Kennilworth Aquatic Gardens and Kensington Orchids, this farm began as a hobby. At first Mr. Thomas, a schoolteacher, gave away his goldfish and water lilies, but soon his interest expanded into a business. Except for the ponds, the garden appears much like any quaint Maryland farmstead. How-ever, the place is truly unique. It claims the largest and most var-ied production of decorative water plants in the world. Besides production ponds, you can see a landscaped area with water gar-dens created as you would find them in a private garden.

Thousands of water lilies, aquatic plants and goldfish are shipped from here each month during the growing season. One of the most fascinating types of ornamental fish is the Japanese carp, koi, that are considered the fish of emperors because of their bril-liant colors and majestic appearance. The water lily's cousin, the lotus, is considered a sacred plant and has been revered for thou-sands of years by the East Indians and the Egyptians.

It is no coincidence that the farm's name seems familiar, par-ticularly to older generations. In the 1930s, the farm was known as Three Springs Fisheries. Then, as now, much of the business was handled by mail order—so much mail that the post office agreed to establish a station on the premises. The question of a name for the station arose, and Mr. Thomas, an opera buff, sug-gested that it be named after Lily Pons, the internationally famous French opera star of the time, since the farm was often called Lily Ponds anyway. Miss Pons actually attended the ded-

Lotus blossom seed head.   *Richard L. Berman*

ication of her name to the post office. The farm has been known as Lilypons ever since. If you would like to learn more about water lilies and water gardens, this is the place to come.

The water gardens are open free to the public. The best time to visit is Memorial Day through Labor Day. Children particularly delight in seeing the thousands of goldfish and koi, while adults are generally more interested in the water lilies. An unusual number and variety of shore birds are attracted here, making this prime bird-watching territory during the migratory periods. Because the hatchery rotates ponds, draining them serially, it provides the unvegetated, muddy areas needed by these birds for feeding.

How To Get There: From the Capital Beltway (I-495), take I-270 northwest to MD 80, Exit 26. Turn right (west, toward Buckeystown) on MD 80 and go 1.5 miles. Turn left (south) on Park Mills Road; and continue three miles to Lillypons Road; turn right and proceed 0.5 mile. There will be signs to guide you to the entrance on the right. Open March 1 through October 30 10:00 A.M.–5:00 P.M. daily, except Easter Sunday and July 4th. Open November through February 10:00 A.M.–4:00 P.M. Monday through Saturday, except Thanksgiving Day and December 24 –January 2. If you would like to visit November through March, it is best to call ahead to check on hours and availability of stock. Special celebrations include Lilypons Days in June, Lotus Blossom Festival in July and Koi Arts Festival in early September.

For Additional Information:
Lilypons Water Gardens
P.O. Box 10
Buckeystown, MD 21717-0010
(301) 874-5133
(800) 999-5459

Little Bennett Regional Park

Little Bennett, located along the Little Bennett Creek in northernmost Montgomery County, is the single largest wooded area in the county, with almost 4,000 acres. Many small streams cross the primarily wooded land, with coniferous and mixed hardwood forests. Parts of Little Bennett are managed as meadows and scrublands, which provide a wide range of habitats for the park's diverse wildlife. Most of Little Bennett is undeveloped natural areas, which can be seen by the extensive network of wide, well-maintained and marked trails.

Little Bennett is a great place to see wildlife from the trail. Many owls nest here, particularly the great-horned owl and screech owl. Woodcocks can be seen in their courtship displays. Warblers are plentiful, particularly in their spring migration, along Little Bennett Stream and the surrounding valley. Wild turkeys can be seen year-round. Other birds commonly seen in the park include mallard ducks, turkey vultures, red-tailed hawk, red-shouldered hawk, hummingbirds, northern flicker, pileated woodpecker, downy woodpecker, eastern kingbird, eastern phoebe, Acadian fly catcher, eastern wood-pewee, barn swallows, chickadees, thrushes, eastern bluebirds, many warbler species, meadowlark, scarlet tanager, red-winged blackbird, indigo bunting, many sparrow species, robins, bluejays and more.

The park supports large populations of deer, foxes, raccoons, opossums, rabbits and a variety of small mammals. Allegheny mound-builder ants have constructed two-to-three-foot-tall anthills throughout the park. Butterflies are plentiful in season.

The park's diverse habitats support some unusual and rare wildflowers, not found elsewhere in Montgomery County. The park has plant and animal species not found in areas south of here. Due to budget cuts, the nature center was closed in 1991, however a program of activities is available each Saturday during the camping season; refer to the Nutshell News.

Hiking

There are numerous trails throughout Little Bennett. A trail map is available at the campground entrance station for $1.00.

Camping

The park has 91 campsites, available for a fee by reservation, and a small store. Contact the campground office for reservations.

How to Get There: From the Washington Beltway, take I-270 north to Exit 18, Route 121 Clarksburg Road. Exit northeast on Route 121. At the first light, Frederick Road, Route 355, turn left. You will see large signs for the park entrance on your right. It should be noted this entrance does not connect to Clarksburg Road, which goes through the southern portion of the park. Likewise, to reach the northern portion of the park by car one must enter further north along Route 355. Contrary to most published maps, only Clarksburg Road can actually be driven entirely across the park. The other roads are closed to vehicle traffic in the center of the park to protect animal habitat and because the roads are frequently flooded.

For Additional Information:
Little Bennett Regional Park
23701 Frederick Road, Clarksburg, MD 20871
(301) 972-6581 (Park Manager)
(301) 972-6581 (Campground Office)
http://www.mncppc.org

London Town

The historic London Town, one of the "lost towns" of colonial Anne Arundel County, is a National Historic Landmark near

Annapolis on eight acres of forested countryside and riverfront slopes which has been developed into a series of natural woodland gardens. Thousands of wildflowers delight nature lovers. Visitors may wander along walkways that lead through masses of daffodils, magnolias, ferns and azaleas during the spring. Rhododendrons, conifers, viburnum, herbs, camellias and holly are also found here among native trees and shrubs. During the summer, profuse displays of day lilies glorify the landscape. Along the shoreline of the South River, which forms the northern boundary of the gardens, is a marsh garden. Four walks have been designed to display native plants. The Spring Walk is crowded with 20,000 narcissus, magnolias and early flowering perennials. The Azalea Glade has masses of evergreens and rhododendrons including all species of azaleas native east of the Rocky Mountains. The Winter Garden is designed around plants that flower in the winter, ornamental bark and colorful foliage. The Wildflower Walk includes only shade-loving American wildflowers. There are two flowering seasons when the garden is particularly interesting, mid-March through July and September through January. Lectures on horticulture and special garden tours can be arranged in advance.

The house, a National Historic Landmark built circa 1760, has been authentically restored to interpret a colonial tavern and residence. London Town is currently the site of one of the largest archaeological excavations in Maryland. Researchers and historians are uncovering the lost town of London, which was established in 1684. Visitors can tour the dig site and hands-on archeology is offered periodically during the warm months.

How To Get There: From Washington, take US 50 east to MD 424 (Davidsonville exit) and turn right (south). At MD 214, turn left, and continue onto Stepney Lane (one block past the intersection of MD 214 and MD 2). Turn left on Stepney Lane (this becomes Londontown Road) and continue to the end of the road. The gardens are also accessible from the water. Boats may dock free of charge opposite Buoy 15 on the South River (about 6 miles inland from Chesapeake Bay). Open 10:00 A.M.–4:00 P.M. Monday—Saturday; and NOON–4:00 P.M. Sunday. The admission to house and gardens is $3.50 for adults, $3.00 for seniors and $2.00 for students 6-18 years old.

For Additional Information:
London Town Publik House
839 Londontown Road
Edgewater, MD 21037
(410) 222-1919
http://www.historiclondontown.com

Louise F. Cosca Regional Park and Clearwater Nature Center Herb Garden

One of the most popular regional parks in Maryland is the Louise F. Cosca Park near the small town of Clinton. Located on 500 acres, it attracts thousands of visitors annually, primarily because of the outstanding Clearwater Nature Center located there. Two of the center's most popular permanent attractions are a pool of fish and turtles and the Natural Treasures of Prince George's County Exhibit Hall. Other exhibits related to wildlife and nature change periodically. A ramp at the nature center accommodates visitors in wheelchairs. The gently rolling terrain, heavily wooded with at least 67 different species of trees, makes it appealing during the hot summer months, but many people visit the park year-round. It offers camping, hiking, picnicking, nature hikes, bird-watching and fishing.

During the summer, you may rent rowboats and paddle boats to explore the lake and to fish and search for catfish, largemouth bass, trout and bluegill. Occasionally, wild duck and Canada geese stop here to rest during the fall migration. A unique habitat nearby called the Suitland Bog hosts a variety of carnivorous plants. The pitcher plant, thread-leafed and intermediate sundew, ten-angled pipewort, rose pink and many other interesting plants grow here. Numerous special activities are scheduled by the park throughout the year including Birds of Prey Day, Turtle Derby Day and evening campfire programs. There are creek hikes, night hikes and insect hikes, all personally guided by a qualified naturalist. Nature arts and crafts sessions are staged also.

Hiking

Most of the hiking here is confined to nature trails winding through the park. Some five miles of foot and bridle trails are open year-round.

Camping

A family campground with 23 wooded sites and two group sites is available year-round. Parking spaces, tent sites, fireplaces, picnic tables and a children's play area are provided. Water and modern heated restrooms, including hot showers, are also available. Camping permits are issued on a first-come basis for no more than 14 days.

Picnicking

Hundreds of picnic sites are provided with tables and grills. Some have running water close by. No ground fires are permitted.

Fishing and Boating

A 15-acre lake is located within the park, and boats may be rented during the summer months. Fish include catfish, largemouth bass and bluegill. A Maryland fishing license and a trout license are required for persons 16 and older.

How To Get There: From the Capital Beltway (Exit 7A), take MD 5 south toward Waldorf. Turn right on Woodyard Road (MD 223) and continue to Brandywine Road (MD 381), then left (south) to Thrift Road. A right turn here will lead you to the park. Open 7:30 A.M. to dusk, year-round. Nominal fee for nonresidents of Montgomery and Prince George's counties during the summer.

For Additional Information:
Park Manager
Louise F. Cosca Regional Park
11000 Thrift Road
Clinton, MD 20735-9764
(301) 868-1397 or 868-3336
(301) 297-4575 or 297-4805 (Nature Center)

Maryland Science Center

The Maryland Science Center, located at Baltimore's Inner Harbor, offers three floors of hands-on exhibits, a five-story IMAX movie theater, and the world-famous Davis Planetarium. All of the Science Center's exhibits encourage the visitor to get involved. Try your hand at the activities featured in the Energy Place, Hubble Space Telescope, Science Arcade and Chesapeake Bay exhibits. Experienced demonstrators present concepts of physics, optics, sound, electricity, zoology, and chemistry on the Demonstration Stage every hour. There is even a K.I.D.S. (Keys into Discovery of Science) Room, specially designed for children ages three through seven. Visitors to the Science Center's IMAX Theater are drawn into the action by the theater's five-story, 75-foot-wide screen about four times a day on weekdays and seven times a day on weekends–call for specific times. Davis Planetarium presentations examine the mysteries of the universe and feature star shows and special effects.

The Crosby Ramsey Observatory on the Science Center's roof holds regular public sessions to observe the night sky, including views of the Sun, Moon, planets and stars through an 8-inch diameter telescope. Special observing events are held for eclipses and comets. The telescope also transmits images to the Davis Planetarium Theater for audiences to view. Guide your own sky viewing by calling the Starline phone, below.

How To Get There: Take I-95 to the MD 395 downtown exit. Turn right onto Conway Street and then right onto Light Street. The Science Center is located on the northeast corner of Light Street and Key Highway, on the south shore of Baltimore's Inner Harbor. Plenty of paid parking space is available within walking distance of the Science Center.

The Science Center is open 10:00 A.M.–5:00 P.M., Monday through Friday; Saturday and Sunday 10:00 A.M.–6:00 P.M. Extended summer hours: Monday through Thursday 10:00 A.M.–6:00 P.M.; Friday, Saturday and Sunday, 10:00 A.M.–8:00 P.M. The entrance fee is $9.75 for adults; $8.00 for ages 13-18 and over 50; $7.00 for children ages 4-12. Admission includes the exhibits, IMAX theater and planetarium.

For Additional Information:
Maryland Science Center
601 Light Street
Baltimore, MD 21230
(410) 685-5225 (24-hour information line)
(410) 962-0223 (TDD)
(410) 545-5918 (Starline 24-hour night sky viewing information)

McCrillis Gardens and Gallery

McCrillis Gardens and Gallery is a five-acre estate with over 750 varieties of azaleas, plus many varieties of rhododendrons and rare showy tree species such as dawn redwood, Japanese snowbell, stewaria, China-fir and Japanese umbrella-pine. The garden was given to the Maryland-National Capital Park and Planning Commission by William and Virginia McCrillis in 1978 and is managed by the staff of Brookside Gardens. McCrillis Gardens must be seen in azalea blooming season, which usually starts in early April and continues until early June; rhododendrons are at their best in mid-May, but may still be in bloom as late as July; perennials add interest into the summer.

The gardens are open daily 10:00 A.M. to sunset; the gallery is open Tuesday-Sunday NOON–4:00 P.M. while exhibitions are on display. No parking on the grounds; no food or drink; no pets, audio devices, bicycles, or bare feet are allowed.

How To Get There: Take the Washington Beltway to Exit 36, Old Georgetown Road, south (Bethesda). Turn right on Greentree Road and proceed about a mile. McCrillis Gardens is on the left, just past the intersection of Greentree and Burdette. There is no parking in the facility and very limited on-street parking during the week before 4:00 P.M.; after 4:00 P.M. and on weekends, parking is available across the street at the Woods Academy School.

For Additional Information:
McCrillis Gardens and Gallery, c/o Brookside Gardens
1500 Glenallen Ave.
Wheaton, MD 20902
(301) 365-1657 or 217-6850
(301) 949-8230 (Brookside Gardens)

McKee-Beshers Wildlife Management Area

McKee-Beshers Wildlife Management Area (which includes Maddux Island) is a 1,960-acre tract of bottomland lying in the Potomac River floodplain. Once used for farming, the land, now owned by the Maryland State Forest & Park Service, an agency of the Department of Natural Resources, is managed primarily for game species—white-tailed deer, fox, squirrel, waterfowl and wild turkey. Hughes Hollow is part of McKee-Beshers Wildlife Management Area accessible from Hunting Quarter Road, is particularly good for bird-watching. Kentucky warblers, woodcocks, green herons, broad-winged and red-tailed hawks, purple finches and a variety of bluebirds can be expected in their respective seasons. Bird-watching, photography and hiking are encouraged. The mixture of field and forest dotted with swamps and small creeks creates an inviting environment for wildlife. Tree and hedgerow plantings, water impoundments and various nesting structures have been added to increase the area's attractiveness to wildlife. Hunting is permitted in all of the area; no hunting is allowed on Sundays.

How To Get There: From the Capital Beltway (I-495), take the River Road (Potomac, Maryland) exit north. Follow River Road for approximately 15 miles, through the town of Seneca. The Wildlife Management Area may be entered through Old River Road, Hughes Road or Sycamore Landing Road. Maps of the area are available at the Gwynnbrook Work Center, below. If possible, it is best to write in advance for the map. No entrance fee.

For Additional Information:
Area Manager
3740 Gwynnbrook Ave.
Owings Mills, MD 21117
http://www.dnr.state.md.us/publiclands

Merkle Wildlife Sanctuary and Visitor Center

The Merkle Wildlife Sanctuary and Visitor Center, under the jurisdiction of the Maryland Department of Natural Resources, consists of about 1,670 acres of open water, field, woodland and marsh along the Patuxent River in Prince George's County. The sanctuary has the largest Canada geese wintering population on the western shore of the Chesapeake bay. A number of osprey and some bald eagles nest here. Numerous smaller birds and other waterfowl also frequent the area. The visitor center has two-story high windows to view the birds and features a variety of wildlife exhibits. This is an excellent place to visit from October through early March to see the migratory waterfowl.

Merkle Wildlife Sanctuary affords visitors an opportunity to learn about the Patuxent River environment and how to protect it. Naturalists work with visitors and school groups to provide an understanding of the relationship between land management, fish, and wildlife habitat and the Patuxent River. Bird watching and hiking are permitted on designated seasonal trails. Groups can schedule interpretive nature programs during the week; public programs are offered on the weekends. A quarterly schedule of programs is available upon request. Some programs involve nominal fees and may require advance reservations.

The principal activities here are hiking, photography and bird-watching. But before doing these you should check with the nature center staff.

Driving Tour

The Chesapeake Bay Critical Area Driving Tour provides an opportunity for visitors to explore the sanctuary grounds. The tour extends from Patuxent River Park at the end of Croom Airport Road and ends at Merkle. It is accessible at either end only for hiking and biking on Saturdays (January–September) between 10:00 A.M. and 3:00 P.M. On Sundays, it is open to vehicles only from 10:00 A.M. to 3:00 P.M.; traffic is one-way from the Patuxent River Park (see listing below).

How To Get There: From the Capital Beltway (I-495), take MD 4 east to Upper Marlboro. Turn right (south) on US 301. Follow US 301 to MD 382 (Croom Road) and turn left 4.0 miles to Saint Thomas Church Road. Turn left and follow the signs 2.8 miles to Merkle. The grounds are open to the public every day from 7:00 A.M. to sunset. The visitor center is open weekdays 10:00 A.M.–4:00 P.M.; weekends 10:00 A.M.–6:00 P.M., April 1–October 31 or 10:00 A.M.–5:00 P.M. (November 1–March 31). The visitor center is closed on major holidays.

For Additional Information:
Manager
Merkle Wildlife Sanctuary
11704 Fenno Road
Upper Marlboro, MD 20772
(301) 888-1410
http://www.dnr.state.md.us/publiclands

Mt. Briar Wetlands Preserve

Although the preserve is small, only about 30 acres, it is one of Maryland's unique non-tidal wetlands. It has a great variety of wetland wildlife and attracts other wildlife from the adjoining farms. Water flows from seepage springs at the north end of the preserve, saturating the soil. The soil is a silty clay loam with moderate acidity, with a predominance of *sphagnum* moss; sphagnum is normally associated with colder climates and is considered an indicator of high wetland quality. The prevalent plant species include common cattail (*Typha latafolia*), spicebush (*Lindera benzoin*), flowering rush/arrowhead (*Sagittaria*), and duckweek (*Lemna*); in addition there are several rare or endangered plant species here. This lush area has 29 tree species, 81 grasses, 16 shrubs and vines, 4 moss species, 36 bird species, plus other animal life. One can see unusual insects, not seen anywhere else in the area, such as a leaf moth that perfectly imitates a dead tree leaf and a white-yellow-black "two-headed" caterpillar, that the author saw on one visit.

One can view the wetland from over 2,400 linear feet of floating boardwalk with rope rails and three observation decks, which were erected by the Maryland Conservation Corps crews in 1987-1988. Adjacent fields are mowed on alternating years to provide an open grassy "managed meadow", with some short grass and some taller grass habitat. There are no restrooms, water, maps or attendants at the site. Mosquitoes, however, are plentiful, so don't forget to put on insect repellent.

How To Get There: Take I-270 north from the Capital Beltway to Frederick, Maryland; exit on US 340 southeast and go 11 miles to MD 67; go north about 7 miles to Rohersville, turn left on Rohersville Road (Main St. on some signs); take the first right on Millbrook Road. The park entrance is about one mile down the road on the right, just past a farm with silos on both sides of the road; go slowly, the site is not well marked. There is a large parking lot and picnic table.

For Additional Information:
Washington County Department of Parks
1307 Potomac Street
Hagerstown, MD 21740
(301) 791-3125

Myrtle Grove Wildlife Management Area

Approximately five miles west of La Plata, Maryland, is a wooded wildlife area with a small stream wandering through it that offers an opportunity to observe an excellent variety of creatures. Squirrel, white-tailed deer, quail, rabbit, ducks and Canada geese, woodcock and a great variety of songbirds, raptors, wild turkey, bobwhite quail, woodpeckers, marsh birds and hummingbirds can be found. Muskrat, mink, otter, red and gray fox, as well as numerous bats and moles make their home among Virginia pine, various oaks, hickory, beech, tulip poplar, dogwood, hornbeam, sweet gum, mountain laurel, pawpaw and various club mosses. Part of the area is a water impoundment for waterfowl, and during their fall migratory period great numbers of ducks and geese stop here, sometimes to spend the winter. Bald eagles are frequent visitors.

Myrtle Grove is the oldest management area in southern Maryland. It has grown to 900 areas from the original 754 acres, which were purchased in 1929 for $5,000. You may notice selective cutting of trees, road daylighting (cutting trees to allow sunlight to reach the ground), planting of food plots, mowing and the maintenance of hedges to benefit wildlife. There is a

23-acre lake, three green tree reservoirs and a moist soil impoundment at Myrtle Grove. All are man-made and managed for wildfowl and fishing. The green tree reservoirs are wooded swamps where the water level is raised during the fall and winter to allow migratory waterfowl to rest and feed there. The water levels are lowered in the spring and summer to keep the trees alive and produce food for wildlife. Recently several areas were cleared and the reservoirs were planted with Japanese millet and sorghum to attract waterfowl.

Myrtle Grove is used both as a stocking area for endangered wildlife and as a data collection area to monitor environmental conditions. A food production survey has been taken over the past several years by counting acorn on different types of oak trees. Gypsy moth collection boxes are placed in the area to measure infestation. The eastern tiger salamander has been reintroduced here. Myrtle Grove is one of only three designated target-shooting areas open to the public in the entire state. It has the only firearms range on any wildlife management area. Use of the range is very heavy, especially on weekends. On some days over 100 recreational shooters use the area; a permit is required to use the range.

Hiking

A network of trails bisects the area. Maps are available from the manager's office at the work center. All the trails are over relatively flat terrain and can be most rewarding when combined with wildlife watching. The area is open for hunting during the appropriate seasons.

Fishing

Freshwater fishing for largemouth bass, bream or bluegill and catfish is available. A Maryland state fishing license is required for persons 16 and older.

How To Get There: From the Capital Beltway (I-495), take MD 5 south to MD 301. Continue south on 301 to La Plata, and turn right (west) on MD 225. Myrtle Grove is on the north side of MD 225 about 5 miles west of La Plata. No entrance fee.

For Additional Information:
Area Wildlife Manager
Myrtle Grove Wildlife Management Area
5625 Myrtle Grove Road
La Plata, MD 20646
(301) 743-5161

Department of Natural Resources
Maryland Wildlife Service
Tawes State Office Building
Annapolis, MD 21401
(410) 260-8540
http://www.dnr.state.md.us/publiclands

Nanjemoy Marsh Sanctuary

(Also Nanjemoy Creek Heron Great Blue Heron Sanctuary
and Nanjemoy Creek Environmental Education Center)

Nanjemoy Marsh Santuary is now closed to the public except
for scheduled field trips led by the Nature Conservancy and the
Southern Maryland Audubon Society. However, we consider it
so exceptional, we thought readers, especially dedicated birders,
might want to join one of those groups to go on the trips.

Located in Charles County, just east of the Potomac and
abuot 30 miles south of Washington, is the enchanting Nanjemoy Marsh Sanctuary. Established and maintained by the
Southern Maryland Audubon Society, it contains 58 acres of
outstanding tidal marsh habitat and is a great bird-watching
area. During the spring, droves of red-winged blackbirds come
this way, many pausing to build nests. The great blue heron
feeds here, and you may also see the green heron, an occasional common egret, red-tailed hawk, osprey and even a bald eagle.
No eagles are known to nest here, but there are some nesting in
nearby areas; osprey do nest in the marsh. Muskrats and raccoon are plentiful but during the summer months so are mosquitoes. Marsh has long been known as one of the most productive and fertile environments on earth. Trails lead through
the marsh, but because it is a delicate area, it is open to the public only on a limited basis. The Southern Maryland Audubon
Society received title to the land in 1991, then marked and
cleared a foot trail along the shoreline.

The nearby 288-acre Nanjemoy Creek Great Blue Heron Sanctuary, owned by The Nature Conservancy, is closed to all visitors to protect the approximately 900 great blue heron pairs that nest there, making this the largest great blue heron nesting colony on the east coast north of Florida; the numbers of birds and exact location vary from year to year. The preserve also shelters the rare Virginia wild ginger, at least four species of wild orchids, fox, mink, otter and rails. The only way to visit the sanctuary is to be a Nature Conservancy member and be selected through a lottery for one of the few guided trips sponsored each year by the Maryland/DC Nature Conservancy; this spectacular day trip itself is worth the price of a Maryland Nature Conservancy membership. The Nanjemoy Creek Environmental Education Center, also nearby, sponsors ecology programs for area school children; it is available only to educational groups, by reservation.

How To Get There: The Marsh sanctuary is located along Nanjemoy Creek, south and east of MD 6 in Charles County, off Taloe Neck Road, not far from the town of Bryans Road. Please contact the warden before visiting the sanctuary. He will give more specific directions at that time as well as advise you on particular delights to look out for at different times of the year. No entrance fee.

Contact the owners, below to arrange to go on a scheduled trip to the Great Blue Heron Sanctuary. Nature Conservancy trips are limited to members, but this trip alone is worth the price of membership. The Nature Conservancy is probably the country's leading non-profit, non-government organization that acquires and preserves vast areas of important wildlife habitat; every nature lover should consider membership.

For Additional Information:
George Wilmot, Volunteer Warden
Nanjemoy Marsh Sanctuary
6722 Amherst Road
Bryans Road, MD 20616
(301) 375-8552

Southern Maryland Audubon Society
P.O. Box 181
Bryans Road, MD 20616

The Nature Conservancy
Maryland & District of Columbia Chapter
2 Wisconsin Circle, Suite 300
Chevy Chase, MD 20815
(301) 656-8673
http://www.tnc.org

Nanjemoy Creek Environmental Education Center
(301) 743-3526 (educational groups only)

National Aquarium in Baltimore

The National Aquarium, in Baltimore's Inner Harbor, is the next best thing to strapping on scuba tanks and diving in all seven seas, a few rivers, and some ponds in a single afternoon. Opened in 1981, the Aquarium houses over 10,000 living aquatic species in more than 2,000,000 gallons of water in numerous separate habitats. On your self-guided tour, you are "immersed" in the sights, sounds, smells and—in a few exhibits—feels, of living aquatic environments. A one-way moving escalator takes visitors on a journey from the depths of the ocean to the top canopy of a rain forest. You will walk quite a distance, so dress appropriately with comfortable shoes.

Visitors begin their tour in Maryland with four exhibits on the state's aquatic habitats: an Allegheny Mountain pond, a tidal marsh, the coastal beach and the Atlantic Shelf. Stop off in the movie theater to see a multimedia show on aquatic life and habitats of the Chesapeake Bay. Continue through the Surviving Through Adaptations gallery, where you'll see large aquariums with venomous lionfish, luminescent "flashlight fish", colorful anemones, artfully camouflaged fish and more. Each exhibit is an example of animal adaptation to a specific environment. See fossil fish projected on the walls. Go through a California marine kelp forest and a Pacific coral reef. See the Sea Cliffs exhibit, which recreates the cliffs of Heimay, Iceland. Here arctic aquatic birds—puffins, guillemots and razorbills—preen themselves on land and "fly" through the water for fun and fish-food; you can see the underwater bird aquabatics through an underwater viewing window located in the Sea Cliff's pool wall. Next is the Children's Cove, where children of all ages can handle horseshoe crabs, sea urchins, starfish and other tolerant creatures.

Jungle sounds lure the visitor up a long narrow passage to emerge in the middle of a South American tropical rain forest under a 64-foot tall glass pyramid. Visitors walk a path through the jungle, as exotic birds fly, walk and paddle around you without barriers. Amongst the tropical foliage are scarlet ibis, blue-crowned mot-mots, sun conures, iguanas, two-toed sloths, two lion tamarins and dozens of other exotic tropical creatures. At the exit of the Rain Forest exhibit are a series of small "hidden life" enclosures; look very closely to find the well-camouflaged frogs, snakes and lizards in each.

Two popular attractions of the Aquarium are the 335,000-gallon **Atlantic Coral Reef** and the 220,000-gallon **Open Ocean** exhibit; both feature a diver's-eye view of large (and not so large) marine species. The coral reef tank, the largest of its kind in the US, has about 3,500 colorful reef fishes. Three times daily a scuba diver enters the tank to feed schools of fish, rays and a hawksbill turtle. The Open Ocean is probably the most memorable exhibit, especially for children. Visitors will be circled at eye-level by living sharks, including hammerhead sharks, lemon sharks, sand tiger sharks, sandbar sharks, nurse sharks, plus schools of hatchetfish, rays and other smaller fish, who, strangely, don't seem to mind living among these voracious predators.

The **Marine Mammal Pavilion**, which almost doubles the size of the aquarium, opened in December of 1990. The highlight of the Marine Mammal Pavilion is the 1.2 million-gallon habitat for bottlenose dolphins, with the world's largest acrylic windows for observing the underwater activity. Visitors can see a 20-minute educational presentation on marine mammals "Dolphin Discoveries: Life Beneath the Waves" in the 1,300-seat amphitheater surrounding the marine mammal habitat. Other features of the new Marine Mammal Pavilion include the Discovery Room, which houses a collection of marine artifacts for visitors to examine, a gift shop, food court and Exploration Station.

Exploration Station is a series of new high-tech exhibits that give the visitor the view of life from the marine animals' point of view. Life-size seals and manatees swim alongside. In another exhibit, the visitor can hear and see the world as a whale does. In another, one gets the predator's view of how difficult it is to catch evasive prey; and there's more.

Changing Exhibits are changed every year or so. **Venom: Striking Beauties,** on display until January 2000, features over 40 species of venomous spiders, snakes, insects, fish, and lizards.

Visitors learn what's myth and what's to fear. The animal assassins include Australian taipan–the world's most deadly snake; the deadly stonefish, the black mamba, gila monsters, beaded lizards and blue ring octopus; also some scary but not as deadly creatures such as cowkiller and bullet ants, tarantulas, black widows, giant centipedes and scorpions.

Hours, Tickets, Lines and Membership: The Aquarium's winter hours (September-May) are 10:00 A.M.–5:00 P.M. daily, and 10:00 A.M.–8:00 P.M. Fridays; summer hours (May 15–September 15) are 9:00 A.M.–5:00 P.M. Monday–Thursday, 9:00 A.M.–8:00 P.M. Friday–Sunday. Tickets to the Aquarium are currently $11.95 for adults; $10.50 for seniors, and $7.50 for children (3–11); children under the age of 3 are admitted free. Plan to spend several hours to see and appreciate everything.

The Aquarium is Maryland's premier tourist attraction, pulling in over 1.5 million visitors a year. So, it's no surprise that waiting lines for the Aquarium can be quite long, sometimes exceeding 30 minutes, especially on weekends, holidays and throughout the summer. The best times to visit, when lines are shortest, is late afternoon and evening. There are three good alternatives to waiting in line. Coupons for a specific entry time may be obtained from the outdoor reservations booth on the date of your visit, but these sell out fast. Advanced tickets for a specific time and date can be obtained with a small surcharge from TicketCenter outlets, by calling (202) 432-0200 in the Washington area or (410) 481-6000 in Baltimore.

The best alternative to waiting in the lines is to become a member of the Aquarium. Members get free admission through a members-only entrance with no waiting, plus you help support the continuing operation of the Aquarium. You can join at the members' entrance. Memberships range from $32 for individuals to $63 for a family, per year.

How To Get There: Take either I-95 north or the Baltimore-Washington Parkway (I-295) north to Baltimore; take the Inner Harbor exit. Make a right on Conway Street, left onto Light Street, then right onto Pratt Street (one way). The route to the Aquarium and Inner Harbor complex is very well marked. On-street parking can be difficult to find on any day, so be prepared to pay downtown rates for commercial parking garages. Space can usually be found in parking garages on Pratt Street across from the Aquarium and on Piers 5 and 6 just past the Aquarium.

The Aquarium has facilities for handicapped, including wheelchairs; advance arrangements are recommended. Baby strollers are not allowed inside for safety reasons and must be checked at the stroller check desk in the lobby; baby backpacks are available for loan.

For Additional Information:
The National Aquarium in Baltimore
Pier 3
501 East Pratt Street
Baltimore, Maryland 21202-3194
(410) 576-3800
(410) 576-8238 (Fax)
http://www.aqua.org

National Colonial Farm and Ecosystem Farm

Walking through the National Colonial Farm one gets a sense of an earlier era when the hillsides of Maryland were dotted with small-scale, low-income homesteads. The National Colonial Farm, located across from Mount Vernon in **Piscataway Park** (described elsewhere), features 100 acres of cultivated land including corn, wheat and tobacco fields, a museum garden, a kitchen garden, a woodlands trail, a chestnut grove and a wildlife pond. A small part borders the Potomac River. The farm teaches people how life was lived on a typical colonial-era family tobacco farm. Interpretive staff in 18th-century dress, use 18th-century tools and techniques to work the farm, with many of the same crop species that would have been raised then. Several circa 1780 farm buildings have been restored and are open to the public including the farm home, tobacco barn, smokehouse, out-kitchen.

The new **Ecosystem Farm** is an educational demonstration of high productivity agriculture with environmentally sound sustainable harvest practices. A solar powered electric system powers the irrigation system and an electric fence to keep deer from eating the crops.

The pond is particularly interesting during the fall migration of waterfowl when Canada geese and several species of ducks stop to rest and sometimes to winter. It is stocked with bluegill and largemouth bass, which share the waters with snapping turtles. A self-guided woodland trail displays the trees and plants that provided food for colonists during the Revolutionary War. The pawpaws, persimmons, black walnuts, hickory nuts, blackberries, raspberries and wild strawberries are still being eaten by visitors. Occasionally white-tailed deer, rabbit and raccoon are seen along this trail. The American Chestnut grove, containing hundreds of trees, is a part of a major research project aimed at producing a blight-free chestnut tree through seed mutation. Also on the farm is an area in which edible wild foods are grown. The Saylor Memorial Grove has a sheltered picnic area in a wooded setting and a boat pier that offers a panoramic view of Mount Vernon across the Potomac River. The pier was formerly used by a ferry from Mount Vernon across the river, but now is used for public fishing.

Nearby is the Native Tree Arboretum, with 125 species native to southern Maryland.

How To Get There: From the Capital Beltway (I-495) take Indian Head Highway (MD 210) south about 10 miles to Livingston Road. Turn right onto Bryan Point Road. Follow Bryan Point Road for 4 miles to the farm parking lot on the right. Open everyday except Mondays, Christmas, Thanksgiving and New Year's Day 10:00 A.M.–4:00 P.M. in spring and summer; Call about reduced hours in fall and winter. Admission to the farm is $2.00 for adults $0.50 for children (3-12).

For Additional Information:
The National Colonial Farm
Accokeek Foundation
3400 Bryan Point Road
Accokeek, MD 20607
(301) 283-2113
http://web.gmu.edu/bios/potomac/af

Oxford

Sometimes one finds surprising natural attractions in the most unexpected places—such as the tiny hamlet of Oxford on Maryland's Eastern Shore. It is loaded with history, including the home of Robert Morris, a close friend of George Washington, who, it is claimed, financed the Revolutionary War in large part. But this is also a fine place to visit the waterfront, to watch a wild mallard duck raising her young during the summer months and to catch blue crabs from the clear waters. You can sit by the waters of the Tred Avon River under great maple and oak trees in the small city park, and enjoy the solitude and serenity. A stroll around town will lead you past big boxwood, pecan trees and, on the town's main street, a huge trellised grapevine, said to be the largest in Maryland. It was planted around 1810 and still produces fruit. A free public beach area offers an opportunity to cool off during warm summer months.

How To Get There: From Washington, take US 50 east across the Chesapeake Bay Bridge to Easton; pick up MD 333 southwest to Oxford where the road comes to a dead end. You may wish to take the small toll ferryboat over to Bellevue on your return trip.

For Additional Information:
Talbot County Chamber of Commerce
805 Goldsborough Street
P.O. Box 1366
Easton, MD 21601
(410) 822-4606
http://www.talbotchamber.org

Maryland Department of Economic and Employment
    Development
Office of Tourism Development
217 E. Redwood Street
Baltimore, MD 21202
(410) 333-6611

Oxon Hill Farm

Overlooking the Potomac River a few miles south of Washington, in Prince George's County, is Oxon Hill Farm. The farm periodically schedules events where, under supervision, visitors can help milk a cow, press cider, collect warm eggs from the nest, shell corn and pick apples at this turn-of-the-century working farm. Seasonally, interpreters demonstrate planting crops and shearing sheep. Hayrides are often offered, as are demonstrations of animal care, traditional crafts and rural culture. A hay barn, feed room, equipment shed, and workroom are open to the public. Machinery and equipment are displayed and demonstrated. Cows, chickens, horses and pigs wander around the pens and fields. In the spring, newborn lambs, chicks and calves can be seen. In May the sheep are sheared, and in July a steam-powered threshing machine threshes the wheat crop. In the fall, the farmer picks the corn and cuts the sorghum cane. Many varieties of vegetables are raised in the garden, some of which you might not recognize. You can walk along the self-guided woodlot nature trail through the forest and orchard. Although the trail is only one-half mile long, it is sloped and is too rough for baby strollers and wheelchairs. The farm is administered by the National Park Service.

How To Get There: Take Exit 3A (Indian Head Highway) south from the Capital Beltway (I-495). Bear right off the exit ramp onto Oxon Hill Road. The farm is 100 yards to the right; look for the sign. Open daily year-round: 8:00 A.M.–4:30 P.M.; closed Thanksgiving, Christmas and New Year's Day. No entrance fee. Call to see when activities are scheduled.

For Additional Information:
Oxon Hill Farm
c/o National Capital Parks-East
1900 Anacostia Drive, S.E.
Washington, DC 20020
(301) 839-1176
(301) 839-1177 (tape of activities)

Patapsco Valley State Park

One of the largest state parks in the greater Washington area is a pristine stream valley park containing some 15,000 acres along the scenic Patapsco River. Steeped in both human and natural history, it is one of the finest and most interesting parks in the greater Washington area. The Patapsco Valley State Park begins upstream about seven miles from the river's mouth in the Chesapeake Bay and averages only one-half mile in width. Nearly all the surrounding terrain is heavily wooded.

First discovered in 1608 by Capt. John Smith, the Patapsco

River was named Bolus for the nodular deposits of red clay near its mouth. The name Patapsco is derived from an Indian tongue, but its exact meaning is unclear. Warring bands of Susquehannock Indians raided the first settlements along the river, but the Europeans eventually planted the land in corn, tobacco and, ultimately, in wheat. In 1772 the Ellicott brothers built the first flourmill on the Patapsco near the present site of Ellicott City. The enterprise flourished, and Baltimore soon became one of our country's major exporters of wheat.

The river figured in conflicts too. During the Revolutionary War, Lafayette and Rochambeau crossed the Patapsco with their armies. It was at the mouth of the Patapsco that Francis Scott Key wrote "The Star-Spangled Banner" during the War of 1812. Later, during the Civil War, Union troops guarded the Thomas Viaduct against sabotage by Confederate sympathizers. In 1828, part of the first 13 miles of the Baltimore & Ohio Railroad were laid through the Patapsco River canyon, becoming the first railroad to the West.

The Patapsco's water quality has vastly improved since the 1970s (and the clean water legislation) to the point where water quality is now very good and safe for all recreational uses. In fact, breeding of local fish species has been very successful. The stream is beautiful in this section of Maryland. Winding through a steep and narrow canyon that it carved thousands of years ago, the Patapsco drops across the fall line separating the rolling Piedmont Plateau from the level Coastal Plain. Ancient crystalline rocks, millions of years old, are exposed in this area making it a fascinating place for amateur geologists. The dense forests of river birch, sycamore, beech, tulip poplar, maple, oak and dogwood shelter a damp floor where numerous ferns and flowering shrubs grow. In spring, masses of May apple, dogtooth violet and bloodroot dot the landscape, but wildflowers can be found here almost any time of the year. You can also see the red and gray fox, white-tailed deer, raccoon, striped skunk and wood duck as well as a variety of turtles, snakes and lizards. Blue herons and kingfishers are common along the river. Beavers can frequently be sighted, with an occasional otter. Salamanders are found along the river bank and camp woodlands.

The Avalon Area contains a two-mile drive along the river to a 200 foot long suspended pedestrian bridge over the river. A River of History Visitor Center is planned to open in the summer of 1999.

In the Hilton area, picturesque dogwood glades paint the landscape in white during springtime. A beautiful overlook of the Patapsco River valley is found in the Hollofield area. Morning is the best time to go there, especially if you plan to take photographs. In the McKeldin area, there is a big pool with singing rapids, where the river widens to punctuate the remotest and most untrammeled area of the park with five miles of beautiful trails.

Outdoor Adventure programs are offered almost year-round; these include hiking, nature walks, and canoeing, among other things. Call the park for a schedule.

Hiking, Bicycling and Horseback Riding

About 27 miles of improved hiking trails exist in the park, but they are varied and challenging, in many instances paralleling the river. Spring, fall and winter months are the best for hiking since the humidity is high during the summer months. The park offers many miles of unimproved horseback trails. The Avalon and McKeldin areas and the various side roads leading through the park area are excellent for bicycling. No rentals of horses or bikes are available in the park. The two-mile Grist Mill recreational trail is paved and handicapped accessible.

Camping

Camping is allowed at the Hilton and Hollofield area; both offer hot showers and laundry tubs. Mini-cabins are available in the Hilton area. Reservations are available. Regularly scheduled nature walks and evening campfires are held during the summer season.

Picnicking

Extensive picnic grounds are located at various sites in the park. Shelters, including some that handle up to 250 people, may be reserved beginning the first working day of January. Call early. The park is trash free (meaning no trash containers or pickups are provided), so plan to haul out your own trash.

How To Get There: From Washington, Take I-95 north to I-695 (the Baltimore Beltway) west to Exit 15, Route 40 west three miles toward Ellicott City. Follow signs on Route 40 to the park headquarters where you may obtain maps and information about all areas of the park. A nominal entrance fee is charged weekends only March through October, except for the Avalon Area, which requires a fee seven days a week. Prospective visitors are advised to call ahead to confirm opening dates and times.

All developed park areas offer handicapped accessibility to picnic sites, comfort stations, and camping.

For Additional Information:
Park Manager
Patapsco Valley State Park
8020 Baltimore National Pike
Ellicott City, MD 21043-3499
(410) 461-5005

Maryland Department of Natural Resources
Forest and Park Service
Tawes State Office Building
Annapolis, MD 21401
(410) 260-8186 (business hours)
(410) 260-8888 (other hours)
http://www.dnr.state.md.us/publiclands

Patuxent River Park and Jug Bay Natural Area

The Patuxent River is the longest river entirely within the state of Maryland, and its drainage area occupies approximately one-tenth of the state's total land area. Although the water level varies, it is on average the deepest river in the state.

The upper segment of the river flows through low, wooded hills of the Piedmont. Soils here are mostly stony and several major streams and valleys feed into its waters. The waters flow through several major population centers, such as Columbia, Laurel and Fort Meade, and then pass the Patuxent Wildlife Research Center. The sandy, highly erodible soils of the Coastal Plain characterize the middle portion of the Patuxent watershed. About 50 miles from the headwaters of the river the narrow gorge broadens into Jug Bay, which is three miles long and one-half mile wide at its widest, and then narrows again before opening into the Chesapeake Bay. Most of the basin's 6,700 acres of wetlands lie along this section. Finally, the river meets the Chesapeake Bay where the average water depth varies from 20-30 feet to as much as 130 feet at Point Patience, one of the deepest spots in the bay. Here the river is almost two miles wide.

The Maryland-National Capital Park and Planning Commission manages the open space lands of the Patuxent River Park as "limited-use natural areas". The 2,000-acre Jug Bay Natural

Area, a heavily wooded with sycamores, beeches, oaks, maples and other mixed hardwoods, is home for white-tailed deer, raccoon, pileated woodpecker, red-tailed hawk, opossum, red fox and squirrel. Wood ducks, otter and beaver may be spotted by patient observers. Along the nature trails and boardwalks through the marsh and swamps one can see unusual plants, such as orchids and wild rice and some 12 species of ferns. Hollies, viburnums and mountain laurel form a thick undergrowth to the second-growth forest. The woods are full of wildflowers during the spring and summer.

Overall, Jug Bay is one of the finest areas in the state for bird-watching. Of the 374 birds recorded as being observed in Maryland, over 250 have been sighted in Jug Bay. More than two dozen species of waterfowl, including thousands of Canada geese, spend some portion of the fall and winter here. Bald eagles, ospreys, blue herons and a variety of hawks are sometimes seen here also. The many varieties of birds are attracted by the extensive wild-rice marshes in Jug Bay. Spatterdock, pickerelweed, arrow arum and cattails grow in the bay attracting red-winged blackbirds and Virginia rails. These birds eat the seeds from the wild-rice plants by sitting on the stalks or jumping up to eat from the bent over plants. Because wild rice falls off the stalk very easily, migrating waterfowl are able to eat the grain from the soft ground.

Boat ramps, fishing areas and trails for horseback riding, nature walks and hiking are open to the public year-round, but, again, by special use permit only. Volunteer programs are offered for individuals and groups in wildlife management, environmental repair, reforestation, trail construction and nature study. At Patuxent Village the interpretive staff tells the story of life along the river. In this reconstructed pioneer village, visitors tour the smokehouse, the log house, the hunting, trapping and fishing shed and the Jug Bay tobacco packing barn. You learn by demonstration how meat was prepared and preserved, how logs were skinned and cabins and barns built, how the river was fished, and how the land was farmed. Another aspect of the historical interpretive programs offered at the park is the W. Henry Duvall Tool Museum. This collection of over 1,000 antique tools and implements of early colonial life on the river complements the Patuxent Village exhibit. It is open Sundays 1:00 –4:00 P.M. and by reservation Tuesday through Saturday.

A **Chesapeake Bay Critical Area Driving Tour** has been developed, which allows visitors to drive 4 miles through the Patuxent River Park and the Merkle Wildlife Sanctuary past educational displays, observation towers and scenic overlooks on the Mattaponi Creek. The one-way tour begins at the entrance to the Jug Bay Natural Area off Croom Airport Road. The route circles Croom Airport and then crosses Mattaponi Creek into Merkle. The driving tour is open to the public on Sundays 12:00–3:00 P.M. or by advance reservation for groups.

Hiking

The park contains a variety of trails including a half mile of boardwalk and eight miles of hiking and horseback-riding trails. In the Black Walnut Nature Study Area, boardwalks leading through the marsh and swamp combine with trails through the woods to provide a fine opportunity to observe the fragile wetlands of the Patuxent. Naturalists lead hikes devoted to plant and animal identification, natural history, folklore and much more. Observation blinds located at the river's edge provide an excellent place to observe waterfowl such as ducks, Canada geese, or whistling swans. The best time to see them is from October to February. Nature hikes are given year-round by advance reservation.

Camping

A number of isolated semiprimitive tent campsites are available by advance reservation. Ground fires are permitted if weather conditions allow; firewood is furnished at sites. Bring water containers. Camping is open from April through October. There is a nominal fee.

Fishing and Boating

The Patuxent River offers excellent fishing from boat or bank for largemouth bass, perch, catfish and many others. A Maryland fishing license is required for persons 16 and older. Three boat ramps are available for those with a special use permit for which there is a charge. The permits are available at the park office.

Canoeing and Kayaking

Canoes and kayaks are available for rent both for downriver trips and for paddling at Jug Bay. The downriver trip is a five-hour, eight-mile paddle from Queen Anne Bridge to Jug Bay. Reservations must be made in advance. Guided tours aboard the *Otter*, a pontoon boat, are available for groups from April through October. The tour is lead by naturalists who explain marshland ecology. The tours are by reservation only, with a minimum of eight persons needed for the one-hour trip.

How To Get There: From the Capital Beltway (I-495), take MD 4 east to Upper Marlboro, then turn right (south) on US 301 and proceed 1.3 miles to Croom Station Road. Turn left there, and follow it to the end. Turn left (east) on Croom Road (MD 382) and continue to Croom Airport Road. Turn left again, and follow this road east, bearing right at the curve, to the park entrance road.

For Additional Information:
Patuxent River Park
16000 Croom Airport Road
Upper Marlboro, MD 20772-8395
(301) 627-6074 or 888-1410

Maryland-National Captial Park and Planning Commission
Department of Parks & Recreation
6600 Kenilworth Ave.
Riverdale, MD 20737
(301) 699-2407
(301) 699-2544 (TTY)
http://www.mncppc.org

Patuxent River State Park

Serving as a green buffer corridor in a densely populated metropolitan region, Patuxent River State Park lies along the Patuxent River between Howard and Montgomery counties. The long, narrow park begins near the river's headwaters not far from the Frederick County line, then continues downstream for about 12 miles. Along the way it adjoins Triadelphia and Rocky Gorge reservoirs, which supply most of the water for Montgomery and Prince George's counties.

Most of the park's 7,980 acres consist of gently rolling farmland with much of the tree cover found close to the river.

The Washington Suburban Sanitary Commission, which administers Triadelphia and Rocky Gorge reservoirs, has designated a portion of reservoir lands for such activities as picnicking, fishing, horseback riding and boating; permits are required for everything but picnicking. An azalea garden near Brighton Dam, which impounds the Triadelphia Reservoir, is open to the public daily 8:00 A.M.–7:00 P.M. for several weeks each spring, usually late April through early May. The Brighton azalea plantings contain over 22,000 plants and are a very popular springtime spot. On one recent Mother's Day over 6,000 visitors came to the gardens.

Hiking and Horseback Riding

Hiking in Patuxent River State Park is very popular. There is a one-half mile nature walk. Horses are prohibited on the nature trail. The Maryland State Park Service has provided an excellent educational brochure designed for use along this self-guided trail. About 28 miles of horseback trails are available—along wooded ridges, through open meadows and floodplain lands, crossing and recrossing the river and its tributaries. Horseback riding is also permitted during daylight hours on designated lands surrounding Triadelphia and Rocky Gorge reservoirs; contact the Washington Suburban Sanitary Commission for a permit. Trails on reservoir land may be closed during wet weather in order to protect the watershed from erosion.

Fishing

The Patuxent River between MD 27 (Ridge Road) and MD 97 (Georgia Avenue) and the Cabin Branch from Hipsley Mill Road downstream to the Patuxent River have been designated as a special trout stream management area restricted to "catch and release" fishing; check on regulations with park rangers.

Fishing is also allowed from boats and along the shoreline at Triadelphia and Rocky Gorge reservoirs; a state fishing license is required to purchase a permit from the Washington Suburban Sanitary Commission office (see address below) or at Brighton Dam. Reservoir fishing is permitted daily between March 1 and December 15 from sunrise to one hour past sunset. Be sure to check where fishing is allowed; recreational use of the reservoirs and their shorelines is limited to officially designated areas.

Hunting is permitted at Patuxent River State Park during the fall and winter months. Check with the park office for designated hunting areas and the dates that the park allows hunting.

How To Get There: From the Capital Beltway (I-495), follow Georgia Avenue (MD 97) north. The park office is located at

11950 Clopper Road, Gaithersburg, Maryland. To reach Brighton Dam and Triadelphia Reservoir, take Brighton Dam Road east from the town of Brookeville, which lies along Georgia Avenue. Rocky Gorge Reservoir (also known as the T. Howard Duckett Reservoir) is crossed by US 29; follow it northeast from Exit 23 of the Capital Beltway. No entrance fee.

For Additional Information:
Park Manager
Patuxent River State Park
11950 Clopper Road
Gaithersburg, MD 20787
(301) 924-2127

Office of Communications
Washington Suburban Sanitary Commission
14501 Sweitzer Lane
Laurel, MD 20707
(301) 206-8100

Patuxent Research Refuge and National Wildlife Visitor Center

The Patuxent Research Refuge and Wildlife Research Center, located along the Patuxent and Little Patuxent rivers in Laurel, Maryland, is uniquely both a National Wildlife Refuge and a research center. It is an environmental education facility and recreational area as well. The Refuge was created in by President Franklin D. Roosevelt in 1936 as the country's first national wildlife experiment station, with 2,670 acres. In 1975, an additional 2,000 acres was added. Then in 1991 and 1993, 8,100 acres of Fort Meade, known as the North Tract, were transferred to the Refuge, making it one of the largest undeveloped tracts in the Washington area. The 12,750 acres are managed for habitat diversity for resident and migratory wildlife.

The Refuge's primary mission is research support for the protection and conservation of wildlife and wildlife habitats. Three focuses of the research have been migratory birds, environmental contaminants and endangered species (the most famous of which are the cranes and condors). Research also includes the investigation of the status and trends of biological resources. Until recently, the facility was entirely off-limits to the public. Much of it, including all the research facilities and animal shelters, still is, except for the North Tract and the National Wildlife Visitor Center.

The **National Wildlife Visitor Center**, is a premier environmental and ecology education facility, almost a museum of ecology. There are exhibits on environmental issues, bird migration, endangered species, and endangered habitats. Also featured is the research conducted by the Department of the Interior scientists, and the scientific tools and techniques they use. In addition to a very large and modern exhibits complex, the center has a large auditorium, classrooms, a book shop, seasonal open-air tram rides and a series of outdoor trails.

Selected areas of the **North Tract** are open for wildlife observation, hiking, biking, fishing, horseback riding, and (only as permitted) hunting. The North Tract is a large forest of mostly upland oaks and pines and bottomland hardwood forests along the Patuxent and Little Patuxent rivers. There are large areas of wetlands including bogs, oxbow marshes, meadows, and small lakes, making this ideal habitat for numerous species. Birding is excellent—at least one bald eagle pair nests here. Mallards, black ducks and wood ducks and Canada geese reside year-round. Gadwall, widgeon, ring-necked duck, and green and blue-winged teal are migratory transients. Pileated woodpecker, barred owl, red-shouldered hawk and bobwhite quail breed here. Wetland mammals include beaver, mink, raccoon, muskrat and otter. Upland species include gray fox, red fox, southern flying squirrel and occasional bobcat sightings. Numerous species rare or endangered in Maryland are found here. The large expanse of undeveloped land serves as a shelter island in a sea of urban development. A wildlife viewing tower overlooking a man-made wetland area provides an opportunity for a bird's eye view of the site.

Although visitors are allowed every day, we advise limiting your North Tract visits to Sundays (when hunting is always prohibited) during the hunting season (September 1 to January 31). Even when hunting is prohibited, you may hear gun shots from the nearby rifle and pistol ranges. Hikers and wildlife watchers are advised to visit only those areas specifically authorized on the public use permit and to stay on well-used trails; there may be unexploded ordnance in the refuge from its previous use in weapons training. There is an approximately six-mile drive through the North Tract that provides views of the major habitats and access to 10-12 miles of hiking trails leading to marshes and lakes. For information on a variety of nature programs, call the North Tract office.

How To Get There: To reach the visitor center, take the Baltimore-Washington Parkway (I-295) 3.6 miles north of the Beltway to the Powder Mill Road Exit. Turn right (east) on Power Mill Road and go 1.8 miles to the entrance on the right.

To reach the North Tract, take the Baltimore-Washington Parkway to MD 198 east, go 1.9 miles and turn right (just before entering Fort Meade) at Bald Eagle Drive. Go one mile down the improved dirt/gravel road to the visitor contact station. All visitors must check in and get a day use permit. The North Tract is open 8:00 A.M.–4:30 P.M. daily, but hours vary seasonally. No admission fee.

For Additional Information:
U.S. Fish and Wildlife Service, Patuxent Research Refuge
10901 Scarlet Tanager Loop
Laurel, Maryland 20708-4027
(301) 497-5760 (general information)
(301) 597-5593 (TDD only)
(410) 674-3304 (North Tract Visitor Contact Station)
(410) 674-4625 (TDD only)
http://www.gorp.com/gorp/resource/us_nwr

Piney Run Park

Piney Run might be classified as a typical county park, but it also has some interesting natural features. Located some 25 miles west of Baltimore in the southeastern portion of Carroll County, it has a beautiful 300-acre lake with scenic coves and crystal-clear water nestled in 500 acres of hardwood and pine forest. The earthen dam impounding the creek was built to protect Carroll County from flooding and to provide a municipal water supply and a recreation area. During the fall and winter months, the area is excellent for bird-watching and observing wildlife. Canada geese occasionally come here, as well as several species of migrating ducks. Rabbit, squirrel and raccoon live in the area, as do opossum, the barred owl, red-tailed hawk and various songbirds, many species coming to feed on the autumn olive and crab apple in the park.

Hiking and Skiing

Approximately five miles of hiking trails weave through the park. Trail maps are available at the entrance. You can see a large variety of birds, wildflowers, ferns, trees and shrubs in season. The Field Trail is especially attractive to bird-watchers because the area is ideal habitat for birds. The Lake Trail offers a scenic panorama of the reservoir while the Inlet Trail is designed for the rugged individual who wants to get away from civilization. All hiking trails double as cross-country skiing trails when the snow depth allows. The following are all circuit trails:

Field Trail	0.7 mile
Inlet Trail	3.5 miles
Indian Trail	0.25 mile
Lake Trail	0.5 mile

Boating and Fishing

There are boat ramps, and fishing is good to excellent. Large-mouth bass, striped bass (rockfish), catfish, trout and tiger muskellunge are stocked. Mid-spring and early fall are the best times to fish. Only non-gasoline-powered boats, canoes, sailboats and rowboats may be used on the lake; a boat pass must be purchased at the gate. Daily and seasonal boat passes are available. No boats are allowed from November through March. Canoes, rowboats and pedal boats can be rented. Shoreline fishing is permitted, but anglers are advised to be certain they carry out what they bring in; littering is not tolerated. A Maryland fishing license is required for all anglers ages 16 and above.

Picnicking

Some 100 tables and grills are provided for picnickers, many of them in shade areas. No ground fires are permitted. Four picnic pavilions may be reserved for an additional fee.

Nature Center

The Piney Run Nature Center provides visitors with an excellent introduction to the wondrous world of nature. Visitors can see examples of the lake's fish in a 150-gallon aquarium, observe thousands of honeybees in an indoor glass hive and enjoy many of the hands-on nature exhibits. Park naturalists are available to answer questions or provide suggestions for enjoying the park. Programs are scheduled throughout the year. From April through October the Nature Center is open Tuesday through Saturday 10:00 A.M.–5:00 P.M. and Sunday 1:00–P.M. to 5:00 P.M.; closed Mondays.

How To Get There: The park is approximately 40 miles from Washington. From Exit 16 of the Baltimore Beltway (I-695), take I-70 west to MD 32. Turn right (north) and proceed to MD 26 (Liberty Road), then turn left there. Proceed 2 miles, then turn left onto White Rock Road. At Martz Road, turn left again to the park. Open April through October, 6:00 A.M. until sunset daily. The entrance fee is $4.00/car for Carroll County residents, $5.00/car for non-residents and an additional $3.00 for cars towing a boat; seasonal passes available. Off-season, November through March, visitors may park outside the gate, hike, fish from the bank or visit the Nature Center. No boats are allowed in the lake during this period.

For Additional Information:
Park Manager
Piney Run Park and Nature Center
30 Martz Road
Sykesville, MD 21784-8125
(410) 795-3274

Piscataway Park

Piscataway Park, which lies approximately 19 miles south of the District of Columbia line in both Prince George's and Charles counties. It includes seven miles of riverfront across the Potomac River from Mount Vernon and preserves virtually the same wooded, panoramic vista that George Washington himself might once have seen. The 1,500 acres that currently make up the park hug the shoreline of the Potomac River and the mouth of Piscataway Creek along its southern shore. The National Park Service also holds scenic easements on some 3,000 acres of private land on the hills above the park, thus ensuring some limited control over changes in its environment. Piscataway consists of cultivated fields, tidal swamps and marshes and wooded thickets. White-tailed deer, gray fox, opossum, raccoon, squirrel and some 218 species of birds live here or use the area. Piscataway Creek's tidal wetlands are prime habitat for mink, otter and muskrat and provide nesting areas for the wood duck and osprey. A boardwalk gives visitors a view of marsh life and is especially interesting in the winter when bald eagles are frequently seen. The stream itself has been noted as a significant herring run.

At present, the other public use facilities within the park are the Marshall Hall of the Marshall Plantation, Fort Washington Marina on the Potomac, the **National Colonial Farm and Ecosystem Farm** (described elsewhere) and the Hard Bargain Farm. Hard Bargain Farm is an operating farm maintained jointly by the National Park Service and the Alice Ferguson Foundation. It is managed as an environmental study area for elementary school students and other groups interested in the ecology of the area; it is open by reservation only, primarily for school groups.

On the northern side of Piscataway Creek, embracing a portion of the Potomac River shoreline, is **Fort Washington National Historical Park**. The first fort ever built to protect the nation's capital stood here (the present fort was constructed after its predecessor was destroyed by American forces to prevent capture by the British in 1814). Under the jurisdiction of the National Park Service, the fort occupies a 341-acre parkland that offers strolls through the woods and picnic sites.

Hiking

You are permitted to hike or bird-watch on the grounds and from the boardwalk, but no formal trails have yet been developed. Two walks branching out of the picnic area near the park entrance are sometimes overgrown, but easy to follow. At low tide, most the of the Potomac shoreline is accessible for hiking.

Canoeing and Boating

Piscataway Creek provides three miles of canoeing waters. Boat launching is possible in the park from the end of Bryan Point Road (canoes only) and Farmington Landing at the end of Wharf road. The State of Maryland is planning to develop additional marina facilities including a small convenience shop.

How To Get There: From the Washington Beltway (I-495), take MD 210 (Indian Head Highway) some 10 miles south. (Indian Head Highway is the Maryland extension of the District's South Capitol Street.) Turn right onto Bryan Point Road for 4 miles to the park entrance. Open year-round, dawn to dusk. Welcome Center Hours 10:00 A.M. to 4:00 P.M. daily, closed Mondays; December 15-March 15, open weekends only. Admission is $2.00 for adults, $.50 for children, $5.00 maximum per family.

For Additional Information:
Piscataway Park
National Capital Parks–East
1900 Anacostia Drive, S.E.
Washington, DC 20020
(301) 763-4600

Robinson Neck-Frank M. Ewing Preserve

The Robinson Neck–Frank M. Ewing Preserve, is one of the Nature Conservancy's (Maryland/DC Chapter) largest, covering a total of some 920 acres in Dorchester County, about half pine forest and half brackish tidal marsh. Identified as some of the most valuable marshland in the Chesapeake Bay region by the Smithsonian Institution's Chesapeake Bay Natural Areas study of 1974, the preserve is an exceptional black duck nesting area. It also shelters the endangered Delmarva fox squirrel (much larger than the common species) and bald eagle. In addition, the preserve provides a home for large populations of heron species, egrets, rails and other migratory waterfowl. Several species of ducks breed here. Migratory songbirds inhabit the upland forest, which is dominated by loblolly pines with an understory of American holly and wax myrtle and extensive poison ivy ground cover. The tidal marsh flora includes common or Olney three-square bulrush, narrowleaf cattail, needlerush and saltmarsh cordgrass.

The preserve is open to the public year-round for bird-watching and nature walks. Long pants to guard against the abundant poison ivy, waterproof shoes and insect repellent are advised. January through March, when the ground tends to be dryer and the leaves are gone from the poison ivy, is the best time for access to the dry interior habitats—you may observe muskrat, deer and wintering waterfowl. May, when the spring migration is at peak, is the best time for bird-watching. Summer brings flowering plants and marsh grasses, but warm weather and wetlands mean lots of biting insects. September and October bring the fall migrating birds, especially warblers and puddle ducks. November and December bring diving ducks to the creeks and geese to the fields. A self-guided interpretive nature trail starts at an old logging road, veers off into a pine woods, alternately crossing through marsh and woods, ending at the tidal marsh of Slaughter Creek, where bald eagles, osprey and marsh hawks can often be seen. Bring waterproof footwear and binoculars.

How To Get There: From Washington, take US 50 east, across the Chesapeake Bay Bridge, and south through Cambridge. Just east of Cambridge, turn right on MD 16 and head southwest 16 miles to the Taylors Island Bridge over Slaughter Creek. Take the first left after the bridge onto Robinson Neck Road. Proceed 2.7 miles to a grassy road on the left blocked by a cable gate. Park next to the preserve entrance sign without blocking the road or along the road shoulder to the left of the gate. Walk down the grassy road 600 for about 0.75 mile and enter the woods. A trail guide is available from the Nature Conservancy.

For Additional Information:
The Nature Conservancy
Maryland /District of Columbia Chapter
2 Wisconsin Circle, Suite 300
Chevy Chase, MD 20815-7065
(301) 656-8673
http://www.tnc.org

Rock Creek Regional Park and Meadowside Nature Center

Beyond the northern boundary of the District of Columbia, Rock Creek Park becomes Rock Creek Regional Park, containing some 2,700 acres. In Maryland, the park is administered by the Montgomery County unit of the Maryland-National Capital Park and Planning Commission. It contains many of the same natural aspects of Rock Creek Park in Washington (described elsewhere). Two man-made lakes, Needwood and Frank, were constructed between 1964 and 1966. **Needwood Lake** has 74 acres of surface water. It is designed to accommodate families, organized groups, fishermen, picnickers and boating enthusiasts. Fifty-four acre **Lake Frank** is suited to environmental education, nature study and more passive forms of recreation. The outstanding Meadowside Nature Center is accessible to the handicapped and offers many special programs. Thirteen nature trails traverse a variety of habitats.

A wildlife management demonstration area, showing the natural and artificial means of creating a sanctuary for a variety of animals, has been established at the nature center to show visitors how to set up their own backyard wildlife sanctuaries. It includes bird feeders, birdbaths, birdhouses and special plants that produce food for wildlife. Many trees here are centenarians. A walnut grove includes a tree that is 11 feet in circumference. Unique in the area is a stand of mature white pine.

The **Meadowside Nature Center** provides a number of interesting sites to visit. A collection of log buildings illustrates the lifestyle of early Americans who farmed in this area. The farmstead includes a log cabin made of hand-hewn local oak and hickory logs, a smokehouse, a root cellar and herb and vegetable gardens. A guide to the buildings describes their use and is available at the nature center. There are also a cemetery, a covered bridge and hummingbird and butterfly gardens. There are 7.5 miles of trails in and around the Meadowside Nature Center designed to cover a variety of habitats including meadows, woods, ponds, lakes and streams. A half-mile trail runs along a stream to the Muncaster Mill ruins, the site of the stone foundations of the Muncaster lumber and gristmills. The longest trail, the Lakeside Trail, is 3.13 miles around Lake Frank, a 54-acre man-made lake created for flood control. A marsh and several small ponds are located nearby for environmental studies of fish, insects and small mammals. Meadowside Nature Center itself contains three self-guided exhibits that delight youthful visitors. Legacy of the Land has an earthen tunnel and underground cave that provides children with an opportunity to look at the world from a fish's point of view. There is an Indian wigwam where you can play Indian games and dress up like Indians or settlers. The Curiosity Corner discovery room offers animal skins and furs to touch, recorded nature sounds to listen to, and some reptiles and amphibians to see. Free nature films are typically shown every Saturday at 11:00 A.M., 1:00 and 3:00 P.M. A complete listing of all the programs offered by the Maryland-National Capital Park and Planning Commission Nature Cen-

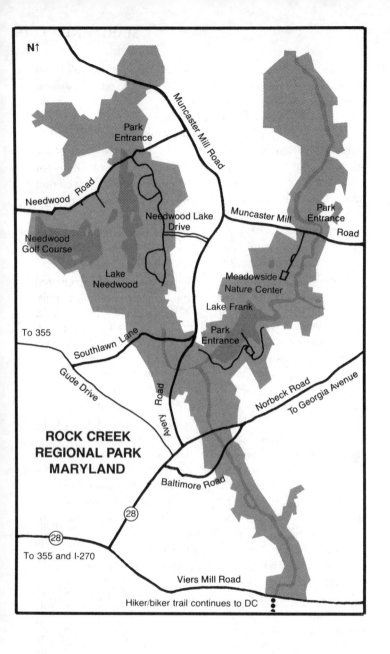

ters in Montgomery County is available in the *Nutshell News* brochure, which can be picked up at any of the nature centers.

Hiking

Hiking trails lead around each of the lakes, but most of the trails are found in the Nature Center area. Thirteen different trails traverse the area around the Meadowside Nature Center (see descriptions of some above). Check with the Nature Center for a trail map.

Bicycling

Bicycling is allowed only on the wide, paved paths designated for bicycles. There is an extensive network of hiker/biker trails, starting at Lake Needwood and going southeast along Rock Creek 14 miles to the District line, connecting to Rock Creek Park in the District (see listing Rock Creek Park under the District of Columbia and Bicycling in the Appendix).

Boating and Canoeing

Rental rowboats, canoes and pedal boats are available at Lake Needwood from May to Labor Day. No boats are permitted on Lake Frank.

Picnicking

Picnic tables are available at Lake Needwood with grills nearby. Shelters, restrooms and drinking fountains available. Picnic shelters can be reserved by calling 301-495-2525.

How To Get There: To get to the Nature Center take the Capital Beltway to Exit 21 (Georgia Avenue-MD 97) north to Norbeck Road; turn left on Norbeck Road, then turn right on Muncaster Mill Road. Follow Muncaster Mill Road until you reach Meadowside Lane. Turn left, and follow signs to the Nature Center, located at the end of the road. Other sections of the park are accessible from the many roads that cross it. The park is open sunrise to sunset daily. Meadowside Nature Center is open 9:00 A.M. to 5:00 P.M. Tuesday through Saturday and closed on Sundays and Mondays; No entrance fee.

For Additional Information:
Park Manager , Rock Creek Regional Park
6700 Needwood Road
Rockville MD 20855
Manager's Office (301) 948-5053
Boat Shop (301) 762-1888
http://www.mncppc.org

Naturalist Meadowside Nature Center
5100 Meadowside Lane
Rockville, MD 20853
(301) 924-4141

Saint Clement's Island and Potomac River Museum

Saint Clement's Island, located in the Potomac River off the southern shore of Saint Mary's County, was the site of the landing of the first Maryland colonists in 1634. At that time, it was approximately 400 acres in area and a haven for wildlife. Today, it has been reduced by erosion to an area of about 40 acres. Though it has seen a long and varied history of human use, it has recently been returned to its natural state and is under the jurisdiction of the Maryland Park Service. It has also been designated a National Historic District. The island's sparse vegetation consists of wild pear, cedar, maple, oak, pine and various other species of flora common to tidewater. Rabbits, reptiles, rodents and many types of waterfowl, mostly migratory, can be seen on Saint Clement's. Osprey nest and rear their young on this island and nearby lands, and the great blue heron lives here as unmolested as when men first saw the area. Although a few deer have been observed swimming to Saint Clement's from the mainland, they do not remain long because protective cover is lacking.

You can take boat trips to the island from the public dock at the Potomac River Museum, located on the Maryland shore across from Saint Clement's. It is best to check the schedule beforehand for departure times. Advance reservations are necessary. The boat normally runs NOON–5:00 P.M. Saturday and Sunday from Memorial Day weekend through Labor Day, however, it is out of service until the fall of 1998 or spring of 1999. There is a $1.00 charge for adult admission to the museum.

Charter trips for groups of 45 or more are available on weekends with advance reservations. Casual dress is advised. Visitors may go ashore to view the wildlife and historical exhibits. The entire tour lasts approximately two hours.

Picnicking

Picnic tables and pavilions are provided at designated areas on the grounds of the museum and St. Clement's Island. No fires are permitted at the museum, but barbecue pits are provided on Saint Clement's Island.

How To Get There: From Exit 36 of the Capital Beltway take MD 5 south and southeast to Morganza. Turn right on MD 242, and follow it to its end. Signs will point the way to the museum from here. The museum is open daily from March 25 through October 1, weekdays 9:00 A.M.–5:00 P.M. and weekends from NOON– 5:00 P.M. October 2 to March 24 it is open Wednesdays through Sundays 12:00–4:00 P.M. Nominal fee. Please call ahead to see if and when the boat is running.

For Additional Information:
Saint Clement's Island–Potomac River Museum
Colton Point, MD 20626
(301) 769-2222

Sandy Point State Park

On the western shore of the Chesapeake Bay is Sandy Point State Park, a little piece of land that offers some of the best birding opportunities in Maryland. Nearly every bird found in Maryland has been sighted at Sandy Point. It is not hard to see why. Currents have moved the sand into the bay attracting migratory birds to its relatively short (4-mile) east-west crossing. In addition, Sandy Point contains a surprising number of different habitats making it hospitable to a large number of different birds. Beaches, ponds, open water and woodlands all attract birds to this little park. Shorebirds, including plovers and sandpipers, visit the park in the spring and summer. Waterfowl arrive in late October to January and many remain over the winter. The best time to look for birds is during stormy weather when the wind is blowing to the northeast in fall and southeast in spring, and after a rain when birds can be seen in the pools that collect in grassy areas and on the beach and parking lots. Canada geese, as well as black mallard, old squaw and canvasback ducks come this way in great numbers. During the late fall and winter the Arctic snow bunting stop here. The great blue heron, green heron and common egret are sometimes seen, and osprey fish the offshore waters. Two peregrine falcons have begun nesting on the Chesapeake Bay Bridge feeding on the pigeons that live there. They can be observed from the park.

The botanist will find a variety of marsh and aquatic plants, including spartina grasses. At one time during the early 1800s Sandy Point was known for its access to an inexhaustible supply of seaweed, called "sea ore" by the early settlers. It was much in demand as a fertilizer. In 1833, Baptist Mezick, a Baltimore businessman, purchased the property and operated a wharf. A pond in the park still bears Mezick's name. The 680-acre parkland offers a playground, refreshment stand, showers and toilets, a swimming beach, surf fishing and picnicking facilities. A more recently purchased tract of 137 acres adjoining the park will be kept as a natural area for study of flora and fauna; it includes a mature stand of yellow poplar, oaks, white pine, holly and dogwood.

Fishing

Fishing is a major pastime here for rockfish, perch, spot and bluefish. Surf fishing is excellent. Crabbing during the hot summer months is also popular. A Chesapeake Bay fishing license is required. A license may be purchased at the park's marina facility. Boats may be rented at the marina, and there is a bait-and-tackle shop. The park's launching ramp will accommodate most boats.

Picnicking

The park has a first-class shaded picnic area with tables, grills and drinking water. Picnic shelters are available only by reservation.
How To Get There: From Washington, take US 50 east. The park entrance is just east of Annapolis, off US 50. The entrance fee is $2.00 weekdays, $3.00 weekends per person during the summer months.

For Additional Information:
Sandy Point State Park
1100 East College Parkway
Annapolis, MD 21401
(410) 974-2149

Seneca Creek State Park and Seneca Creek Greenway Trail

Seneca Creek State Park occupies about 6,609 acres in Montgomery County northwest of Washington and has some of the best (separate) hiking and mountain biking trails in the area. It follows Seneca Creek for some 12 miles, from west of Route 355 to the Potomac River. The park is a composite of beautiful woodlands and stream valley, where Great Seneca Creek flows between sheer cliffs and around interesting rock outcroppings. Other streams and brooks join the creek within the park, as it hurries to join the Potomac at a little town called Seneca. This is one of Maryland's newest parks. There are hiking trails, sheltered picnic areas, open picnic areas, bird-watching, fishing, hunting, boating and a disc golf course. In the open fields and dense woods, you can hunt wild creatures with your camera or binoculars. Horseback trails are available in undeveloped areas of the park. An orienteering trail teaches map and compass reading. Winter brings opportunities for cross-country skiing, and sledding. Wild turkey, white-tailed deer, bobcat, raccoon, opossum, fox and the cottontail rabbit live here. Birds include the cedar waxwing, bluebird and several species of tanagers, orioles and hawks, as well as owls. For several thousand years, the Seneca Valley was occupied by Indians who established several villages there. The site of the oldest Indian dwelling in Maryland, dating back to 10,000 BC, is within park boundaries. When European settlers arrived in the late 1600s and early 1700s, they found thriving Indian villages with extensive farming areas. As the settlers moved in and the Indians moved out, fields were planted in tobacco, grains and cultured apple and peach trees. Gristmills were established and some of their remains are visible today. One unique feature of this park is the earthquake fault line found here—the only one in Maryland.

Hiking, Biking and Horseback Riding

Seneca Creek State Park has some of the best hiking and biking trails in the area. There are marked trails throughout the park area. Five trails lead through the park and each is assigned a color to guide you. Mink Hollow is 1.5 miles long and crosses many different habitats including a small marsh and a pine forest. It is moderately easy to walk and connects the dam with the picnic shelters. The Long Draught trail is 2.5 miles long and follows the Long Draught Branch through forested areas. The Great Seneca Trail (1.25 miles) follows the Great Seneca Creek. There are several rocky areas that make this trail mod-

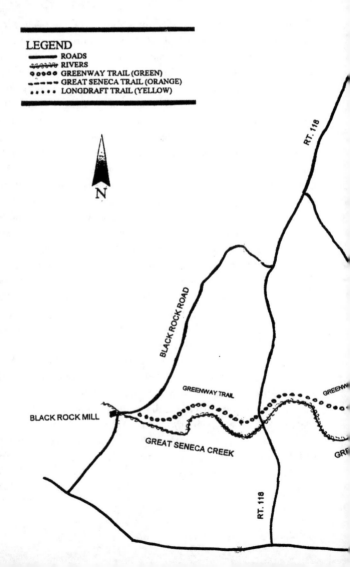

LEGEND
ROADS
RIVERS
○○○○○ GREENWAY TRAIL (GREEN)
▬▬▬▬ GREAT SENECA TRAIL (ORANGE)
• • • • LONGDRAFT TRAIL (YELLOW)

N

RT. 118

BLACK ROCK ROAD

GREENWAY TRAIL

GREENW

BLACK ROCK MILL

GREAT SENECA CREEK

GR

RT. 118

erately difficult. It connects the Visitor Center with the dam. A popular trail is the Lake Shore trail (3.7 miles long), which encircles Clopper Lake and crosses several old farms that become seas of wildflowers in season. Finally the Old Pond trail (.3 mile long) is a short section of trail which follows a small spring, passes a pond and connects the Visitor Center with the Great Seneca Trail. Several miles of park roads offer excellent biking. Lake Shore, Long Draft and Mink Hollow trails are open for mountain biking, except when they are muddy or wet.

The new **Seneca Creek Greenway Trail** is one of the best hiking trails near Washington for near-wilderness hiking to see and hear nature in relative solitude, in all seasons. The trail,

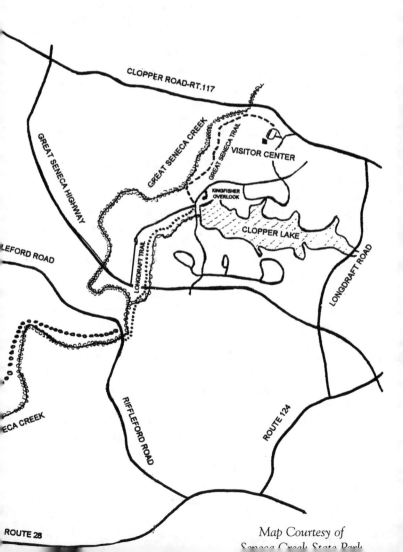

Map Courtesy of
Seneca Creek State Park

still a work-in-progress, runs along the Great Seneca Creek from the Great Seneca Highway to the Potomac River. Only foot traffic is allowed; no bikes or horses. At the east end, one can access the trail from the developed area of the park (see How To Get There), taking the yellow blazed Long Draft Trail from its start near the Clopper Lake dam, under the Great Seneca Highway, past the Wetland Area and Observation Deck, and along the gravel road to Riffle Ford Road. At Riffle Ford Road, hikers turn right to cross Seneca Creek at the bridge, then cross the road to the trailhead. You can also park on the wide paved shoulder of Riffle Ford Road, where it crosses the creek and start west from there; the Greenway trail is blazed in teal green. Be aware that there's a skeet shooting range nearby, so you may hear gunfire, but the trail is protected by a high berm. The trail runs west through beautiful, relatively undisturbed stream valley, 2.5 miles to Darnestown-Germantown Road (another potential starting point) and then 1.3 miles to Black Rock Mill on Black Rock Road. **Black Rock Mill** is a historical stone gristmill, with the remains of the 3-story stone building and mill still visible; you can park in a small parking lot at Black Rock Mill or cross the bridge over the creek and park on the right near the trailhead. The stream valley between Riffle Ford Road and Black Rock Mill is quite beautiful with much wildlife. The round trip from Black Rock Mill to Clopper Lake Dam and back can be hiked in four hours. To reach Riffle Ford, Darnestown-Germantown or Black Rock Roads, take I-270 to Route 28, exit 6 west, past Quince Orchard Road, then turn right on one of them until you cross the creek; the trailhead is marked by signs. The trail west of Black Rock Mill, across Route 28 and River Road to the Potomac is mostly walkable, but was not completed at press time. Call the park before hiking the trail after heavy rains, as the Seneca Creek can overflow it's banks, flooding the trail.

The new **Schaeffer Farm Trail System** consists of about 10 miles of multi-use trails designed specifically for **mountain biking** and horseback riding. These trails were constructed by volunteers and have been designed to minimize impact on the environment that they pass through. To get here take I-270 to Clopper Road, Route 117 west, past Route 118 to Schaeffer Road, turn left. Go about 2 miles past the ballfields, to the sign at a farm entrance on the left (on a sharp right bend in the road). Take the left driveway that leads to the parking area. The trails are open sunrise to sunset. Bikers must yield to all; hikers must yield to equestrians.

Volunteers constructed the majority of both the Greenway

Trail and the Schaeffer Farm Trail System. If you would like to volunteer to help finish and maintain the trail, call the park for more information.

Boating and Canoeing

A 90-acre lake provides excellent fishing for largemouth bass, crappie, catfish and sunfish. Boating facilities are available to boaters and fishermen. Canoeists can use the lake, but they may prefer to float in quiet Seneca Creek. The best time for canoeing is in the late winter and spring. From July until November, the water level is likely to be so low as to require frequent portages. The creek wends its way through a stand of 300-year-old cypress trees. It is an excellent spot for photography. Canoes, rowboats and pedal boats are available for rental, and pontoon boat tours are given every weekend during the summer and by reservation for groups.

How To Get There: From the Capital Beltway (I-495), take I-270 northwest to Gaithersburg and exit at Exit 10, Clopper Road. Continue west on Clopper Road, which leads through the Gaithersburg section of the park. Watch for state park signs. Nominal entrance fee.

For Additional Information:

Park Manager
Seneca Creek State Park
11950 Clopper Road
Gaithersburg, MD 20878
(301) 924-2127
http://www.dnr.state.md.us/publiclands

Seth Demonstration Forest

Seth Demonstration Forest, consisting of only 125 acres, is a woodland managed for timber and educational benefits. Though it lies a few miles beyond the 50-mile radius we use in this book, it is located not far off US 50, a major north-south route on Maryland's Eastern Shore that leads to several other attractions within our designated radius. If you feel the desire to stop and explore a cool green woodland, Seth State Forest provides a convenient place for doing just that. There are no organized activities and no improved facilities here, but there are birds aplenty sharing the woods with white-tailed deer, squirrel and rabbit. And in the spring and summer, the forest floor is made resplendent by an abundance of wildflowers. Pleasant walking trails throughout the area lead through stands of pines and mixed deciduous hardwoods.

How To Get There: From Washington, follow US 50 east, across the Chesapeake Bay Bridge and south through Easton. About one mile out of Easton, turn left (north) onto Dutchmans Lane, then left (north) again on Doverneck Road. The woods up the road on the left mark the beginning of Seth Demonstration Forest. Forest property is marked on all boundaries with bright yellow paint blazes.

For Additional Information:
Project Forester
Seth Demonstration Forest
150 Deep Shore Road
Denton, MD 21629
(410) 479-1623

Regional Forester
DNR, Forest Service
201 Baptist Street, Suite 22
Salisbury, MD 21801-4979
(410) 543-6745

Smallwood State Park

Bordering the south shoreline of Mattawoman Creek, not far upstream from its junction with the Potomac River, Smallwood State Park consists of nearly 465 scenic acres in Charles County and includes the Sweden Point Marina facility and the Mattawoman Natural Environmental Area. The entire creek and the rural, primarily wooded lands that adjoin it, have been recognized by the scientific community as an important natural area. Extensive wooded swamps throughout the flood plain provide excellent habitats for muskrat, fox, beaver and otter. In addition the swamps are noted for a large number of nesting wood ducks and mallards. Many other types of birds feed here including the great blue heron, the kingfisher and red-winged blackbird. There is also a very rare type of lotus not usually found in the Washington Capital Region.

The park is named after General William Smallwood, the highest ranked Revolutionary War Officer from Maryland and the fourth governor of Maryland (1785-1788), who once made his home here. His plantation was a meeting place for famous Americans during the founding of the country. Smallwood's reconstructed plantation house and burial place may be seen by visitors. Another interesting historical feature is the burial ground for approximately 20 of General Smallwood's slaves and indentured servants. Their graves bear no names, but many of them are known to have been born on the land and to have died here without ever once leaving the vast 5,000-acre estate. Sweden Point is a state-run marina offering complete boat-launching facilities with six launching ramps providing access to Mattawoman Creek and the Potomac River. The Mattawoman Natural Environmental Area is made up of a number of small parcels of undeveloped land and marshland throughout the Mattawoman Creek basin that are available for hiking and fishing.

Hiking

There are approximately 2.5 miles of trails throughout the park. Trail maps can be picked up at the concession or park headquarters. The trails lead to bottomlands along the creek. In the spring, colonies of May apples intermingle with jack-in-the-pulpits and a bevy of wild flowers. Ferns of many types blanket the ground throughout the year. Opossum, squirrel, raccoon and red fox venture forth to consume the ripe fruit of the paw-paw. Hikers will also see the river birch, the only member of the birch family found at low elevations in the South. Other species include wild black cherry, sweet cherry, sweet gum, hickory sycamore, white and red oaks, as well as tulip poplar. At one point along the trail, the honeysuckle is gradually engulfing nearby trees. Birdwatchers find many species to observe.

Picnicking

There are approximately 20 picnic sites throughout the park. They are furnished with grills and tables, and are available on a first-come first-serve basis. Playground equipment is located at the entrance to the campground. There are three shelters for rent that accommodate from 50 to 125 persons.

Camping

The campground is open mid-April to mid-October with 16 sites equipped with electricity and 4 mini-cabins.

How To Get There: From Exit 37 of the Capital Beltway, take MD 210 (Indian Head Highway) south and west to Potomac Heights. (Indian Head Highway is the Maryland extension of the District's South Capitol Street.) Turn left on MD 225 (watch for signs to Smallwood State Park) and follow it to Mason Springs. Turn right there onto MD 224 and continue for 4 miles to Sweden Point Road and turn right. Follow it into the park.

The park is open year-round with limited facilities during the winter season. The park is open from October 1–October 31, 7:00 A.M. to sunset; November 1–March 31, 8:00 A.M. until sunset; April 1–April 30, 7:00 A.M. to sunset; May 1–September 31, 6:00 A.M. until sunset. Smallwood's reconstructed home is open on Sundays (May to Sept.), 1:00–5:00 P.M. An entrance fee is charged from the first of May to the end of September.

For Additional Information:
Park Superintendent
Smallwood State Park
c/o Merkle Wildlife Sanctuary
11704 Fenno Road
Upper Marlboro, MD 20772
(800) 784-5380 or (301) 888-1410

Smithsonian Environmental Research Center

On the Rhode River seven miles south of Annapolis is the Smithsonian Environmental Research Center, an educational and scientific research center operated by the Smithsonian Institution. It encompasses 2,700 acres of forests, abandoned fields, marshlands, active farms and even islands within the Chesapeake Bay. The staff varies from 90 to 120 persons conducting scientific research on the Rhode River and the land surrounding it. This area, representative of southern Maryland, presents a full range of habitats and animal populations for study. The scientific research program is designed to study the dynamics of an estuarine watershed ecosystem and to clarify the effects of past and present human activities on this system. The education program is intended to improve the quality and effectiveness of outdoor environmental education and to convey the scientific research findings to the public. As a part of the Smithsonian Institution, the center is open to the public Monday–Friday 9:00 A.M.–4:30 P.M.

Hiking

A 1.5 mile self-guided Discovery Trail provides an introduction to the natural environment that makes up the Maryland coastal plain. The trail is flat and passes through fields, forests and marshlands. A pamphlet available at the Administration Building explains the numbered stations located along the trail. The Java Historic Trail includes registered archaeological sites with side loops of 1-2 miles passing recreated prehistoric Indian campsites, European farming settlements between the 1600s and 1800s and recent farming development (just before the Smithsonian acquired the land). There is also a marshland boardwalk.

Canoe, Boat, and Facility Tours

The Muddy Creek Canoe trip is a guided tour given most weekends, by reservation only. Canoes and a guide are provided for $2.50 per person. The Rhode River Boat Trip, aboard the Center's 45-foot research vessel, explores the Rhode River and Chesapeake Bay. A naturalist explains the ecology of the area and student groups can take measure indicators of the water quality at various points along the route. The boat trip is by reservation only.

Tours of the center's nature research setting are conducted periodically, by reservation, led by trained staff members. The tour gives visitors the opportunity to see the research sites where scientists are studying the environment. Reservations are required. For specific times and dates call the center between 8:30 A.M. and 4:30 P.M. Monday through Friday. Weekday tours for groups are available upon request. Boat and canoe tours for groups are also a part of the program. There is a $4.00 charge for the tour.

How To Get There: From Washington, take US 50 east to MD 424 (Davidsonville exit) and turn right (south). At Davidsonville, turn left (east) on MD 214 and go about 5 miles to MD 468. Turn right (south) and go 1 mile to Contees Wharf Road, then turn left (east) and go about 1 mile to the center, which lies along the southern shore of the Rhode River.

For Additional Information:
Education Department
Smithsonian Environmental Research Center
P.O. Box 28
Edgewater, MD 21037
(301) 261-4190
education@serc.si.edu
http://www.serc.si.edu

Visitors Information Center
Smithsonian Institution
1000 Jefferson Drive, S.W.
Washington, DC 20560
(202) 357-2700

Soldiers Delight Natural Environment Area

Soldiers Delight was once part of an Indian hunting ground. Today, it is a secluded natural area where one may study and commune with nature. Containing some 2,000 acres in the west central portion of Baltimore County, Soldiers Delight is one of the few serpentine grasslands remaining in the Old Line State. Amateur and professional botanists and geologists will find much of great interest. Chromite and many other minerals are found in the area. In fact, this is one of the first places in the world where chromite (used to produce the chrome on your automobile bumper) was mined. The year was 1818, and the chrome mines were worked extensively by the Tyson family of Maryland for more than 60 years. Mule teams hauled the ore to the Elkridge Landing on the Patapsco River. From there, it was shipped to many parts of the world. Not until vast deposits of chrome ore were discovered abroad did the mines close down, but they reopened briefly during World War I when the metal was needed for the manufacture of steel.

Soldiers Delight is unusual, beginning with the soil. It is weathered from serpentine, a metamorphic rock comprised mostly of hydrous magnesium silicate (more popularly known as serpentine). Because the soils contain such high levels of nickel and magnesium, only certain plant species can adapt to their toxic effects. Characteristic among these are blackjack oak, post oak and Virginia pine (a recent invader not native to the ecosystem), all able to survive on shallow soils and low moisture. The area was originally a vast open prairie with oak copses (oak savanna), but is now succumbing to pine woodland, though efforts at prairie restoration are underway.

Other plants include little and big bluestem, Indian grass, turkeyfoot, common beardgrass and various other grasses, sedges and rushes characteristic of midwestern prairies. The rare vanilla-scented holygrass and tufted hairgrass are found nowhere else in Maryland. Also growing here are the bird's-foot violet, gray goldenrod, serpentine aster, sandplain gerardia and blazing star. In the fall, one can find quantities of fringed gentian, a large purple flower.

Long-tailed salamanders hide in the chrome mine passageways, while raccoons, opossums, deer mice, rabbits, fox and white-tailed deer roam the barrens. Birds include chickadees, nuthatches, woodpeckers, titmice and hawks, as well as black and turkey vultures. The prairie warbler and towhee nest here. The woodcock, red-winged crossbill and cardinal also inhabit the area; quail are sometimes seen.

Soldiers Delight, because of its interesting background and unique natural qualities, became the target project of a citizens' committee formed in 1959 to preserve the area. In the spring of 1965 another organization—Soldiers Delight Conservation, Inc.—was incorporated to raise the money needed to purchase the land. A check was presented to the state in 1969, and the following year acquisition began. A visitor center includes a classroom, exhibit room, and other facilities.

Hiking

Several miles of marked hiking trails extend throughout the area and afford the best way to experience the park. Visitors are requested to stay strictly on the trails because of the fragile nature of the area. No horseback riding or bicycling are allowed. No camping facilities are available, only day use is allowed. The primary object here is to preserve the natural features, since they are fragile. This is a place to view, study, appreciate—then leave just as you found it.

Rockhounding

Although no collecting or disturbing the rock formations is permitted, those who enjoy studying rocks will find this a remarkable place to visit and observe. The rocks crop out everywhere and, where broken, invariably present the bluish-black massive appearance so typical of serpentine. Chromite, chalcedony, deweylight, kamererite, magnesite, picrolite and talc are found here. The ultimate origin of the serpentine is the earth's upper mantle, thought to be created by sea-floor spreading and possibly lithospheric plate collision.

How To Get There: Take the Baltimore Beltway (I-695) to I-795; exit at Franklin Blvd. (west); merge to the right onto Church Road, go to the end; turn left on Berrymans Lane. Go .5 mile, turn left onto Deer Park Road; go 1.5 miles to the visitors center. No entrance fee.

For Additional Information:
Soldiers Delight Natural Environment Area
5100 Deer Park Road
Owings Mills, MD 21117
(410) 922-3044

Maryland Department of Natural Resources
Forest, Park and Wildlife Service
Tawes State Office Building
Annapolis, MD 21401
(410) 260-8700
http://www.dnr.state.md.us/publiclands

Sugarloaf Mountain

Most people do not think of mountains in connection with our nation's capital, but just 30 miles from Washington is Sugarloaf Mountain. Jutting above the peaceful rural landscape of lower Frederick County to an elevation of 1,282 feet, Sugarloaf is an outpost of the Appalachians. The mountain was discovered by a Swiss explorer who named the mountain Sugarloaf after the solid "loaf" of sugar that was sold during colonial times. In 1969 Sugarloaf Mountain was designated a Natural

Landmark on the National Register of Historic Sites because of its geological interest and natural beauty. Located in the heart of a 3,000-acre privately owned preserve, it was acquired as part of the estate of Gordon Strong. It is open to the public for the enjoyment and appreciation of its wild environs.

Once Sugarloaf was at the bottom of an inland sea, but internal pressures forced it upward to a height far above what it is now. Some scientists believe that the Appalachian Mountains were twice as high as they are now, but have been worn down over time to their present height. Sugarloaf is a monadnock, that is an isolated rock left by erosion of the region around it. The mountain is topped by a plate of quartzite composed of sands of quartz cemented together with silica. The quartzite is 200 feet thick and very hard, creating cliffs and boulders around the sides of the mountain.

During the Civil War, Union forces maintained a watchtower and signal station atop the mountain to monitor Gen. Robert E. Lee's crossing at White's Ferry and his advance toward Antietam. In 1899, Gordon Strong bicycled from Washington to Frederick while on vacation. He was so impressed with Sugarloaf Mountain that he bought the land and built a home he called "Stronghold". In 1926 he decided to share the natural beauty of the terrain with the public. Even President Franklin D. Roosevelt came to visit and so liked the setting that he wanted to acquire it for a presidential retreat. Strong would not sell, but he showed the president the spot that is now Camp David in Catoctin National Park. Sugarloaf Mountain is now administered by Stronghold, Inc., a non-profit foundation established by Gordon Strong. One of the programs of the foundation is a campaign to save the American chestnut tree, nearly wiped out by blight years ago. Thousands of American chestnut seedlings have been planted here, and efforts are underway to develop a blight-resistant tree.

Hiking and Horseback Riding

Sugarloaf Mountain has a complex of fine trails, some leading to a 180-degree view of the area. Over an acre of level ground at the summit supports a sparse growth of stunted oak trees. The Bull Run Mountains far to the south can be seen on a clear day. Since the mountain breaks off into a sheer cliff on the south and west sides, the view here is unobstructed. Horse trails also have been developed and are well maintained.

Picnicking

Picnic tables and restrooms are located near the parking lot. Tables are provided at several other picnic areas as well.

How To Get There: From the Capital Beltway (I-495), take I-270 northwest to MD 109 and turn southwest. Continue to Comus Road and turn right there; watch for direction signs. No entrance fee.

For Additional Information:
Information Officer (Stronghold, Inc.), Sugarloaf Mountain
7901 Comus Road
Dickerson, MD 20842
(301) 874-2024 (Frederick)
(301) 869-7846 (from metro DC)

Information Officer
Tourism Council of Frederick County
19 East Church Street
Frederick, MD 21701
(301) 663-8687

Tuckahoe State Park

Tuckahoe State Park is located nine miles west of Denton on the Eastern Shore. Tuckahoe Creek, which runs through the length of the park, is a quiet, pristine country stream, bordered for most of its path by wooded marshlands. Areas of secluded beauty abound. Containing some 3,800 acres the forest is filled with pawpaws, red maples, red and white oaks, mockernuts, river birches and tulip trees. The park features the Adkins Arboretum—500 acres displaying the flora and fauna of Maryland. Three trails, each a mile long, represent the three regions in Maryland with characteristic forests. At present, the park offers family camping, youth group camping, picnicking, fishing, boating and canoeing, as well as bird-watching and hiking.

Hiking

Hiking trails that wander through the park include the Piney

Branch Trail, the Woodland Nature Trail, the Physical Fitness Trail, the Lake Trail, and trails within the Adkins Arboretum. Check with the park superintendent for the latest information.

Camping

Thirty-five campsites are available for tent or trailer camping. The camping area features a central bathhouse with showers and toilets. Potable water and a dump station are available, but individual campsites do not have hookups. Pets, on leash, are allowed. Sites are taken on a first-come, first-served basis.

There are four youth group areas each accommodating 25 people, available by reservation only.

Fishing and Boating

A 60-acre lake offers opportunities for boating, canoeing and fishing. Two-thirds of the lake is flooded woodland and the rest is cleared. The wooded portions provide the best fishing. Large-mouth bass, crappie, pickerel, bream and catfish are found here. A Maryland state fishing license is required for persons 16 and older. There are canoe rentals. A concrete boat ramp is available with ample parking for cars with trailers. No gasoline-powered motors are permitted, giving the lake a quiet, pristine atmosphere excellent for canoeing.

Picnicking

There are two picnic areas: one on Cherry Lane and another on Crouse Mill Road near the lake. Both have restrooms and are open April 1 to October 31. No ground fires are allowed.

How To Get There: From Washington, take US 50 east, across the Chesapeake Bay Bridge, to MD 404 near Wye Mills. Take 404 east to MD 480 and turn left (north) there. When you get to Eveland Road, turn left into the park. No entrance fee at present.

For Additional Information:
Park Manager
Tuckahoe State Park
13070 Crouse Mill Road
Queen Anne, MD 21657
(410) 820-1668

Maryland Department of Natural Resources
Forest and Park Service
Tawes State Office Building
Annapolis, MD 21401
(410) 260-8186
(800) 830-3974
http://www.dnr.state.md.us/publiclands

U.S.D.A. Beltsville Agricultural Research Center

At Beltsville, just a short distance northeast of Washington, is the U.S.D.A. Beltsville Agricultural Research Center covering 7,000 acres. About one-half of the acreage remains in a near-wilderness state, with fine hardwood forests covering rolling hills laced with small streams. Other portions are divided into experimental pastures, orchards, gardens and cropland. About 650 buildings housing research laboratories, greenhouses, barns, poultry houses, shops and offices are located here. There are more than 2,000 large domestic animals—cattle, sheep, hogs—and some 1,300 turkeys. Some of its accomplishments include the modern blueberry, strawberry, hog, turkey and disease resistant potatoes.

The center is responsible for research on insect controls, agricultural satellites, biotechnology and human nutrition. The National Agricultural Library houses two million books and periodicals about agriculture and science. It is the largest agricultural library in the world. Also located here are the National Fungus Collection, the National Parasite Collection and the Systematic Entomology Collection. Over 28 million specimens of insects and mites are preserved here. Tours are by appointment only and visitors must report to the Visitor Center when they arrive. No hiking trails are provided, but this is a fine place to bird-watch, glimpse other types of wildlife or to bicycle on the many narrow roads through the area.

How To Get There: From the Capital Beltway (I-495), take US 1 north, and turn east on Powder Mill Road (MD 212) to the ARS National Visitor Center, Log Lodge Road, Building 302; open 8:00 A.M.–4:30 P.M. weekdays except holidays.

For Additional Information:
USDA ARS National Visitor Center
Building 302, BARC-East
Agricultural Research Center
Beltsville, MD 20705
(301) 504-9403

Watkins Regional Park and Nature Center

Covering more than 1,000 acres in Prince George's County, Watkins Regional Park offers something for almost everyone. In addition to six miles of color blazed hiking trails, the park's attractions include a nature center, picnic areas, children's playground, some camping facilities, a miniature railroad, hay rides, the Old Maryland Farm, indoor and outdoor tennis courts, and athletic fields. The Old Maryland Farm features an assortment of farm animals and demonstration gardens.

Open year-round, the Watkins Nature Center offers exhibits of local flora and fauna. The extensive variety of programs here includes night hikes, fall migration bird walks, snake-feeding demonstrations, evening campfires, school programs and day camps. The forest cover is primarily hardwood, containing such common species as oaks, hickories, tulip poplar, sour gum, sweet gum, birch, beech and dogwood. In the moist bottomlands is an abundance of May apple, paw paw trees, Solomon's seal, Indian cucumber root and bloodroot.

Among the 30 species of birds you may observe are the red-bellied woodpeckers, wood thrush, mockingbird, nighthawk and Carolina wren. Other wildlife includes the gray flying squirrel, opossum, raccoon, rabbit and white tailed deer. At Christmas, Watkins Regional Park features the Festival of Lights, an exhibit of lighted trees, shrubs, roadways, specially built displays and buildings in the park. Watkins Regional Park is operated by the Maryland-National Capital Park and Planning Commission.

How To Get There: From the Capital Beltway (I-495), take MD 214 (Central Avenue) east to MD 193 (Watkins Park Drive) and turn right (south); continue for about one mile. The park entrance is on the right. Both the park and the nature center are open year-round.

For Additional Information:
Watkins Nature Center
301 Watkins Park Drive
Upper Marlboro, MD 20774
(301) 249-6202
TTY (301) 699-2544
Fax (301) 249-3231

Wildfowl Trust of North America

The Wildfowl Trust of North America is probably the best place in the area to observe and study Chesapeake Bay wildfowl close-up. All of the migrating aquatic wildfowl species and most shorebird species possible to see on the bay have been seen here. The 500-acre site, known as Horsehead Wetlands Center is located just below Kent Narrows on the Eastern Shore. It is a unique wetland ecosystem, enhanced by man with several small freshwater ponds, providing ideal waterfowl habitat. The site includes six distinct marshland habitats listed by the Smithsonian as "critical to be preserved". Wood duck, northern pintail, gadwall, shovelers and blue-winged teal are among the captive waterfowl collection, but you wouldn't know it to look at them, as they paddle free with their mates on the ponds uncaged; the fences keep people and foxes out. The captive ducks attract wild migratory ducks and geese, who naturally feel comfortable with their fellow waterfowl and like the protected habitat and occasional free lunch.

Visitors can view the birds in several ways. For rainy days there is an attractive viewing gallery with a window wall overlooking a large pond inhabited by waterfowl indigenous to the Chesapeake region. A pair of trumpeter swans is also housed here. Once present on the Atlantic flyway, the trumpeter's call has not been heard on the Chesapeake for nearly 200 years. A program to reintroduce the trumpeter swan to the Chesapeake by teaching birds to migrate using an ultralight was begun in 1997. The viewing gallery also includes a gift shop. A one-mile woodchip pathway leads through the three exhibit/breeding areas for different regional wildfowl: Chesapeake Bay, Prairie Potholes and Alaska Wetlands (featuring the emperor goose). You pass a woodland pond, visible from an observation blind that has been developed as a nesting site for wood ducks; this trail also passes a hummingbird and butterfly garden, planted with flowers attractive to man, bird and bug. Another trail leads past a 10-foot-high wall of *phragmites* grass, a field of milkweed and a forest of loblolly pines to the 10-acre Lake Knapp; here viewing towers and blinds allow one to see egrets, herons and osprey. The lake is a veritable motel for birds, with enclosed wood duck platforms on short poles and open osprey platforms on tall poles.

Seasonal highlights of the Wildfowl Trust are as follows: March–May, nesting waterfowl, songbirds, osprey, spring wildflowers, and fox kits; May–July, ducklings, young osprey, butterflies, hummingbirds, fawns and turtles; August–October, ducks in eclipse plumage, egrets, herons, swamp wildflowers, and shorebirds; November–February, winter waterfowl migrants, deer, red fox, bald eagles, and winter songbirds.

The Wildfowl Trust, founded in 1979, is a private, non-profit conservation organization dedicated to the preservation of wetlands and wildlife through the best examples in education, conservation and research. Guided tours and lectures are available.

How To Get There: Take Route 50 east from Washington toward Annapolis; continue on Route 50 over the Chesapeake Bay Bridge ($2.50 toll, eastbound only) across Kent Island. Just after crossing the Kent Narrows bridge, take Exit 45 on Route 18 into Grasonville. Follow Route 18 east (left) past the Grasonville Firehouse, turning right onto Perry Corner Road (there is a very small sign for the Wildfowl Trust at the corner). The entrance is about .5 mile on the right. Drive down the gravel road about a mile to the parking lot. Stop at the visitor center, the round building across the road from the parking lot. No pets or smoking allowed; small entrance fee ($3.00 adults, $2.00 seniors, $1.00 children). The Wildfowl trust is open 9:00 A.M. to 5:00 P.M. every day except December 24 and 25, Thanksgiving, and New Year's.

For Additional Information:
The Wildfowl Trust of North America
P.O. Box 519
Grasonville, MD 21638
(410) 827-6694

William Paca Garden

The great houses of the 18th century in and around Annapolis had terraced gardens with arbors and boxwood mazes. None survived to modern times. Such was the case of the 2-acre gardens of William Paca, one of the signers of the Declaration of Independence and Revolutionary Governor of Maryland. The garden he maintained behind his Georgian home in the late 1700s was described by early travelers as the most elegant in Maryland's capital city. In the 19th century it was covered by tons of landfill, and in the 20th century it was obliterated by a hotel, parking lot and bus station. In 1965, when Historic Annapolis Foundation purchased the Paca House, its imaginative preservationists proposed that the garden be re-created. In their excavations they actually found remnants of the original gardens and decided to restore it. Enough of Paca's garden wall emerged from the diggings to indicate the locations of the five gracefully proportioned terraces of the original gardens. It took years to restore and re-create them, but the gardens prove that no matter how disturbed a piece of land is, it is possible to save it.

Paca was so proud of his garden that he had Charles Willson Peale paint his portrait with the garden in the background. Later, this became an important instrument revealing the original design of the garden. Paca's design allows the garden to be appreciated in all seasons, not just the spring and summer when the flowers are in bloom. The evergreens and the strong design make the garden look attractive all year long. Within the hedges lie four garden rooms: a holly parterre, a boxwood parterre, a flower parterre and a rose parterre. In the center of the holly parterre is a Governor William Paca holly (Ilex opaca) grown from a cutting taken from a holly at the Governor's Wye Island plantation. Beyond the four parterres lie the pond in the shape of a fish, crossed by a Chinese Chippendale bridge and a wilderness garden planted with native trees and shrubs. Considerably less formal than the upper portions of the gardens, the lower reaches are romantic and natural in spirit. Amid the formal plantings are vegetables, herbs and fruit trees. Only trees, shrubs, flowers and other plants known in William Paca's time adorn the gardens.

How To Get There: From Washington, take US 50 east to Annapolis. The garden is located in the center of Annapolis between Prince George and King George streets. The entrance to the garden is at 186 Prince George Street; open daily all year except Christmas Eve, Christmas and Thanksgiving days: 10:00 A.M.–5:00 P.M. Monday through Saturday and 12:00–5:00 P.M. on Sunday. In the winter, the garden closes at 4:00 P.M. The house is open during the same hours. The entrance fee for house and garden is $7.00 for adults, with discounts for seniors, children and tour groups. The house only is $5.00; garden only, $4.00.

For Additional Information:
William Paca House and Garden
186 Prince George Street
Annapolis, MD 21401
(410) 263-5553   (800) 603-4020

Woodend and the Audubon Naturalist Society

In Chevy Chase, northwest of Washington and adjacent to Rock Creek Park, there is a remarkable wildlife sanctuary called Woodend, headquarters of the Audubon Naturalist Society of the Central Atlantic States. The ANS was founded in 1897, as a membership organization dedicated to increasing the public awareness of natural history and the importance of preserving our natural resources. Such luminary conservationists as Theodore Roosevelt, Rachel Carson, Justice William O. Douglas and Roger Tory Peterson have been local members. Small but unique, Woodend contains 40 acres of unusual plants and wildlife and a fine nature trail. It is an excellent year-round birding spot. The mowed fields near the mansion are ideal habitat for American goldfinches, Carolina wrens and house wrens. The Canadian hemlock forest farther along the path is a favorite resting place for Carolina chickadees, white-throated sparrows, pine siskin and screech owls. Common flickers, rufous-sided towhee, yellow-throat, yellow-rumped warbler, house finch and cardinals are common along the edge between the field and the woods. Finally, as you enter the dark deciduous woods you will hear the eastern wood peewee, tufted titmouse and several types of woodpeckers.

Other wildlife abound as well— gray squirrel, raccoon, deer and flying squirrel. In a small pond on the premises are wood frogs, bullfrogs, salamanders, crayfish and numerous other aquatic creatures. Occasionally you may spot a hawk or a red fox. Pileated woodpeckers visit the area, too. The self-guided trail begins just west of the main house. It is .75 mile long and can be walked in 45 minutes. A highlight of the trail is "the grove", a group of tall eastern hemlock, which is so quiet that it has become a popular place to hold weddings. Birds congregate here during the winter months, for these trees provide a great source of food and protection from stormy weather and predators.

A number of different types of trees are located at Woodend—beech, maple, ginkgo, elm, black walnut, hickory, oak and sassafras. There are also some very thorny shrubs, known as Hercules' club or the devil's walking stick. One of the most unusual trees found here is the *Franklinia altamaha*, which grows just below the greenhouse and bears large, white, magnolia-like flowers in the fall. Naturalist William Bartram found this species in Georgia in 1765 and brought a specimen back to the world-renowned botanical gardens established in Pennsylvania by his botanist father, John. Bartram named his plant in honor of his good friend, Benjamin Franklin and the Georgia river along which he had discovered it. The species has not been seen in the wild since, though it is believed to still grow wild along some lonely remote stretches of the Altamaha. Thus it is possible that all the Franklinias in the world today are direct descendants of the Bartram's transplant. The Franklinia may be seen below the greenhouse. There is also a formal garden, sunken garden, two ponds bursting with aquatic life and a small spring-fed stream.

Woodend is a place where you come to notice and study nature in miniature—the small things you normally would pay little attention to elsewhere, such as counting the rings in a dead tree stump or watching a butterfly or a grackle feed. It is also a place to listen to the music of spring peepers, to the hammerings of industrious woodpeckers, to the lovely trills of resident songbirds. The mansion, which serves as the headquarters building, is the former private estate of Capt. and Mrs. Chester Wells. It was named after Mrs. Wells's family estate in her native Australia. Mrs. Wells willed Woodend to the Audubon Naturalist Society upon her death.

The ANS operates a bookstore at Woodend. It offers a comprehensive selection of natural history and conservation titles, binoculars, bird feeders, birdseed and nature-related gift items.

The ANS sponsors a wide variety of educational programs for children and adults. These include college-level field biology courses given in conjunction with the U.S. Department of Agriculture, children's programs, adult weekend nature forays and long distance nature trips. The *Audubon Naturalist News*, a newspaper containing information on natural history, and local conservation issues, is published 10 times a year. *The Voice of the Naturalist* is a recorded message about unusual bird sightings that changes weekly. Finally, the popular Audubon Lectures are an annual series of lectures held downtown at the National Museum of Natural History. Co-sponsored with the Smithsonian Resident Associates the lectures are an excellent way for people with an interest in conservation to meet people with like interests.

How To Get There: From the Capital Beltway (I-495), take Connecticut Avenue south to Manor Road and turn left on Manor Road to Jones Bridge Road; turn right on Jones Bridge Road and then turn left on Jones Mill Road. The entrance is 0.25 mile down Jones Mill Road on the left. From Washington, take Connecticut Avenue north and turn right on Manor Road (not far beyond East-West Highway). Take a right on Jones Bridge Road and a left onto Jones Mill Road. Go about .25 mile and watch for the sign on your left. The Woodend grounds are open from dawn to dusk. The Woodend bookstore is open Monday through Saturday 10:00 A.M.–6:00 P.M., Thursdays until 8:00 P.M. and Sunday noon–5:00 P.M.

For Additional Information:
Audubon Naturalist Society
8940 Jones Mill Road
Chevy Chase, MD 20815
(301) 652-9188
(301) 652-3606 Bookstore
http://www.AudubonNaturalist.org

Wye Island Natural Resource Management Area

Tucked away in a recess of the Chesapeake, between the Wye and the Wye East rivers, is one of the finest islands in the bay. Located off Maryland's Eastern Shore in Queen Anne County, Wye Island was purchased in large part by the state in the mid-1970s. Today, Wye Island Natural Resource Management Area (NRMA) is maintained by the Maryland Department of Natural Resources, State Forest and Park Service. Although it has been farmed for years, the island has many outstanding natural qualities. Aside from the farming, it retains much of its original flavor. Virgin timber still stands on the island, and there are many wooded bays and inlets where white-tailed deer browse. Some people say bobcat are still found on the island.

Wye Island is 4.4 square miles of a unique tidewater area that has undergone little irreversible change since early colonial times. Much of the area seen from the six miles of roads on the island consists of fields of corn and soybeans separated by tangled hedgerows. Occasional small tracts of deciduous timber—oaks, maples, gun, sassafras and sycamore—are made almost impenetrable by heavy growth of shrubs and vines; these provide excellent cover for a great diversity of wildlife. The island has some 30 miles of shoreline, along which nesting osprey are found. Occasionally eagles are sighted, and some may be nesting on the island. Fox, raccoon, groundhog, muskrat, cottontail rabbit, gray squirrel and numerous shorebirds live here, along with the highly endangered Delmarva fox squirrel. The little green heron, egret, great blue heron, red-tailed hawk, fish crow, barred owl and the great horned owl also inhabit the island, some only during the migration season. A few pileated woodpeckers have been sighted.

One of the most impressive portions of the island is the School House Woods area, a 30-acre tract of virgin forest open enough to walk through easily from the road to the waters of the river. Great white oak, red oak, hickory and gum trees are found here. The state plans to maintain the island in a near-natural state, continuing the agricultural operation but using best management practices. The timber band and grass buffer strip around the island's shoreline has been widened in an effort to curtail shoreline erosion. The state will also attempt to maintain the island primarily as a nature preserve and study area. Recreational use will be in the form of low-impact recreation. However, the area does allow limited hunting for deer and goose in season.

Boaters may circle the island in shallow-draft boats and view the wildlife along its shore. The shoreline is deeply indented by numerous tidal creeks and inlets. Landings are discouraged, but if they are made boaters are urged to treat Wye Island with the care such a fragile area deserves and to leave nothing behind but footprints. The same is recommended for those who use this property from the land side. No fires are permitted and, at this writing, the area is open on a daily basis from sunrise to sunset.

Hiking

Two trails have been developed on the island, but there are six miles of little-traveled gravel roads ideal for hiking and wildlife watching.

How To Get There: From Washington, head east on US 50, across the Chesapeake Bay Bridge. About 12.5 miles beyond the eastern terminus of the bridge, before you reach Wye Mills, turn right on Carmichael Rd. This same road dead-ends on Wye Island. Open daily from sunrise to sunset. No entrance fee.

For Additional Information:
Wye Island N.R.M.A.
632 Wye Island Road
Queenstown, MD 21658
(410) 827-7577
(410) 827-9675 fax
(When writing for information, please include self-addressed, stamped envelope)

Wye Oak State Park

On Maryland's Eastern Shore, near the little community of Wye Mills, is the stately Wye Oak, largest white oak tree in the entire United States and Maryland's official "living symbol" of the state tree. Measuring 95 feet tall with a spread of 165 feet, it has a trunk more than 52 feet in circumference at its widest girth. The tree is believed to be more than 400 years old. Pictures, descriptions and measurements of the oak are recorded in the Hall of Fame of the American Forestry Association in Washington, DC. Located on publicly owned land, the Wye Oak is now a part of Wye Oak State Park.

The tree has received the greatest of care, and today it is in excellent health. The origin of the buttressed roots that form the oak's wide base is a matter of conjecture. One explanation offered is that an old country store was once located on its site, and horses tethered to the tree by customers bruised the roots by stomping their hoofs. This resulted in malformed root growth that eventually developed into huge burls. The park in which it stands includes only 29 acres and offers little else in the way of natural attractions. There are, however, several structures of historical interest nearby; they are described in the free state park brochure.

The Maryland Department of Natural resources has sold seedlings raised from the champion oak following years when it drops acorns. To inquire call 1-800-TREESMD.

The brick one-room schoolhouse by the Wye Oak is the 2nd oldest in Talbot County, dating back to colonial times. It has been restored inside and out and furnished to look as it did when used as a schoolhouse in colonial days.

How To Get There: From Washington, take US 50 east over the Chesapeake Bay Bridge to MD 662. Turn right (south) on MD 662 and continue through the town of Wye Mills. Wye Oak State Park is just south of Wye Mills on the right. Open daily, all year. Admission free.

For Additional Information:
Wye Oak State Park
13070 Crouse Mill Road
Queen Anne, MD 21657
(410) 820-1668

Maryland Department of Natural Resources
Forest, Park and Wildlife Service
Tawes State Office Building
Annapolis, MD 21401
(410) 260-8186
(800) 830-3974
http://www.dnr.state.md.us/publiclands

Talbot County Chamber of Commerce
Court House
Eaton, MD 20601
(410) 822-2807

Zekiah Swamp

Undoubtedly one of the finest natural areas within the greater Washington area is Zekiah Swamp in southern tidewater Maryland. Its dense chambers, woven around the beautiful Wicomico River headwaters, cover some 70,000 acres. In a 1974 study of the Chesapeake Bay region, the Smithsonian Institution designated this 16-mile-long swamp as an area deserving top ecological priority because of its uniqueness in this state and its rich natural treasures. And rich it is, sheathed in lush, jungle-like forest, cloaked with mist rising from damp mysterious sanctuaries. The Zekiah Swamp was once a tribal center for the Sacayo Indians, who later moved to the headwaters of the Potomac and eventually became extinct. The dense vegetation creates an eerie aura of mystery. Rising lights created by swamp gas, along with the mystical sounds of the insect and wildlife world at night, have given birth to many of the legends that surround the swamp even to this day. In the vicinity of the town of Allens Fresh, the swamp waters emerge from the uniform swamp valley and meander through vast wetland areas before contributing their flow to a 15-mile-long tidal river that empties into the Potomac. Not far from the river is the Newburg Talbot Terrace Scarp, one of the few inland cliff-like areas remaining in Maryland's coastal plain.

Bald eagles have been known to nest at the edges of the swamp, and there is a variety of hawks and other birds, including the barred owl, pileated and red-bellied woodpeckers and the turkey vulture. Occasionally, the great blue heron, green heron, common egret and yellow-crowned night heron are sighted here.

In the brackish waters of the swamp's lower reaches, osprey, Wilson's snipe, Canada geese and a concentration of other migrating birds winter over. White-tailed deer, raccoon, opossum, beaver, otter, muskrat, fox and many species of small animals thrive in these lush environs and bobcat are occasionally reported. For anyone who enjoys studying insects, this is the place to come. Many insects seen at the insect zoo in the Smithsonian Institution's National History Museum (described elsewhere) have been collected in Zekiah Swamp. The caddisfly, dragonfly nymphs, glass shrimp beetles and the long-bodied, rare pelecinid wasp dwell here. One of the greatest entomological finds in the recent past was a viceroy larva. Probably no other place in the greater Washington area has a more primeval setting or provides a better opportunity to explore and observe wildlife in its natural environment. But much, of course, depends upon the person visiting here. Except for the headwaters of the swamp, which lie within the Cedarville State Forest, and 400 acres, where tidal and fresh waters meet that are state owned, the swamp is privately owned by various farmers and is not open to the public. However, the Maryland Forest, Park and Wildlife plans to buy 5,000 acres around the entire length of Zekiah Swamp.

You might wish to consider a canoe float on the Allens Fresh Run and the Wicomico south downstream to the Potomac. The wide portions of the Wicomico offer some interesting wetlands on both sides of the river. The privately owned land in the swamp is not open for exploration. A small path leads from just before the bridge over Zekiah Swamp on the north side, through a small parcel of state-owned lands a short distance into the swamp. Most of the swamp can only be observed from the road where Routes 5 and 6 cross it, about five miles east of Route 301. Do not wander far into Zekiah without someone who knows the area personally; it is large and mostly wetlands, with few permanent trails or landmarks.

Sight-Seeing

A good route is MD 232 on the east side of the swamp; it runs in a generally north-south direction from MD 382 south to MD 234 and parallels portions of the swamp. In addition, there are several roads that penetrate and dead-end within the swamp. The swamp may be explored a short distance from the bridges that cross it on MD 5 near Bryantown and MD 6 near Dentsville. Other good views may be obtained near Allens Fresh and in the **Cedarville State Forest**. To reach Allens Fresh, take MD 301 south to MD 234 east, an access to Allans Fresh is 1-1.5 miles on the right. Park rangers at Cedarville and Merkle Wildlife Management Area are knowledgeable about the swamp and will be glad to answer any questions.

Merkle Wildlife Management Area staff has offered canoe trips through Zekiah periodically between April and November; call them to see if any are scheduled. In addition, the Sierra Club and other hiking/nature organizations occasionally have Zekiah trips.

How To Get There: Zekiah Swamp is one of the largest natural features in the area but one of the most difficult to find and see. From the Capital Beltway (I-495), follow MD 5 south and east to Bryantown, which is near the swamp, and inquire for directions locally. A visit to Cedarville State Forest is a good way to start your exploration (this area, including directions on how to get there, is described elsewhere.

For Additional Information:
Merkle Wildlife Management Area
(301) 888-1410   (800) 784-5380

Cedarville State Forest
(301) 888-1410

Southern Maryland Recreational Complex
11704 Fenno Road
Upper Marlboro, MD 20772
(301) 888-1410

Maryland Department of Natural Resources
Forest and Park Service
Tawes Office Building
Annapolis, MD 21401
(410) 974-3771 (business hours)   (410) 461-0053 (other hours)

Bill Thomas

NATURAL ATTRACTIONS
IN VIRGINIA

VIRGINIA AND WEST VIRGINIA

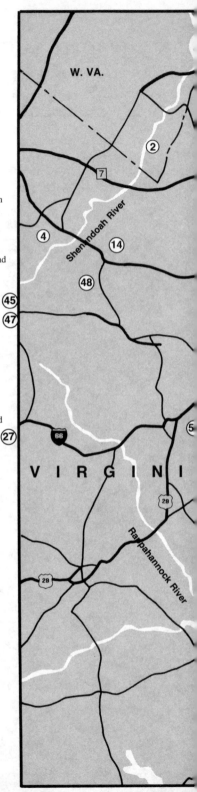

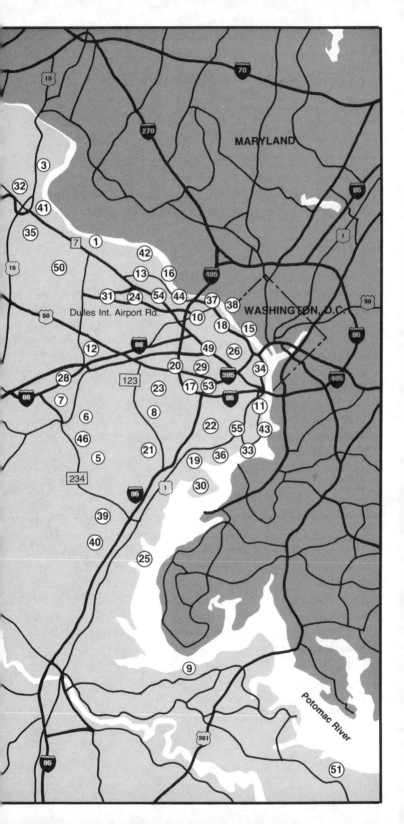

Algonkian Regional Park

Located amid some fine wooded scenery along the Potomac shore near the Louduon-Fairfax county line, Algonkian Regional Park offers boating, hiking, picnicking, fishing, swimming and bird-watching. You can also play golf or go boating on the Potomac River. Though this park offers more to those seeking recreation than it does to nature lovers, the trails are good for hiking, and bird-watchers report sightings of unusual species along the river.

Hiking

Two trails follow both the high and low banks of the Potomac River. A nature walk, which currently meanders through some seasonally swampy woods, will soon be rerouted when the park's recreational facilities are expanded. Bird-watchers in particular will find these paths appealing.

Boating

Boating on the Seneca Lake section of the Potomac River is a popular pastime here. A boat-launching ramp in the park provides public access.

Picnicking

Picnic tables, scattered informally under the trees along the shoreline, offer scenic views of the Potomac. There is also a large covered pavilion and smaller shelters, which may be reserved for group outings.

How To Get There: From Exit 10 of the Capital Beltway (I-495), take VA 7 west for about 11 miles to VA 637. Turn right and drive 3 miles to the park entrance. Park open year-round, from dawn to dusk. No entrance fee for residents of northern Virginia; nominal fee for nonresidents.

For Additional Information:
Algonkian Regional Park
47001 Fairway Drive
Sterling, VA 20165
(703) 450-4655

Northern Virginia Regional Park Authority
5400 Ox Road
Fairfax Station, VA 22039-1022
(703) 352-5900

Appalachian National Scenic Trail

**APPALACHIAN TRAIL
NORTHERN VIRGINIA**

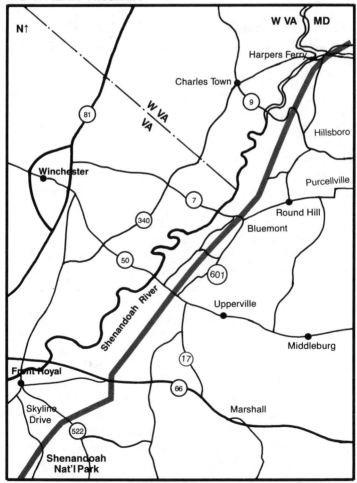

See the entry under Maryland for the history, overview and maps of the Appalachian Trail. A portion of the Appalachian Trail was rerouted in 1986 to pass through Harpers Ferry, West Virginia and by Jefferson Rock. Jefferson Rock is the precise location where Thomas Jefferson is supposed to have stood and exclaimed that the view was "worth a voyage across the Atlantic." The rock itself would have long ago toppled into the village below, geologists say, except for some red sandstone supports placed under it about 1860. The Appalachian Trail now follows a footbridge across the Potomac River, where it crosses the C&O Canal National Historical Park and Towpath Trail leading either west to Cumberland, Maryland, or east along the north side of the Potomac to Washington, DC.

Ball's Bluff Regional Park

Ball's Bluff Regional Park is known as a superb area to view wildflowers in a quiet, undisturbed setting between Leesburg and the Potomac River. The Northern Virginia Regional Park Authority acquired 170 acres of land around the small Ball's Bluff Battlefield National Cemetery and developed it into a park. Interpretive signs along the trail lead the visitor through the historic Civil War Battle.

The habitat runs from river bottomland to hardwood forests to rocky cliffs. The bottomland is among the best places in the area to see myriad Virginia bluebells (the state flower). Other wildflowers found in the area include jack-in-the-pulpit, white trout lily, harbinger-of-spring, wild ginger, twinleaf, cutleaf toothwort, squirrel-corn, Dutchman's-breeches, wild geranium, bloodroot, spring beauty, star chickweed, green violet and yellow corydalis. In the upland area, saxifrage and rockcress can be found. There are a number of rare or endangered species at Ball's Bluff, which are protected by law. Under no circumstances should you disturb or remove any plant or animal matter.

Ball's Bluff is the site of the Civil War Battle of Ball's Bluff fought on October 21, 1861; some believe that this battle was a turning point in the war, with the humiliating Union defeat here precipitating a change in Union leadership and strategy. The Battle resulted in the first Congressional investigation into the conduct of the War. Ball's Bluff National Cemetery is the second smallest national cemetery in the United States. Relic hunting or removal of any material is strictly prohibited.

Hiking

A wonderful two-mile circuit trail goes through Ball's Bluff; it is recommended at any season. The trail is partially unmarked, but fairly easy to follow; it can get muddy and slippery when wet. The trail starts at the end of the gravel road and goes down a moderately steep incline to the Potomac River. Turn left and travel west along the river about 0.8 mile with the high bluffs on your left. As you approach a large ravine ahead, the bluffs taper down. Go left (don't cross the ravine) and back up a moderate upgrade on the path along the top of the bluff. This passes through upland oak hickory woods, going along the high bluff overlooking the river with great vistas of the Potomac River and Maryland farmland. The trail returns to the left rear side of the cemetery (as you face the cemetery entrance). In wet weather, you might want to go the other direction, staying just on the bluffs.

There are no restrooms, water fountains, maps nor full-time park personnel at Ball's Bluff. No admission charge.

How To Get There: From the Washington Beltway, take Virginia Route 7 toward Leesburg. Just before Leesburg, take the Route 15 bypass north (toward Maryland). Turn right on Battlefield Parkway and left on Ball's Bluff Road. The park is located at the end of the street.

From White's Ferry (crossing from Maryland); take White's Ferry Road to Route 15, turn left (south); Battlefield Parkway will be on your left in about 1 mile.

For Additional Information:
Balls Bluff: 1-(703) 729-0596
Northern Virginia Regional Park Authority
5400 Ox Road
Fairfax Station, VA 22039-1022
(703) 352-5900

Blandy Experimental Farm and Orland E. White Arboretum, State Arboretum of Virginia

Blandy Experimental Farm belongs to the University of Virginia (UVA). It is located about 50 miles west of Washington near Boyce, Virginia. It consists of about 700 acres and contains the 170-acre Orland E. White Arboretum, a collection of over 5,400 trees and shrubs representing over 800 species and varieties, many of them labeled. This is the only mature arboretum on limestone soils in the mid-Atlantic region and has one of the most diverse plant collections in the southeastern U.S. The arboretum's collections were planted according to the Engler-Prantl taxonomic scheme, a systematic plan in which plants are organized from the most primitive to the most advanced families according to the prevailing theory of plant systematics at the time the arboretum was first organized. A new theory of plant organization and systematic scheme replaced the Engler-Prantl scheme, but for obvious reasons the collection could not be readily rearranged. Thus the collection offers an interesting study of the history of plant taxonomy.

The collection includes over 80 percent of the genera of north temperate conifers, about 50 percent of the world's pine species, 25 percent of the known fir species, hemlocks, spruces, cedars, larches, sequoias, dawn redwoods and a large grove of ginkgo. (The *Ginkgo biloba*, or maidenhair tree, is the only surviving member of a very primitive tree family from the Mesozoic Era, 180 million years ago; it is a large, beautiful species immune to most tree diseases.) Species or genera represented include oaks and beeches, chestnuts, elms, birches, alders, ironwoods, mulberries and magnolias; rose family trees include apples, hawthorns, cherries, quinces and cork trees; pea family plants including locusts and Kentucky coffee tree; boxwoods, 18 species of maple; and olive family plants including ashes. The list is too long to even summarize. Over 50 families of flowering woody plants are represented.

There are certain to be flowers from early spring on and fall colors last until late November. In addition to woody plant collections, the arboretum also has meadows and ephemeral wetlands, providing diverse habitats for bird-watching. White-tailed deer, red fox and hawks also frequent the meadowlands.

Graham F. Blandy, a New York stockbroker, bequeathed nearly 700 acres of his estate, named "The Tuleyries," to the University of Virginia upon his death in 1926. The Blandy Experimental Farm, so named in keeping with Blandy's bequest, remains to this day an active UVA research facility. Within the farm is the 170-acre Orland E. White Arboretum, named after Professor White, the first director of Blandy Farm. The arboretum was declared the official State Arboretum of Virginia by the General Assembly in 1986. It is open to visitors from dawn to dusk everyday, but the office is open only 9:00 A.M.–5:00 P.M. weekdays. A picnic area, water fountain, public telephone and restrooms are available.

Late April is one of the best times to see the rose and magnolia displays, as well as a field of naturalized daffodils. In late spring, the marshes bloom with yellow iris. In July, the meadows are almost totally golden with *Galium verum*, yellow bedstraw. The fall is wonderful with the autumn colors in a wide variety of trees. Volunteer-maintained herb and perennial gardens add sources of seasonal interest and color, particularly in spring and fall.

Trails

There is a visitor pavilion with maps available for three self-guided walking tours, ranging from 0.2 mile (30 minutes) to 1.2 miles (2 hours), and a 3-mile loop drive. In addition, there is a new Virginia Native Plant Trail. Watch out for poison ivy along the paths. Guided tours are available to non-profit groups with an appointment.

Educational Programs

Educational programs for the public at the arboretum include a series of spring and fall workshops on horticulture, ecology and botanical arts, university accredited summer courses in botany and ecology, a scientific summer seminar series and a school tour program. In addition there are a number of special events. Programs are announced in season brochures and in *Arbor Vitae*, the arboretum newsletter.

How To Get There: From Washington, take I-66 west to Route 17 north (toward Winchester, don't take 17-Business); at Route 50, turn left (west) at the light. Take Route 50 across the Shenandoah River bridge; from the bridge go 4 miles to the "Virginia State Arboretum" sign and make the next left to Blandy.

For Additional Information:
Blandy Experimental Farm &
The Orland E. White Arboretum
Route 2, Box 210
Boyce, VA 22620
(703) 837-1758
http://www.virginia.edu/~blandy

Bull Run Marina and Fountainhead Regional Parks

These two adjacent parks are located on scenic Lake Occoquan, an extension of Bull Run Creek that widens considerably before eventually joining the Potomac River. An observation deck in Fountainhead Regional Park affords a spectacular view of the park. While both parks primarily offer water sports, there are also some impressive woodlands. Ferns, laurel, dogwood, hemlock, hickory, oak and pine cover the hillsides. Some of the hemlock date back more than 200 years.

The parks shelter a profusion of wildlife, including wood duck, osprey, bluebird and several species of hawks. During the spring and fall, many migratory waterfowl stop over, while the marsh provides a nesting place for wild ducks and geese. White-tailed deer, bald eagle, beaver and wild turkey occasionally are seen; raccoon, turtle and squirrel are plentiful.

Picnic tables are scattered under trees overlooking the water. Nature trails wind around the lake over heavily wooded hills and ravines. There is a new 4.5 mile Mountain Bike Trail, (see below) Fountainhead offers boat and motor rentals. Rental canoes and group canoe trips are provided at Bull Run Marina. Fountainhead Regional Park boasts a new accessible seawall pier and a mini-golf course.

Hiking and Horseback Riding

The parks offer some excellent hiking trails through marshland, upland woods and open meadows. The 17.5-mile-long reblazed and repaired Bull Run-Occoquan Trail (described elsewhere) runs through a portion of the parks. Both hikers and horseback riders can use it. The whole trail affords excellent views of Bull Run Creek, Lake Occoquan and stream islands. A trail brochure is available.

Mountain Bike Trail

Fountainhead Regional Park has a new 4.5 mile network of red-blazed trails designated primarily for year-round mountain biking. The trail can be ridden as a loop of two lengths starting at the Fountainhead parking lot, going along the Occoquan River and returning on an inland route. The route involves some hilly terrain, with obstacles, mud, and water crossings. Helmets are required for all cyclists. The trail closes one hour before sunset. No dogs or horses on the trail, please. The trail is open only when dry. Call (703) 250-2473 for trail conditions. A trail map is available.

Picnicking

Excellent picnic facilities are provided in both parks with tables and grill. No ground fires are allowed.

Boating

Twenty-two-mile-long Lake Occoquan is made accessible by boat-launching ramps at both parks. Johnboat and electric motors are available for rental at Fountainhead Regional Park. Bull Run Marina rents canoes and johnboats. Gas motors are limited to 10 h.p.

Fishing

Lake Occoquan, offering fishing for largemouth bass and catfish, is restocked periodically. This is an excellent place to teach youngsters how to fish. Tackle and bait are sold; rowboats and motors can be rented. A state license is required if 16 or older and can be purchased at Fountainhead Regional Park.

How To Get There: To reach Fountainhead, take I-95 south (Exit 4 from the Capital Beltway) and exit at Lorton. Turn right (west) on Lorton Road (VA 642) to Furnace Road (VA 611). Turn right and proceed to Ox Road (VA 123); turn right again. At Hampton Road (VA 647) turn left and follow Hampton Road to the park entrance.

To reach Bull Run Marina, take I-66 west (Exit 9 from the

Capital Beltway) and exit at Fairfax (VA 123). Head south on VA 123 (Ox Road) to Clifton Road (VA 645), and turn right on Clifton to Henderson Road (VA 612). Turn left on Henderson to Old Yates Ford Road. Turn right and follow Yates Ford Road to the park entrance. Fountainhead is open mid-March through November. Bull Run Marina is open the first weekend in April through October on Friday, Saturday and Sunday only. No entrance fee.

For Additional Information:
Northern Virginia Regional Park Authority
5400 Ox Road
Fairfax Station, VA 22039-1022
NVRPA Headquarters (703) 352-5900
Bull Run Marina (703) 631-0549 (weekends)
Fountainhead (703) 250-9124

Bull Run-Occoquan Trail

From its western terminus in Bull Run Regional Park the Bull Run-Occoquan Trail currently extends eastward for about 17.5 miles to a point within Fountainhead Regional Park. It is open to both hikers and horseback riders. Along the way, the Bull Run-Occoquan Trail, also known as the Blue Trail, passes through Hemlock Overlook Regional Park and Bull Run Marina. Hemlock's facilities are used for a group public environmental studies center. The dense forest of hemlocks, for which the park is named, includes many trees more than 200 years old. As you hike downstream from Bull Run Regional Park, you will find the terrain gradually becoming wilder and more beautiful. The gently sloping stream valley gives way to low, sharp hills with wooded groves and rhododendron underbrush. These woods harbor an abundance of wildlife, so walk quietly, watch and listen carefully. A trail brochure is available from the parks through which the trail passes or from the NVRPA

To walk this trail is also to walk through history; this is the site of the First and Second Manassas battles, among the most important Civil War battles. Bull Run was a strategic barrier between forces of the North and South. A railroad bridge which crosses Bull Run at Popes Creek, about midway on the trail, was destroyed several times to prevent its falling into enemy hands;

BULL RUN - OCCOQUAN TRAIL

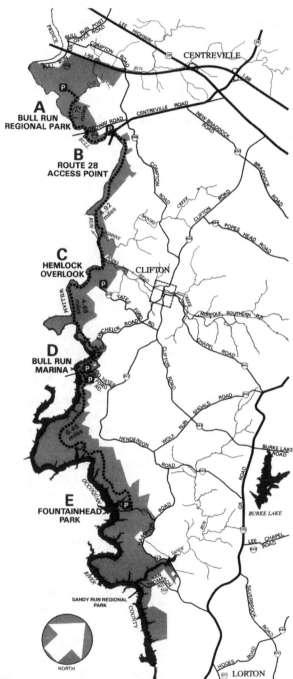

Note: Stream crossings may be difficult or impassable as a result of high water after inclement weather.

Map courtesy of Northern Virginia Regional Park Authority

remnants of the bridge & fortifications remain.

How To Get There: Please refer to the description of Bull Run Regional Park and Bull Run Marina Park for directions on how to gain access to various points on this trail. There is year-round access near the northern end of the trail near Centreville. Take I-66 to Centreville, Route 28 south. After passing Compton Road, take the last driveway on the right before crossing the bridge over Bull Run. Most of the trail is south (left as you face Bull Run) of this point.

For Additional Information:
Northern Virginia Regional Park Authority
5400 Ox Road
Fairfax Station, VA 22039-1022
(703) 352-5900

Bull Run Regional Park

The most comprehensive park in northern Virginia is, without question, the Bull Run Regional Park along Bull Run Creek, just downstream from Manassas National Battlefield Park. It is part of a 5,000 acre tract of woods and meadows, where fields of wildflowers bloom in springtime beside the pools and eddies of a quiet stream. Much of the land remains a primitive and untouched wilderness. A great variety of birds and wildlife is found here, including the pileated woodpecker, dove, quail and even flocks of turkey. The cottontail rabbit, gray squirrel, fox, white-tailed deer, opossum, raccoon and a multitude of aquatic creatures also inhabit the area.

The Civil War buff and historian will find as much here as the naturalist, photographer, casual camper or picnicker. Situated on the Piedmont Plateau, the park possesses a great deciduous forest that offers the ultimate in springtime and autumn scenic beauty. The park also encompasses a low swampy area and meadowland, giving it a variety of ecosystems for nature study. In mid-April the NVRPA naturalists lead the annual Bluebell Walk, one of the area's oldest nature walks. Hikers will see the spectacular beauty of one of the largest stands of bluebells on the East Coast. The park includes an outdoor swimming pool (open from Memorial Day weekend to Labor Day), miniature golf, and a five-mile-long bridle path, a children's playground, an indoor archery range, a skeet and trap shooting center, a spacious special events center, campgrounds, a mini-nature center and a camp store.

Hiking and Horseback Riding

Pick up information and maps at the camp center. There are several park trails. The Yellow and White trails comprise the 1.5-mile Bluebell Nature Loop. Along this path, early spring Virginia bluebells and other wildflowers contribute a frenzy of color to the swampy floor of the forest. You can easily walk it in an hour and a half. Serious hikers should inquire about the historic and scenic 17.5 mile long **Bull Run-Occoquan Trail** (described elsewhere with map) which follows Bull Run Creek, having its western terminus in this park. Riders on horseback may follow the same route. Another bridle trail (5 miles in length) leads from the pool parking lot to Cub Run bridge. A field area on the east side of Cub Run, across the bridge, may also be used for horseback riding when the ground condition is not too marshy, but there is no stable.

Camping

There are 150 tree-shaded family campsites available, 90 of them with electrical outlets. Also provided are a camp store, hot showers, restrooms, laundry facilities and a dump station. Group campsites are available for youth organizations. Reservations are accepted for family sites and required for group camping.

Picnicking

Picnic tables, grills and shelters are available. No ground fires are permitted. Pets must be kept on leashes.

How To Get There: From Exit 9 of the Capital Beltway (I-495), head west on I-66 to exit 52, VA 29 at Centerville. Drive south about 2 miles to the park sign, where a left turn onto Bull Run Post Office Road, VA 621, will lead you to the park entrance. The park is open from mid-March through November, from dawn to dusk.

For Additional Information:
Bull Run Regional Park
7700 Bull Run Drive
Centreville, VA 22020
(703) 631-0550

Northern Virginia Regional Park Authority
5400 Ox Road
Fairfax Station, VA 22039-1022
(703) 352-5900

Burke Lake Park

Fishing at 218-acre Burke Lake is supposedly the best in Northern Virginia, so most visitors come here for just that purpose. This Fairfax County park includes a marina, live bait and tackle shop, boat and life preserver rental and a boat-launching site. The remainder of the 883-acre area is heavily wooded and offers the opportunity to explore, bird-watch or seek out wildlife. No sailboats are allowed on the lake; if motors are used, they must be electric. Vesper Island, in the center of the lake, is maintained as a state waterfowl refuge. Canada geese, ducks and herons visit the area; a good time to see them is in October and November. The herons, however, may stop off at any time of year.

Hiking and Bicycling

Five miles of hiking trails circle the lake. Bicyclists are allowed to use the same paths, so keep an eye out for each other. Beaver Cove Nature Trail, with a length of nearly three quarters of a mile, winds its way through different forest communities. Along the way, you will see evidence of tree-cutting by beavers.

Camping

A family campground with 30 wooded sites is available for tents, recreational vehicles and travel trailers whose maximum length is 25 feet. Sites are allocated on a first-come-first-serve basis. Fresh water, hot showers, restrooms and a dump station are provided, but there are no hookups. The maximum camping stay is seven days. There is a camp store. The campground is open May–September.

How To Get There: Take Exit 5 from the Capital Beltway and follow Braddock Road (VA 620) west. Turn left (south) on Burke Lake Road (VA 645). Proceed 5 miles, and turn left on Ox Road (VA 123) to park entrance. Parkgrounds open daily year-round dawn to dusk. Boat rentals and campgrounds are open only during the summer; call for specific dates.

For Additional Information:
Park Manager
Burke Lake Park
7315 Ox Road
Fairfax Station, VA 22039-1022
(703) 323-6601

Fairfax County Park Authority
12055 Government Center Parkway
Suite 927
Fairfax, VA 22035-1119
703-324-8662
http://www.co.fairfax.va.us/parks

Caledon Natural Area

Caledon Natural Area, located on the Potomac River just west of the Route 301 bridge, is primarily a refuge for eagles and other raptors. Therefore, protection of the eagles is the top priority and much of the area has restricted public access to protect the 120 species of birds found there. These include uncommon migrants such as Canada warbler and gray-cheeked thrush. Other species include white-footed mouse, gray fox and 39 species of reptiles and amphibians. It is a prime summering area for bald eagles and up to 60 have been seen at one time in the area. Of Caledon's 2,579 acres, about 800 acres are mature hardwood forests, with trees averaging 80–100 years old. The park also contains a wide variety of flora, including the rare floating primrose willow.

Caledon was the former estate of Captain John Alexander (for whom Alexandria, Virginia, is named) who purchased it in

1659; his descendants later gave the land to the State of Virginia. Caledon's visitor center is a beautiful turn-of-the-century, white colonial-style house, attractively landscaped. However, it is only open from Memorial Day to Labor Day. The park is open year-round from 8:00 A.M. to sunset.

Hiking and Tours

There are five trails with circuit hikes starting at about one mile. The trails are well marked with little change in elevation. The mature trees above lead to relatively modest plant life below—there is little greenbriar or poison ivy. The trail system is actually a chain of trails, which allow the visitor to take a circuit hike of five different lengths starting and ending at the same parking area; each "link" goes through successively older forests. Maps are found in the picnic area at the trailhead.

A special feature is the ranger-led eagle tour, for which a nominal fee is charged. The guided tour lasts 1.5 hours and is limited to 20 persons. Participants are taken by minibus to prime eagle habitat. Eagle tours are given Saturday and Sunday, June 15 through Sunday of Labor Day weekend. Reservations are recommended; group tour reservations available by request. The tours can be suspended if affecting eagle activity.

How To Get There: From Washington, take I-95 south to Exit 45, Route 3 west, Fredericksburg. Drive through Fredericksburg, possibly stopping to see the many historic sites there. Continue on Route 3 until you cross the Rappahannock River Bridge, turn left on Route 218. Follow Route 218 for about 19 miles; signs for Caledon will be on the left.

From southern Maryland, take Route 301 south, across the Potomac River to Virginia. Turn right at Route 206; go 3 miles to Route 218, turn right (west); Caledon is less than 2 miles on your right.

For Additional Information:

Park Manager
Caledon Natural Area
11617 Caledon Road
King George, VA 22485
(540) 663-3861
http://www.state.va.us/ndcr/parks

Claude Moore Colonial Farm at Turkey Run

In a wooded area in Fairfax County, are The Claude Moore Colonial Farm and the Pavilions of Turkey Run. The 100-acre farm and pavilions are operated by the non-profit, publicly supported Friends of The Claude Colonial Farm at Turkey Run, Inc. in cooperation with the National Park Service. The farm re-creates the world of a poor tenant farmer of the 1770s in this area. The colonial farm family, portrayed by staff and volunteers in period clothing, tills, plants and cultivates the fields by hand just as they were done two centuries ago. The 12 acres that are cultivated include corn, wheat, tobacco, kitchen gardens and an apple orchard. Domestic animals include Red Devon dairy cattle, a quarter horse, Ossabaw Island and razorback hogs, bronzeback turkeys and "Dung Hill" chickens; all are either rare breeds or representative of the 18th-century breeds. A small log house with reproduction period furniture and tools is used for family meals.

Many species of wildlife still roam the woods and meadows of the farm as in the old days. White-tailed deer are seen almost daily and all wildlife creatures indigenous to the Washington area are seen here from time to time—raccoon, opossum, skunk, rabbit, red-tailed hawk and migratory ducks and geese.

Turkey Run Park is a separate location, described elsewhere, found off the George Washington Parkway, nearby.

How To Get There: From the Capital Beltway (I-495,) take VA 193 (Georgetown Pike) east toward Langley. About 2.3 miles on the left side of the road is the farm's entrance sign; follow the signs to the visitor parking lot.

From the George Washington Memorial Parkway, take the VA 123-McLean exit; go 1 mile and turn right onto Georgetown Pike (VA 193) west; turn right onto the access road. Go approximately 0.5 mile; the visitor parking is on the left. The farm is open Wednesday through Sunday, 10:00 A.M.–4:30 P.M., from April through mid-December. The farm is closed on Thanksgiving and during inclement weather. Large groups visiting here should call in advance. Admission is $2.00 for adults, $1.00 for children 3-14 years old and free to members. Alcoholic beverages, pets, bicycles, motorbikes and horseback riding are prohibited in the park.

For Additional Information:
Claude Moore Colonial Farm at Turkey Run, Inc.
6310 Georgetown Pike
McLean, VA 22101
(703) 442-7557

Dyke Marsh

Dyke Marsh is a living remnant of the land that bounded much of the Potomac River two centuries ago. It is the largest remaining freshwater tidal wetland in the Washington, DC area. Unfortunately, in the 1960s, over half of the marsh was mined away for sand and gravel in exchange for other park land. Dyke Marsh contains 385 acres, extending approximately 2.5 miles along the George Washington Memorial Parkway from the Belle Haven picnic area south to Wellington Villa. The name Dyke Marsh comes from the dikes that a 1800s farmer used to try to turn the marsh into farmland. The dikes proved difficult to maintain and they were abandoned. In 1959, Congress set aside this land as an irreplaceable wetland for the preservation and protection of wildlife.

The food and shelter offered by Dyke Marsh attract a wealth of bird life. Over 250 species have been sighted there. Knowledgeable birders call it one of the prime birding spots around Washington, DC. Migratory waterfowl (mallards, Canada geese, wood duck, black duck, pintail, scaup, merganser and ruddy duck), migratory songbirds, herons, egrets, cormorants, coots, terns, gulls, killdeer, sandpipers, bufflehead, red-bellied and downey woodpecker, flickers and raptors (osprey, red-tailed hawk, and bald eagle) are frequently sighted here. (An extensive bird list is available from the Park Service.) The tidal flats offer a world of cattails, great blue herons, muskrats, frogs, reptiles and beavers. Look at the raised section in the middle of the muddy area at the end of the road. Beavers have cut these trees. Also notice the wood-cutting marks made by beavers on the trees throughout the marsh. Arrowhead plant, pickerelweed, European yellow iris and native violet iris, long billed marsh wrens, least bittern and owls still live here, sharing the wetlands with wood duck, turtles and mallards. During July and August the marsh becomes a sea of cattails; there are still extensive beds of the more pollution-sensitive native wild rice. Many species here are making a comeback due to the improvement in

Potomac water quality over the past two decades. Bass are once again seen in the river.

The trail beside the marsh passes through a stretch of bottomland woods including willow, river birch, a variety of gums and oak trees, tangles of wild grape and non-native vines (such as poison ivy). The trail is short (.75 mile long), but it connects to the **Mount Vernon Trail** (described elsewhere). About one mile north of Belle Haven, the parkway crosses Hunting Creek Bridge, commanding a wide view of a tidal lagoon on the west side of the highway. At times, you may catch a glimpse of wading birds foraging in the shallow waters here. Belle Haven picnic area itself puts on a notable show of blooming dogwood in the spring.

How To Get There: From downtown Washington, take Arlington Memorial Bridge, turn south on George Washington Memorial Parkway and travel through the city of Alexandria. As you leave Alexandria, you will cross Hunting Creek. Proceed to the Belle Haven picnic area, about one mile south on your left, where access to the marsh is available by way of a road running three-quarters of a mile through a swamp forest.

For Additional Information:
Superintendent
George Washington Memorial Parkway
Turkey Run Park
McLean, VA 22101
(703) 285-2600
http://www.nps.gov/gwmp

Ellanor C. Lawrence Park

Ellanor C. Lawrence Park in Chantilly is a place to see the history of nature and man in the area. On its 653 acres are found a 200-year-old stone farmhouse, now the renovated Walney Visitor Center, 100-year-old hardwood trees, artifacts from the Civil War, a two-acre lily pond with cattails and willows, a nature trail and a very interesting historic loop trail.

Walney Visitor Center provides numerous educational programs, exhibits, a nature library, a living beehive, demonstration gardens, an amphitheater and live lizard, snake fish and turtle displays. At the visitor center, you can pick up brochures on the historical and the nature trails. The .3-mile Historic Loop Trail guides you past an 19th century dairy (used as a place to make cheese and butter and store perishable foods) and the ruins of an icehouse (to store ice cut from a pond in the winter to preserve food and cool drinks in the summer), the ruins of a tack house and a restored log smokehouse—all evidence of a working farm during the 1800s. You can also observe the land for evidence of erosion caused by runoff after trees were cleared during the Civil War and for agriculture. The best time to see the historical features is when the foliage is at its minimum—in winter before the snows or in early spring before the new growth. You can take a leisurely walk and observe wildlife on the park's three miles of nature trails. Spring is the favorite time for wildflowers. The park is also a good location to view local woodland and meadow bird species.

Parking and picnic tables are provided at both the pond and Walney Visitor Center. The pond is the most accessible fishing spot in the area (Virginia state fishing and licensing requirements apply). Ellanor C. Lawrence Park is also a good location to view local bird and plant species in diverse habitats.

Ellanor C. Lawrence Park grounds are open daily dawn to dusk; the visitor center is open weekdays 9:00 A.M.–5:00 P.M. and weekends NOON–5:00 P.M.; it is closed on Tuesdays; holiday and winter hours may vary.

How To Get There: From the Washington Beltway, take I-66 West to Route 28 north (Exit 53); take the first right off Route 28, which is Walney Road. Walney Visitor Center is about a mile up the road on the left.

For Additional Information:

Ellanor C. Lawrence Park, Walney Visitor Center
5040 Walney Road
Chantilly, VA 20151-2306
(703) 631-0013 (Visitor Center)   (703) 324 3988 (TTY)
(703) 750-1598 (historic property rental information)

Fairfax County Park Authority
12055 Government Center Parkway
Suite 927
Fairfax, VA 22035-1119
703-324-8662
http://www.co.fairfax.va.us/parks

Fraser Preserve

Not far from Great Falls Park in Fairfax County is the 220-acre Fraser Preserve, a combination of upland forest, river-bottom marsh and alder swamp owned by The Nature Conservancy. It is not manicured but an undeveloped area where you can enjoy a look at what the land is like when left undisturbed by man. Walking to the end of the trail, you can scan the broad expanse of the Potomac. Near the entrance are yellow pine and honeysuckle, while deeper in the preserve, on northern-facing slopes that drop down to the Potomac River floodplain, are the large trees. Here great white oaks, maples, sycamores and beeches form the canopy. At the bottom of the slopes, a part of the floodplain, is the alder swamp. The northern boundary of the preserve is formed by the Potomac River, much more pristine-looking here than further downstream because it is upstream from the murky, silt-laden waters found near metropolitan Washington. A small, spring-fed pond—bulldozed out years ago—provides some interesting studies in aquatic life. Frogs, salamanders and even an occasional turtle or water snake are seen here. There also are white-tailed deer, wild turkey, quail, raccoon, cottontail rabbit, gray squirrel and garter snakes on the preserve, as well as numerous species of songbirds and the pileated woodpecker. The springtime displays of wildflowers are especially notable in this preserve.

Hiking

An information kiosk located approximately .5 mile beyond the entrance gate (via the service road) provides information about trail routes and some of the natural features of the preserve.

How To Get There: From Exit 13 of the Capital Beltway (I-495), take VA 193 (Georgetown Pike) west. Approximately 2 miles beyond the town of Great Falls, turn right on Springvale Road (County Road 674), and follow it for approximately 2 miles where it becomes Route 755; shortly thereafter the pavement ends at the Fraser Preserve main gate. Since the main gate on the unpaved service road into the preserve is normally locked, please contact The Nature Conservancy for information about visiting. Open year-round.

For Additional Information:
The Nature Conservancy
Virginia Chapter
1233A Cedars Court
Charlottesville, VA 22903
(804) 295-6106
http://www.tnc.org

G. Richard Thompson Wildlife Management Area

(Formerly known as Apple Manor or Linden)

The G. Richard Thompson Wildlife Management Area sits astride the Appalachian Trail near Linden, Virginia. It is a mostly mountainous area with second-growth hardwoods and some open grasslands. In the spring, this is probably the best place in the region to see millions of large-flowered trillium and lady's-slipper (especially near Gate 6). Other wildflowers include jack-in-the-pulpit, wild ginger, may apple, slender and cutleaf toothwort, bloodroot, spring beauty, columbine and many varieties of violets and asters. In the fall, this is a good area to see wildflowers of the daisy family. The preserve is also rich in fauna; hawks can be seen along the mountain tops in the fall migration.

Several trails traverse the area and may be accessed from parking lots on Route 638, which goes along the high, western side of the park, and Route 688 on the east. There are no restrooms and no overnight camping is allowed. This is a popular hunting area, so Sunday visits (when hunting is illegal) are preferred. It is advisable to wear bright clothing.

How To Get There: From the Washington area, take I-66 west to Route 688 (Markham exit), turn right (north) on 688 to parking areas along the east boundary. Or turn left on 688, to Route 55, right to Linden, right on Route 638 to the west boundary. Route 638 and Ridge Fire Trail form the approximate west boundary for about 3 miles. Trails from parking areas 4, 6 and 7 on the west boundary are good places to start, especially for viewing wildflowers. A trail map is available from the state at the address below.

For Additional Information:
Virginia Department of Game and Inland Fisheries
4010 W. Broad St.
Richmond, VA 23230
(804) 367-1000

George Washington Memorial Parkway and Turkey Run Park

One of the finest drives in the greater Washington area is along the George Washington Memorial Parkway provided you travel it at a time when the traffic is not heavy. The best time, of course, is on weekends and holidays. The parkway, which extends 23 miles from the Capital Beltway (I-495) northwest of Washington to Mount Vernon, parallels the course of the Potomac River. Formerly the parkway along the Maryland side was also named George Washington Memorial Parkway, but it was renamed the Clara Barton Parkway.

Opened in 1932, it includes important shrines and recreation areas and provides access to several major natural attractions. Among them are Theodore Roosevelt Island, Roaches Run (a waterfowl sanctuary where snowy egrets, herons and wild ducks congregate within sight of the road), Lady Bird and Lyndon Baines Johnson Park and Dyke Marsh (all described elsewhere). The parkway curves gently between formally landscaped areas, native forest and undisturbed marshes. Though impressive at any season, it is perhaps most beautiful in the spring and early summer. Then the blossoms on the crab apple and pear trees, forsythia, shadbush, redbud, dogwood, wild azaleas, roses, mountain laurel and varicolored day lilies appear in rapid succession. There are pullover rest areas with stone-walled springs, picnic sites and overlooks above the Potomac River. Along portions of the parkway are paths where you can walk, bird-watch or enjoy the scenery.

Turkey Run Park is located on the high bluffs above the Potomac River, between the Potomac and the Parkway. Spring wildflower viewing of Virginia bluebells, twinleaf, white and yellow trout lilies, among others, is good.

Hiking

A well defined hiking trail in Turkey Run Park follows the shoreline of the Potomac River in places. The bottom lands, rich in plant life, are exceptionally attractive in spring.

How To Get There: From downtown Washington, take virtually any of the bridges into Virginia and follow the signs to the parkway. The exit to Turkey Run Park is located just south of the Capital Beltway (I-495) and the American Legion Bridge.

For Additional Information:
Superintendent
George Washington Memorial Parkway
Turkey Run Park
McLean, VA 22101
(703) 285-2600
http://www.nps.gov/gwmp

Great Falls Park

One of the most outstanding natural areas of the greater Washington area is the Great Falls of the Potomac, just upstream from the city. Here the waters of the Potomac rush and fall as they flow through narrow Mather Gorge, named for the first director of the National Park Service. The area possesses a rugged, primeval beauty. Geologically, it is unparalleled. The giant potholes, the rocky islands, the great boulders and schist rocks—all form a composite not easily forgotten. It is a surprising place, totally unlike the Potomac you see elsewhere in the Washington area. Both upstream and downstream from the falls, the river appears docile, its flow barely discernible, but it is very treacherous. The river shows its true self in the park, becoming a raging torrent a quarter-mile wide and in places 50 feet deep. At full flood, 134,000 cubic feet of water tumble over Great Falls each second. Here, the Potomac drops a total of 76 feet—not in one abrupt fall, but in several that look like a series of rapids. One rule is strictly enforced here; there is absolutely no swimming or wading. The river's currents are extremely hazardous. Children should be watched closely. Drownings are frequent.

Numerous plants and animals live along the banks of the

river and in the park's upland forests and swamp. Please remember that all plants, animals and artifacts in all national parks are protected by federal law, which prohibits removal defacement or excavation. A profusion of spring wildflowers is found here including Virginia bluebells, wild blue phlox, twinleaf, Dutchman's-breeches, squirrel corn, wild ginger, toadshade (sessile trillium), harbinger-of-spring and yellow trout lily. Also of interest is the swamp trail with skunk cabbage, three species of club mosses, ferns and poison ivy. The beaver, wood duck, red fox, broad-winged hawk, muskrat, white-tailed deer, box turtle, cottontail rabbit, gray squirrel and the golden orb spider share the park's environs with skunks, opossum and raccoons. Great oaks, sycamores and beeches thrive here, too. During daylight hours, the call of the pileated woodpecker echoes through the woods while at night barred owls hoot from the trees. This is one of the great birding places around Washington.

The area also has a rich history. George Washington envisioned the Potomac River as a major waterway to the West and, in 1784, helped to form the Patowmack Company. He served as its first president. The company planned to build five canals to bypass the unnavigable sections of the river. Eighteen years later, the canal at Great Falls was completed. During the 26 years that the canal system was in operation, flour, whiskey, tobacco, corn, furs, iron, ore and raw wood materials were poled down the river on flatboats from as far away as Cumberland, Maryland. Business was good and in 1793 "Lighthorse Harry" Lee, a Revolutionary War hero and a friend of Washington's, sponsored a town to be built at Great Falls. He named it Matildaville in honor of his first wife. It thrived until business on the canal began to decline in the 1820s; then it withered and died. It never fulfilled its expectations, but it did have a gristmill, a forge and an inn.

In 1828 the Patowmack Company's commercial rights were transferred to the Chesapeake & Ohio Company, which was organized to build the C&O Canal on the Maryland side of the river. The C&O Canal was a major highway to the West and served to bind the country together with trade and mutual interests. The Canal was soon superseded by the Baltimore & Ohio Railroad, which could carry larger loads more quickly and less expensively than the boats. The ruins of the Patowmack Canal and Matildaville, although reclaimed by nature, are still visible as you hike the trails downstream from the falls. They are particularly noticeable during the winter and early spring months when foliage is absent from the trees. The Patowmack Canal has been designated as a National Historic Landmark,

National Civil Engineering Landmark and a Virginia Historic Landmark. The National Park Service administers the entire area.at the visitor center.

Hiking, Bicycling and Horseback Riding

Bicycle riding is confined to the bike-designated trails, but there is an extensive trail system for day hiking within the park. Some of the trails parallel the river; others cut through the woodlands, cross a swampy area, and then parallel Difficult Run, even beyond earshot of the falls. One hiking trail is an old carriage road. Along the blue-blazed River Trail are places to stop and view the Potomac River and Mather Gorge. The Patowmack Canal trail begins at Wing Dam, near the visitor center, and follows the old canal past the gates, dams, gristmill and iron forge location and is accessible by wheelchair as far as Lock 1. No overnight camping is allowed. Bicyclists and horseback riders should ask for a special map of trails. Bike riding is allowed only on the Old Carriage Road Trail, the Ridge Trail and the Difficult Run Trail. Ranger-led interpretive programs are offered and special programs can be arranged by calling the park.

Hiking and Nature Trails

River Trail	3.0 miles	2 hours	moderately strenuous	begins at picnic ..... area
Old Carriage Trail	2.6 miles	2 hours	quite easy	begins at south parking lot .... restrooms
Patowmack Canal Trail	2.5 miles	1 hour	easy	begins at upper parking lot and follows the canal
Swamp/ Nature	1.8 miles	1 hour	easy	known for wildTrail flowers; follow Old Carriage Road to turnoff
Ridge Trail	3.0 miles	2 hours	easy	through deciduous forest from lower parking lot, follow Old Carriage Trail to turnoff

The best view of Great Falls is from the Virginia side of the Potomac.
Bill Thomas

Fishing

Fishing is not great, but enjoyable. Catfish, bass, carp and a variety of panfish inhabit the waters. Either a Maryland or Virginia fishing license is required.

Picnicking

Picnic grounds are provided with tables and a limited number of grills. No reservations are accepted. Ground fires and alcohol are prohibited.

Rock Climbing

The area is excellent for rock climbing, but dangerous. Only experienced rock climbers should attempt climbing here. Climbers are requested to register at the visitor center or lower parking lot. Proper equipment should be used at all times. Drownings occur annually on the Potomac River and normally involve persons who slip from the rocks into the turbulent river waters.

How To Get There: Take VA 193 (Georgetown Pike) northwest from Exit 13 of the Capital Beltway to VA 738 (Old Dominion Drive) and turn right to the park entrance. Great Falls Park has a minimal entrance fee. A trail map is available at the visitor center.

For Additional Information:
Site Manager
Great Falls Park
c/o Turkey Run Park
McLean VA 22101
(703) 285-2966

Green Spring Gardens Park

Green Spring Gardens is a gardener's delight. The 27-acre park consists of numerous demonstration gardens, a new horticulture center building, the restored 18th-century Manor House, and a wooded stream valley with two ponds. Most of the park and buildings are handicapped accessible.

The 20 theme gardens are of special interest to the garden enthusiast. A Water Wise garden has 150 living specimens with detailed labels and a plant list including Latin name, common name, foliage, bloom season and hardiness; everything one needs to put together a design for a low maintenance garden of one's own. There are several townhouse gardens on replica townhouse plots, showing how beautiful a typical small back yard can be. There's a shade garden, a butterfly garden, an iris garden, and even a swale garden, in addition to the more horticultural veggie and fruit gardens.

The Horticulture Center features a horticulture library open to the public. There are numerous pamphlets, most available for a nominal fee, on many subjects of practical use to the avid gardener such as one on groundcovers for the DC, one of annuals and tender perennials for border gardens in the area, another on hardy perennials, etc. The Horticulture Center has lectures and classes. The attached large greenhouse features a wide range of exotic plants.

One can walk through the woods on the Virginia Native Plant Trail to a pair of ponds, often inhabited by migrating waterfowl.

How To Get There: Take Beltway Exit 6, Route 236, east for three miles to a left at Green Spring Road which leads to the park entrance. The park is open Monday through Saturday 9:00 A.M. to 5:00 P.M., and Sundays NOON to 5:00 P.M.

For Additional Information:
Green Spring Gardens Park & Horticulture Center
4603 Green Spring Road
Alexandria, VA 22312
(703) 642-5173

Fairfax County Park Authority
12055 Government Center Parkway
Suite 927
Fairfax, VA 22035-1119
(703) 324-8662
http://www.co.fairfax.va.us/parks

Gulf Branch Nature Center

An exciting time to visit Gulf Branch is during the spring when the fish make their annual spawning runs up the Potomac River. Herring and shad swim upstream from salt to fresh water, looking for unpolluted creeks and streams in which to reproduce; these can be observed at the mouth of Gulf Branch. At this time, too, the forest of the center and surrounding area is decorated with wildflowers. Jack-in-the-pulpit and bloodroot have grown here since the days of Indian encampments. The voices of the chipmunk, jay and squirrel penetrate the serenity of the daytime forest, while the raccoon, opossum and owl emerge at night. Salamanders and turtles live here too.

Gulf Branch is actually an interpretive center of the Arlington County Parks and Natural Resources Division. The interpretive center has displays and live exhibits that interpret features of the local environment. The center has a living beehive to observe (through glass), and a live copperhead snake. Copperheads are the only venomous snakes found in this area. They can be identified by the hourglass pattern on their backs. The pattern of a snake's skin is the best way to identify it. There are also costumes and a dugout canoe that children are welcome to play in. There are no picnic areas at Gulf Branch, but there are facilities at Glebe Park, which are accessible by trail or road.

Hiking

The main trails are the self-guided Stream Valley Trail, which follows Gulf Branch to the Potomac (0.75 mile long) and the Woodland Trail (0.5 mile long).

How To Get There: From the George Washington Memorial Parkway, just northwest of Key Bridge, take Spout Run Parkway (VA 124) west to Lorcom Lane. Turn right and follow Lorcom Lane northwest to Military Road; turn right there. The nature center is located at 3608 North Military Road. Open year-round: 10:00 A.M.–5:00 P.M. Tuesday through Saturday, and 1:00–5:00 P.M., Sunday; closed Monday and holidays. No entrance fee.

For Additional Information:
Naturalist Staff
Gulf Branch Nature Center
3608 North Military Road
Arlington, VA 22207
(703) 228-3403

Gunston Hall

Overlooking the Potomac River south of Washington stands Gunston Hall, a plantation famed for its architectural beauty, its lovely grounds and its history. It was built in the mid-18th century by George Mason, a statesman and political thinker who is credited with writing the Virginia Declaration of Rights, which has served as a model for the French Declaration of the Rights of Man and our own Bill of Rights. He was a friend of George Washington and Thomas Jefferson and has been called the "Pen of the Revolution." He attended the Constitutional Convention to help draft the Constitution and argued for the elimination of the slave trade and stronger protection of individual rights. When these were not added to the Constitution, he refused to sign it. Today Gunston Hall is owned by the Commonwealth of Virginia and administered by a Board of Regents nominated by the National Society of the Colonial Dames of America. It has been designated a National Historic Landmark. The grounds, which encompass more than 550 acres, offer a combination of formal gardens and wooded countryside that visitors are free to explore. Restored by the Garden Club of Virginia, the gardens contain plants and shrubs actually found in the 18th century. A special feature is the original boxwood hedge planted by George Mason himself. It is now 12 feet high in places. Lord Balfour, a former British foreign secretary, remarked after a visit here during World War I that Gunston boxwood was second only to that at the Vatican. He later wrote from Rome that Gunston's was the finest of all.

Dense woodlands cover the part of the estate that borders the Potomac and a half-mile nature trail leads through the forest to the water's edge. Signs along the way point out some of the variety of trees, including the red cedar, white oak, pecan, tulip poplar, water oak, red maple, beech, black walnut and sassafras. In the spring and summer the flowering dogwood, mountain laurel, lady's-slipper, jack-in-the-pulpit and cardinal flower add the brilliance of their blooms to the landscape. Gunston Hall occupies a portion of Mason Neck peninsula, more than half of which is a public parkland. Two of the estate's neighbors are Pohick Bay Regional Park and Mason Neck National Wildlife Refuge (both described elsewhere). Most of the area has been maintained as much as possible in a natural state, encouraging many species of wildlife to make their home here. A 1.5–2 mile self-guided nature trail has been designed by the Virginia Park Service. A booklet is available at the orientation area. Inhabiting the forests of Gunston Hall today, as during George Mason's lifetime, is the white-tailed deer. Other wildlife includes the Virginia opossum, raccoon, fox, gray squirrel, otter, mink, skunk, rabbit, mallard ducks, the bald eagle and a variety of reptiles. A picnic area is provided under the trees near the parking area.

How To Get There: From Washington, take I-95 south to Exit 163 and follow the signs to Gunston Hall. Open daily, except Christmas Day, Thanksgiving and New Year's Day, 9:30 A.M.–5:00 P.M. The nominal entrance fee includes admission to both grounds and house.

For Additional Information:
Gunston Hall
Mason Neck, VA 22079
(703) 550-9220
(800) 811-6966
historic@gunstonhall.org
http://gunstonhall.org

Hidden Oaks Nature Center

In the middle of Annandale, there is a 52-acre natural oasis called the Hidden Oaks Nature Center. Surrounded by a mixed oak-hickory forest, woodland streams and traces of a Civil War–era railroad, the center provides both educational and recreational facilities. Bird-watching, wild orchids and pink lady's-slipper are the special treats of this park. (Be very careful not to disturb these rare plants, which are protected by law). Excellent exhibits at the nature center focus on the interdependence of man and his environment. Located in Annandale Park, the center contains an athletic field, tennis courts and picnic tables. Most of the park, however, is forested with several nature trails winding through it. The center offers a few live exhibits, displays depicting various aspects of the forest community and a touch-table for a hands-on sensory experience. Nature programs are offered to the public and to groups with prior arrangement. An auditorium, accessible to persons in wheelchairs, is located at the center.

How To Get There: From Exit 6 of the Capital Beltway (I-495), take VA 236 (Little River Turnpike) east to Hummer Road. Turn left (north) there. The center and park are located on the left side of Hummer Road. Open year-round: 9:00 A.M.–5:00 P.M. weekdays, **NOON** to 5:00 P.M weekends and holidays; Open only on weekends during January and February. Closed Tuesday, as well as Thanksgiving, Christmas and New Year's Day. Admission is free.

For Additional Information:
Manager
Hidden Oaks Nature Center
7701 Royce Street
Annandale, VA 22003
(703) 941-1065

Fairfax County Park Authority
12055 Government Center Parkway
Suite 927
Fairfax, VA 22035-1119
703-324-8662
http://www.co.fairfax.va.us/parks

Hidden Pond Park

At Springfield, not far from Washington, is Hidden Pond, a Fairfax County park made up of a variety of lovely fields, tranquil forests and peaceful ponds. Hidden Pond Park and the adjacent Pohick Stream Valley Park are made up of over 400 acres of natural habitat. Tulip poplars, beeches, white and red oaks as well as wildflowers and ferns make up the forests. The key to the park's secrets is the Nature Center, overlooking Hidden Pond; make it your first stop. Live displays and exhibits give the visitor some insight into the ecosystems of the park, such as frog's eggs just laid, caterpillars just hatched, wildflowers in bloom, etc. The nature center has an extensive natural history library and staff to answer nature related questions. Trails along the stream, through the woods, around the one-acre pond as well as a self-guided nature trail, featuring changes in the land wrought by the seasons and climate, provide a good opportunity to explore the area. There is a small sales area with books and items for the nature enthusiast. Other features include a playground and picnic shelter.

How To Get There: From Exit 4 of the Capital Beltway (I-495), head south on I-95 to VA 644 (Old Keene Mill Road). Head west 3 miles, cross Rolling Road, then turn left at the next light onto Greeley Boulevard, which leads to the park. The park is open year-round. The nature center is open 9:00 A.M.–5:00 P.M., weekdays and NOON–5:00 P.M. weekends. Closed Tuesday, as well as Thanksgiving, Christmas and News Year's Day; winter and holiday hours may vary. No admission fee.

For Additional Information:
Naturalist
Hidden Pond Nature Center
8511 Greeley Blvd.
Springfield, VA 22152
(703) 451-9588

Huntley Meadows Park

Huntley Meadows is one of the best parks for viewing wildlife close-up, especially for bird-watching, in the Washington metropolitan area and one of the authors' favorites. Only ten miles from the Capitol this 1,412-acre park, the largest in Fairfax County, is rich with vibrant wildflowers, majestic forests and teeming marshlands. Lying in an ancient river channel, the park is on land flatter and lower than the land around it. Dogue Creek, its tributary Barnyard Run, and Little Hunting Creek run through the area, ultimately finding their way to the Potomac. The impenetrable clay soils that make up the park result in standing water and marshlands; over 500 acres of the park are wetlands.

The diversity of terrain results in one of the greatest varieties of plant and wildlife in the greater Washington area. The activities of beavers (several lodges and dams are visible from the boardwalk) have raised the water level of the park creating new marshes and swamps. In addition to beavers, the park is home to frogs, crayfish, bluegill, raccoon, opossum, river otter, muskrat, white-tailed deer, rabbit and squirrel. Bird species include uncommon varieties such as yellow-crowned night heron, pied-billed grebe, least bittern and American bittern. In addition, you may find red-shouldered hawks, barred owls, herons, wood ducks, mallards, Canada geese, king rails, numerous woodpeckers including the pileated woodpecker, red-winged blackbirds, kingfishers, blue-gray gnatcatchers, barn swallows, tree swallows, indigo buntings, towhees, goldfinches, hummingbirds, warblers and more. Some 500 species of plants have been identified, representing 95 of the 168 plant families known to be capable of growing in this area. More than 200 species of birds (including 70 species of nesting birds), 25 species of mammals, 21 species of reptiles, 16 species of amphibians, 69 species of butterflies and numerous fish and invertebrate species have been found here.

In the springtime, frogs and toads fill the evening air with their songs. Beginning in March and lasting for about six weeks, male frogs give voice to their mating songs, defining their territories and attracting females. Green and bullfrog species breed slightly later. Ten species of frogs and toads are found in the park, each with their own distinctive call. Frog songs can be heard over a mile away and vary with temperature and rainfall. Their mating instincts are stimulated by increased rainfall and temperatures between 55 and 70 degrees. From dusk to midnight, you can hear the frogs singing in the springtime. Soon after they mate, females produce a gelatinous mass containing up to 12,000 eggs, which eventually turn into tadpoles. Tadpoles graduate from gill to lung breathing, while retaining their ability to breathe through their skins. When frightened, frogs flee, play dead, burrow themselves in soil or secrete irritating substances from special glands on their skin. Frogs will die if their skin dries out or if they get so cold their protoplasm freezes, although they can revive if they are trapped in frozen mud even if their bodily processes have stopped. Elegant dragonflies with their rainbow wings and eyes and acrobatic flight fly over the marsh.

In June, a white carpet appears on the marsh with blossoming lizard's tail. In late summer, you will find rose-mallows and cardinal flowers. During the summer, you will find watermeal, a form of duckweed, the smallest flowering plant, on the water. But almost any time of year, especially March through October, there is a great deal of visible animal activity, with seasonal changes in flora.

The wildlife is uniquely visible to the observant visitor at Huntley Meadows, due to 0.6 mile of boardwalk, a wildlife observation tower and a 2-mile interpretive trail. The walk is wide and level, so access is easy. There is always some wildlife in easy view nearby. In warm months frogs and turtles are plentiful. Beaver lodges, dams and channels are within easy view of the boardwalk; it's not unusual to see a beaver or muskrat munching on vegetation only a few feet away. Numerous birds' nests can be seen from the boardwalk or trail; you are almost guaranteed to see many bird species that are unusual elsewhere. Bring your binoculars, observe and listen and you will be richly rewarded.

The Huntley Meadows Visitor Center has an active environmental education program that focuses on the wetland. There is a Nature Detective program for ages 3-5, a Young Explorers program for ages 6-9, a junior naturalists class for ages 9-11, summer camps and various adult/family education classes on such diverse subjects as building nest boxes, identifying amphibians, mammals, insects and plants. Huntley Meadows also offers many guided bird walks. Outdoor programs conducted by the park's naturalists can be arranged for groups of ten or more by calling in advance although these tours are often booked months in advance.

Hiking

The park has over 3 miles of trails and a lengthy boardwalk with a bird-watching tower; most of the path is wide, flat and easily accessible. Definitely take some time and slowly walk the boardwalk and trails. Maps are available at the visitor center.

How To Get There: From Exit 1 of the Capital Beltway (I-495), take US 1 south three miles. Turn right (southwest) on Lockheed Boulevard. About 0.6 mile on the left will be a sign for the park. The park is popular, so it becomes crowded on the weekends and the parking lot can be full.

The park is open year-round from dawn until dark. The visitor center is closed Tuesdays, Thanksgiving, Christmas and New Year's Day. The visitor center hours vary seasonally.

For Additional Information:
Park Manager
Huntley Meadows Park
3701 Lockheed Boulevard
Alexandria, VA 22306
(703) 768-2525

Fairfax County Park Authority
12055 Government Center Parkway
Suite 927
Fairfax, VA 22035-1119
703-324-8662
http://www.co.fairfax.va.us/parks

Lake Accotink Park

Lake Accotink Park is a paradox of a large park with a good sized lake in a highly populated area that is easy to miss and hard to find. The park consists of 482 acres, most mature hardwood upland forest, with 64-acre Lake Accotink on the relatively natural Accotink Creek. Since it does not border a major road, many people who live nearby are not familiar with it. But it's a wonderful, usually uncrowded, place to take a hike in the woods or canoe without a long drive. The lake and nearby marshlands attract migratory waterfowl and a wide variety of other aquatic and avian species.

The park has playgrounds, a miniature golf course, open play fields, picnic areas, four miles of hiking/bicycling trails, boating and fishing.

Hiking

A lovely 3.75 mile hiker/biker trail circumnavigates the park and lake. There are other smaller undeveloped trails within the park.

Boating and Fishing

Lake Accotink has a 65-acre lake with fishing, boat launch, canoe, rowboat and pedal boat rentals. Life preservers and fishing licenses are required. No swimming allowed in the lake and no pets are allowed in boats.

How To Get There: Take I-95 to VA 644 (Old Keene Mill Road) west; turn right on Hanover Avenue; left on Highland Avenue; right on Accotink Park Road to the park entrance on the left. Open dawn to dusk year-round. Pets must be on leash only and no alcoholic beverages are allowed.

For Additional Information:
Lake Accotink Park
7500 Accotink Park Rd.
Springfield, VA 22150
(703) 569-3464

Fairfax County Park Authority
12055 Government Center Parkway
Suite 927
Fairfax, VA 22035-1119
(703) 324-8700
TTY (703) 324-3988
http://www.co.fairfax.va.us/parks

Lake Fairfax Park

Operated by the Fairfax County Park Authority, Lake Fairfax Park offers a variety of activities and some fine nature experiences. The focal point of the expansive grounds is the 18-acre lake, but there also are 476 acres of rolling hills, meadows and woodlands to explore. Weekdays are the best time to visit during summer months since the park is less crowded then. The Water Mine family Swimmin' Pool, Lake Fairfax Park's new theme pool, recreates the excitement of the Old West's Gold Rush with attractions especially tailored to families with young children. Fishing for bluegill and bass is permitted. Paddleboats can be rented for use on the lake. An excursion boat also explores the lake. Numerous birds live here, making it an excellent bird-watching area year-round. Other wildlife includes the gray squirrel, raccoon, opossum, fox, mallard ducks and, during the fall and spring, Canada geese. The Reston Animal Park adjoins Lake Fairfax Park; children may ride an elephant or a camel, visit with baby lions or stroke a newborn bunny.

Hiking and Bicycling

A network of hiking trails extends through the park. One, leading around the undeveloped side of the lake, is little used and offers an opportunity to get away from the crowd; most of the trail is wooded. A 1.5-mile-long fitness trail begins near the parking lot and runs around the athletic fields. You can also hike along several miles of roads leading through the park's picnic areas and campground. Bicycling is permitted on all park roads.

Camping

There are 136 family campsites (76 with electrical hookups) available. There are a dump station, modern sanitary and hot bath facilities, picnic tables, grills and a camp store. There is controlled access with an attendant at the gate during the summer months. Camping is allowed March 1 to December 1, but each visit is limited to seven days.

Picnicking

Picnic tables are available year-round in shady groves near the lake. Grills are provided, but no ground fires are permitted. To reserve a picnic site, call (703) 324-8732.

How To Get There: From Exit 10 of the Capital Beltway (I-495), take VA 7 (Leesburg Pike) west about 7 miles; turn left on VA 606 (Baron Cameron Avenue), then left again on Lake Fairfax Drive to the park entrance. The park is officially open 10:00 A.M. to dark, mid-May through Labor Day. During this period, a small admission fee is charged for nonresidents of the county. The grounds and picnic area, however, are open year-round.

For Additional Information:
Lake Fairfax Park
1400 Lake Fairfax Drive
Reston, VA 22090
(703) 471-5414

Reston Animal Park
1228 Hunter Mill Road
Vienna, VA 22180
(703) 759-3636

Fairfax County Park Authority
12055 Government Center Parkway
Suite 927
Fairfax, VA 22035-1119
(703) 324-8700
http://www.co.fairfax.va.us/parks

Leesylvania State Park

Leesylvania is one of Virginia's newest state parks, opening full time in 1992. It consists of 508 wooded acres, with water on three sides—the Potomac River, the Neabsco Creek and Powell's Creek. Henry Lee II, the father of Henry Lee III, (known as "Light Horse Harry", a cavalry colonel in the revolutionary war and governor of Virginia) and grandfather of Robert E. Lee, lived here; the house no longer remains. There is also the remains of a Confederate gun battery used during the Civil War blockade of Washington. The park offers hiking through hardwood forests and views of water on three sides. Probably due to the damp location, the woods are draped with numerous giant vines hanging from the tree canopy, but don't swing on them; many are poison ivy; others are wild grape. The woods are lovely in the fall. There is a long natural sand beach, with many picnic tables nearby. Swimming, however, is not safe and is prohibited. A visitors center features historical exhibits, a discovery room for environmental education and a gift store.

Hiking

There are four well marked, wide, unpaved loop trails. The Powell's Creek trail runs from the road, just past the park admissions booth two miles over a moderate hill, through a hardwood forest to Powell's Creek; from that point, one can usually see an eagle's nest on the creek. The Bushey Point trail is 1.0 mile long. It connects Powell's Creek trail to the Potomac Beach trail. Potomac Beach trail is a 0.5 mile paved trail that borders the Potomac River through the picnic area and marina. The Lee's Woods historic trail starts at the end of the park road and runs two miles through the historic area; an interpretive brochure is available at the trailhead. Nature and history hikes are conducted by the rangers every Saturday, except during the winter;

call for details. No bicycles are allowed on the trails. No overnight use is permitted.

Boating and Fishing

The park has an excellent boating facility on the Potomac River. It features two paved motorboat ramps, two cranes, two sailboat hoists, and parking for 200 cars with trailers. Boat launching costs $6.00 weekdays and $8.00 weekends. There are many fishing contests; fishing in the waters near Leesylvania is considered excellent. Sailboat races are frequently held nearby. In addition the nearby creeks are good for canoeing. Canoeists can see a beaver lodge in Powell's Creek just above the park. Canoe tours are conducted by the park rangers every Saturday except during the winter; call for details. In addition, there is a park store with snack bar, a gas dock and handicapped accessible toilets and shower.

How To Get There: Take I-95 south from the Washington Beltway about 10 miles to Exit 156 east to Route 1; turn right (south), then take a left at the first light onto Neabsco Road; follow Neabsco Road about two miles to the park entrance on the right. The park is open from 8:00 A.M. to dusk daily. Pets must be kept on a short leash. Many of the facilities, including the rest rooms, are accessible to the handicapped. Entrance fee, $2.00 per car weekdays and $3.00 per car weekends.

For Additional Information:
Leesylvania State Park
16236 Neabsco Road
Woodbridge, VA 22191-4504
(703) 670-0372

Virginia Department of Conservation and Recreation
203 Governor Street, Suite 302
Richmond, VA 23219-2010
(804) 786-1712
(800) 866-9222 (toll free number for brochures)
http://www.state.va/us/ndcr

Long Branch Nature Area

In the center of what once was Arlington's agricultural heartland is the Long Branch Nature Area. Made up of meadow, woodland, stream and ponds, it offers many urban residents a convenient place to escape close to home. When you hear leaves rustling underfoot, a woodpecker drumming, a dragonfly droning over a cattail pond, frogs croaking and crickets chirping, the city seems far away. Two geological formations meet in the park. Along Four Mile Run stream the soft Coastal Plain meets the crystalline rocks of the Piedmont. The plants and animals of both physiographic regions meet and mingle here, increasing the biological diversity of the area. Over 150 species of birds have been sighted here as well as numerous mammals including opossum, muskrat, chipmunk, gray squirrel, cottontail, raccoon and red fox.

The nature center also features a series of theme gardens: native plant garden, fern garden, and children's garden. An environmental education center schedules naturalist-led programs Tuesday through Friday by request. Special nature programs for the general public are offered several times weekly, but reservations are required. Inside the center, a diverse collection of live animal exhibits will educate the visitor. For youngsters, a "discovery room" provides an opportunity to see, feel and smell nature. The gardens, pond, and building are handicapped accessible.

Hiking and Bicycling

A handicapped accessible paved hiker/biker trail winds through the Long Branch stream valley to connect with a section of the 44-mile Washington and Old Dominion Railroad trail and other county bike paths. A spur of the Four Mile Bike Trail also passes through this area. The 0.5-mile woodland trail winds through the nature area with short spurs to the upland meadow, stream and rock garden. The Long Branch spur runs from South Carlin Springs Road through the nature area and down into adjacent Glencarlyn Park where it joins the Arlington County bike trail. From the education center, several short unimproved trails lead through field and forest.

How To Get There: From Exit 6 of the Capital Beltway (I-495), head east on Little River Turnpike (VA 236) to Annandale. Turn left on Columbia Pike (VA 244) and head northeast to South Carlin Springs Road near the Arlington-Fairfax county line; turn left (north). The nature area is at 625 South Carlin Springs, between Glencarlyn Elementary School and the Northern Virginia Doctors' Hospital. Open daily year-round, except Mondays and holidays 10:00 A.M.–5:00 P.M., Tuesday through Saturday; and 1:00–5:00 P.M., Sunday. No entrance fee.

For Additional Information:
Naturalist
Long Branch Nature Center
625 South Carlin Springs Road
Arlington, VA 22204
(703) 228-6535
(703) 845-2654 (fax)

Luray Caverns

Luray Caverns, although well outside our 50-mile range, is included here because of its proximity to Skyline Drive (see Shenandoah National Park listing) and because it is a spectacular phenomenon to witness. Luray with 64 acres of caves and some rooms almost 140 feet high claims to be the largest and most popular cave in the eastern U.S.; it's certainly impressive. The inverted cone-stalactites (which form from the ceiling) and cone-shaped stalagmites (which form from the floor) are created by limestone-laden water dripping into the cave from ground water above. This leaves the calcite deposits that gradually create the many varied formations you see at Luray. Luray is a relatively "fast" growing cavern with a growth rate of about one inch every 120 years. The stalactites and stalagmites eventually merge into columns the full height of the room. Slight variations in other minerals give the formations different colors.

Luray Caverns is a private business and not associated with any government. The first tour starts at 9:00 A.M. daily. The last tour leaves at 7:00 P.M. daily June 15–Labor Day; 6:00 P.M., March 15–June 14 and after Labor Day–October 31; 4:00 P.M. November 1–March 14 weekdays, and 5:00 P.M. weekends. Like most caves, the temperature underground is a constant 54 degrees (F.) year-round, so bring a jacket or sweater and walking shoes. The paths are wide, even and well illuminated and there are no stairs on the tour path. Luray Caverns are handicapped accessible by wheelchair via a chair lift; call ahead to make arrangements.

How To Get There: From Front Royal, at the northern entrance to Skyline Drive (Shenandoah National Park) take Route 340 south about 20 miles and watch for the numerous signs.

From Washington take I-66 west to Route 29 south (Warrenton); at Warrenton take Route 211 west. Luray is 9 miles west of Skyline Drive and very well-marked. (Estimated travel time two hours.) Admission is $11.00 for adults; $5.00 for children 7-13; $9.00 for seniors and active military. Special rates available for groups of 25 or more.

For Additional Information:
Luray Caverns
P.O. Box 748
Luray, VA 22835
(540) 743-6551
http://www.luraycaverns.com

Manassas National Battlefield Park

Twenty-six miles and more than a century away from Washington is the Manassas National Battlefield Park of Virginia. While it was established by Congress to commemorate the two great Civil War battles—First Manassas and Second Manassas—which took place here, the park also has much to offer those who love the outdoors. There are 4,500 acres of equestrian and hiking trails, open meadows, woodlands and several. The battles that took place in this park are also called the battles of Bull Run because that is the name of the major waterway in this area. The area is fragile and the Park Service asks those who visit to be aware of the sensitivity of the area's natural ecosystems and the necessity of maintaining its historic integrity. It once was a place of great suffering and bloody conflict, but today it is a peaceful oasis where you may encounter a great many species of songbirds, the cottontail rabbit, raccoon, opossum, gray squirrel or even a white-tailed deer. Quail, red-tailed hawk, wild turkey and woodpeckers live here too. The area around the park is becoming more and more urban, thereby making Manassas stand out in even greater contrast.

Manassas has a number of habitats that encourage wildlife diversity. There are woods of hemlock, white pine and chestnut oak, meadows and wetlands, including marsh and swampy areas by the Bull Run floodplain. Summer and fall wildflowers are especially nice.

There are three main trails. The Henry Hill Trail is approximately one mile in length and takes approximately 45 minutes. It begins at the visitor center, passes the Henry House and Robinson House sites, then loops back to the visitor center along Jackson's line of battle. The Stone Bridge Trail, which begins at the visitor center, is 5 miles in length and takes 2.5 hours to walk. After following a streambed, this trail retraces the path of the Confederates as they moved to meet the Union threat on the first day. At the end of that day, after 10 hours of fighting, over 900 men lay dead on the fields ending hopes that the war would come to a quick end. The final trail, Deep Cut Trail, also begins at the visitor center, is 6 miles long and takes 2.5 hours to complete; it focuses on the third and last day of the second battle, when the Union troops made a last, desperate attempt to break "Stonewall" Jackson's line. This First Manassas battle, First Bull Run, was fought by raw troops filled with naive enthusiasm for the battle trying to capture a vital railroad junction at Manassas. The Second Manassas battle, Second Bull Run, was fought thirteen months later after General Robert E. Lee had taken command of the Army of Northern Virginia and had driven the Union troops from the outskirts of Richmond. Within two months' time after he had taken over, he had defeated Union troops at Manassas, invaded the North and stood poised to attack Washington, DC. He was finally defeated along Antietam Creek near Sharpsburg, Maryland. The Second Battle of Manassas resulted in over 3,300 dead and was one of the bloodiest battles in the Civil War.

Hiking and Horseback Riding

The park includes 15 miles of hiking trails and a 14-mile-long bridle trail. They pass through a varied terrain that includes woodland, meadows and stream valley. A self-guided auto tour of the battlefield is about 12 miles long and marked by blue tour signs. A pamphlet describing this tour is available at the visitor center for $.50.

Picnicking

A 30-acre picnic ground is provided, with tables and garbage receptacles. No ground fires are permitted.

How To Get There: From Exit 9 of the Capital Beltway (I-495), take I-66 west to Exit 47B, VA 234. Turn north on VA 234 to the park. The visitor center is open daily 8:30 A.M.–5:00 P.M. The grounds are open dawn to dusk. The entrance fee is $2.00 for adults and free for children under 17. National Park Service Golden Eagle and Golden Age passes are honored.

For Additional Information:
Superintendent
Manassas Battlefield National Park
6511 Sudley Road
Manassas, VA 20109
(703) 361-1339
http://www.nps.gov

Mason District Park

In the heart of Fairfax County, not far from Washington, is Mason District Park, with 148 acres of stream valley, rolling meadows and forested hills. The natural area of the park covers 88 of those acres and is blanketed with large oaks, sweet gum, Virginia pine, sycamore, yellow poplar, hickory and a large stand of beech trees. The pileated woodpecker, cottontail rabbit, gray squirrel, raccoon, opossum, white tail deer and numerous songbirds also live or stop here. There is also a wildlife pond where you can get some close-up views of aquatic plant and animal life. Facilities include tennis courts, basketball court, two ball fields, two soccer fields, an amphitheater and a Parcourse jogging trail. The park's facilities are lit until 11:00 P.M. Parking spaces, wheelchair ramps and restroom facilities are provided for persons with disabilities.

Hiking

Several hiking and self-guided nature trails traverse the natural wooded area of the park. None are long, but they are secluded and interesting.

Picnicking

Shaded picnic grounds with tables, grills and water fountains are located here. The picnic area may be reserved for a fee by calling (703) 324-8732.

How To Get There: From Exit 6 of the Capital Beltway (I-495), head east on VA 236 (Little River Turnpike) to John Marr Drive. Turn left .5 mile to Columbia Pike. Turn right and follow to the park entrance on the right. Open year-round.

For Additional Information:
Manager, Mason District Park
6621 Columbia Pike
Annandale, VA 22003
(703) 941-1730

Fairfax County Park Authority
12055 Government Center Parkway
Suite 927
Fairfax, VA 22035-1119
(703) 324-8700
http://www.co.fairfax.va.us/parks

Mason Neck National Wildlife Refuge and Mason Neck State Park

Within 18 miles of the District of Columbia boundary is an area called Mason Neck where majestic bald eagles and thousands of herons nest. The refuge was established primarily to protect a historical roost and nesting area for bald eagles. This unique and small wildlife management area encompasses several distinct ecosystems in an area of only 2,277 acres. Among the most important ecosystems are the upland forests and the vibrant marshes. The wildlife refuge is part of a larger boot-shaped peninsula extending into the Potomac River in southeastern Fairfax County. The peninsula measures 4 miles from top to bottom and occupies some 14 square miles; however, only a portion of this is owned and administered by the U.S. Fish and

Wildlife Service. Bordering the refuge are Pohick Bay Regional Park, Mason Neck State Park and Gunston Hall Plantation. Together with the refuge, they form the Mason Neck Management Area and protect over 6,000 acres for wildlife while providing a wide range of recreational and educational opportunities for the public. Parts of each of these areas have also been left in a wild state.

The peninsula has 12 miles of shoreline, including 4 miles on the Potomac River. Two major freshwater marshes—the refuge's Great Marsh along the Potomac River and the state park's Kane's Creek Marsh on Belmont Bay—provide feeding grounds for numerous species of wildlife. The Great Marsh, encompassing over 285 acres, is one of the largest marshes in northern Virginia and is one of the main attractants to the eagles, waterfowl and other species dependent upon wetlands.

The eagles nest in the upland forest composed of oak, maple, tulip tree, beech, sweet and sour gums, hickory and remnant pines; towering chestnut oaks and beeches edge the shoreline, providing lookout and launch points for eagles and other birds of prey. Eagles are particularly fond of pines or tall "snags" or dead trees along the shore of lakes and ponds. Bald eagles build huge nests that can weigh up to two tons and return to the same nest year after year. The birds begin nesting in December and stay near the nest through the summer until the young birds are able to fly and hunt on their own. Bald eagles are expert hunters, killing their prey with their talons as they swoop down on them or with a swift snap of their powerful beak. They eat mostly fish and waterfowl, although they also sometimes eat small rodents and reptiles.

Inland forests include sweet bay magnolia, willow oak, trailing arbutus, wintergreen, mountain laurel, holly and wild cherry. In the marsh grow wild rice, pickerel weed, spatterdock, rose mallow and yellow iris. Hundreds of American lotus are found along Kane's Creek; when in bloom, the huge flowers and leaves extend almost two feet in diameter. The white-tailed deer, raccoon, muskrat, river otter, cottontail rabbit, gray squirrel, fox and opossum roam throughout the area.

Wildlife activity is greatest during October, November and December, when migratory waterfowl come down the Atlantic flyway. Black ducks, mallards, teal, mergansers, scaup and canvasback ducks crowd the marsh and form rafts in the adjacent river while Canada geese and whistling swans blacken the skies. During summer in the marsh, you will find the snowy egret, blue heron and gulls, along with more than 200 species of other birds. Mason Neck is home to over 1,500 great blue heron nests,

Canada geese in a fall migration stop.   *Richard L. Berman*

one of the largest colonies in the mid-Atlantic region. Due to the extensive wetlands, you will find plenty of mosquitoes as well, so take bug repellent when you visit in warm weather.

Not far south of Mason Neck, near Woodbridge, are two satellite units—Marumsco Refuge, consisting of 63 acres of marsh and Featherstone Refuge, covering 325 acres of marsh and upland forest. Both are administered from the Mason Neck Refuge office and lie along the Potomac River shoreline. Neither is open to the public due to poor access, though Marumsco can be viewed from the abutting Veterans Memorial Park.

Hiking

Group visits are welcome. Only limited trail use is permitted, mostly for bird-watching and photography purposes. Two refuge foot trails, the Woodmarsh trail (3 miles) and the Great Marsh trail (.75 miles) lead visitors through mature forests to viewing points along the Great Marsh. The Woodmarsh trail features an observation platform overlooking a beaver dam. The Great Marsh trail provides the best opportunity to see eagles. Trail guides are available for both trails.

Canoeing

Canoeing as part of a research project or environmental education may be done on a special permit basis, by application at the refuge office. Recreational canoeing is available at the neighboring state park and regional park.

How To Get There: From Exit 1 of the Capital Beltway (I-495), take US 1 south to VA 242 (Gunston Hall Road) about 10 miles. Turn left (east) and go about 4 miles. This will lead directly to Mason Neck. The refuge trails are open year-round during daylight hours. All other portions of the refuge are closed except for research or environmental education (permits required). The refuge office, located in Woodbridge, is open year-round on weekdays.

For Additional Information:
Refuge Manager
Mason Neck National Wildlife Refuge
U.S. Fish and Wildlife Service
14344 Jefferson Davis Highway
Woodbridge, VA 22191
(703) 690-1297

Meadowlark Gardens

Meadowlark Gardens, which opened in 1992, is designed as a living museum of plant life, with 95 acres of beautiful formal landscape and natural beauty. More than two miles of handicapped accessible paved walking trails wind through the park's rolling hillsides and numerous gardens. The park features many specialty gardens including those dedicated to herbs, hostas, Siberian irises, chrysanthemums, daylilies, peonies, azaleas, lilacs, crabapples, flowering cherries, and Virginia native trees. In addition, there is an aquatic garden with a boardwalk. Many of the featured plants are labeled and described making this an educational experience as well. A 1.2 mile mulched nature trail gives a more natural experience at this Northern Virginia Regional Park Authority property.

A visitor center houses a gift shop, restrooms and snack machines. The Atrium, a new indoor garden structure, offers an area for park programs, classes or social events. The Atrium, a new greenhouse-like building for social functions and meetings brings the beauty of the outdoors to the indoors. A calendar of events is available.

How To Get There: From the Washington Beltway, take Exit 10B onto Route 7 toward Tysons Corner. Go 5 miles west on Route 7; turn left onto Beulah Road and drive 1 mile to the park entrance on the right. Meadowlark Gardens is open daily except Thanksgiving, Christmas and New Year's Day:

November to March, 10:00 A.M. to 5:00 P.M.; April and May, 10:00 A.M. to 7:30 P.M.; June to August, 10:00 A.M. to 8:00 P.M.; September and October, 10:00 A.M. to 7:00 P.M.

Admission is $3.00 for adults, $1.00 for children 7-17 or seniors 60 or older, free for children under 7. Annual passes are available. No dogs allowed.

For Additional Information:
Meadowlark Gardens
9750 Meadowlark Gardens Court
Vienna, VA 22182
(703) 255-3631

Northern Virginia Regional Park Authority
5400 Ox Road
Fairfax Station, VA 22039-1022
(703) 352-5900

Morven Park

A tree-lined, mile-long drive makes a picturesque entrance to 1,200-acre Morven Park in the northernmost part of the Old Dominion State. In the first half of this century, the stately mansion served as the home of former Governor Westmoreland Davis; today, the estate is operated by a foundation bearing his name. Mrs. Davis set up a trust fund that provides for continued restoration and the establishment of a nature conservancy program, a carriage museum that features more than 100 horse-drawn vehicles, and the impressive International Equestrian Center, dedicated to horseback riding related activities.

The magnificent Marguerite G. Davis Boxwood Gardens provide a tranquil setting for a picnic lunch or just a lazy day with nature. Observe the wildlife that is surrounded by dense forest as well as open pasture. From the Greek Revival mansion view the Piedmont. If you are here in the spring or summer, you will see flowering plants such as the dogwood, redbud, tulip tree, mountain laurel, Japanese honeysuckle and the pinkster flower at their glorious best. Other varieties of trees and shrubs are scattered about the rest of the estate's grounds. Picnic facilities are available, but Morven Park's beautiful nature trails have been closed.

How To Get There: From Exit 10 of the Capital Beltway (I-495), travel northwest on VA 7 (Leesburg Pike) to Leesburg. When the road forks near the Leesburg Courthouse, bear right to stay on Market Street. Go through historic Leesburg. Take a right onto Morven Park Road, a short distance beyond Leesburg, then a left onto Old Waterford Road. Morven Park is the third gate on the right.

From the Dulles Toll Road & Greenway; take the Toll Road, VA 267 west into Leesburg. At the end of the road, take Route 7 west bypass. Take the second exit for Leesburg (follow exit signs for the Equine Medical Center "VA TECH"). Go right off the exit ramp. Turn left at the first stoplight (Fairview St.) which deadends into Old Waterford Road at the EMC; turn left to Morven Parks' main entrance, the first gate on the right.

House, gardens and carriage museum are open April through October, Tuesday through Friday, noon until 5:00 P.M.; Saturday, 10:00 A.M.–5:00 P.M. and Sunday, 1:00–5:00 P.M. The estate is also open in early December for Christmas tours; call for hours. Entrance fee.

For Additional Information:
Resident Manager
Morven Park
P.O. Box 6228
Leesburg, VA 20178
(703) 777-2414

Mount Vernon

When you visit Mount Vernon, you will realize just how much George Washington loved trees and his landscape. His love of nature influenced him greatly throughout his life. From 1760 to 1788, Washington wrote extensively to record tree plantings, observations of tree habits and growth, and his own experiences with them. He once stated that, if possible, he would have growing at Mount Vernon a specimen of every native American tree and shrub that was beautiful. He planted many of them himself and a great many trees from various climate zones of the country adorn the grounds of Mount Vernon to this day. Until June 8, 1924, 52 trees planted by Washington still stood at Mount Vernon. However, a tornado struck on that day, destroying a great number of them and so seriously injuring several others that they later died. Trees known to have been planted by Washington himself and still standing include the white ash, American holly, English mulberry, hemlock and tulip poplar.

The Mount Vernon Ladies' Association continues to plant trees in Washington's honor. These include tulip poplar, pecan, buckeye, cedar of Lebanon, Kentucky coffee bean trees, white cherry, as well as red cedar, magnolias, maples, oaks and honey locust. There are also some exquisite gardens with flowers and shrubs. The flower garden and kitchen garden symmetrically placed on each side of the bowling green are patterned after the 18th-century designs available to Washington (from English gardening books that he owned). The boxwood hedges have been growing since his day. In 1997, Mount Vernon added a kitchen garden with vegetables, fruits and herbs, based on Washington's writings and the weekly reports of his gardener. You can purchase seeds, boxwood plants or other plants at the museum shop as a pleasant reminder of the natural beauty of Mount Vernon.

Mount Vernon, in George Washington's time sprawled over 8,000 acres, half of which was woodlands; today encompasses 500 acres, 60% woodlands. Recently, the **Mount Vernon Forest Trail** was dedicated to expose visitors to the natural and human history of the area. The trail passes through woods of mature oak and hickory, holly and laurel. Interpretive signs identify interesting facts about the flora and fauna of George Washington's time that still remain today, and that which has disappeared. Signs also explain how essential the woodlands were to colonial plantation life and native American Indians life.

Of course George Washington had to have Cherry Trees,

although the famous story of the chopping down of a cherry tree is considered a myth. Although the original orchards disappeared long ago, as part of the restoration effort, a four acre plot has been restored to its 18th-century status as a fruit tree orchard complete with cherry trees.

How To Get There: From downtown Washington, take one of the bridges leading into Virginia, then follow George Washington Memorial Parkway (Mount Vernon Memorial Highway) south to its terminus. Mount Vernon is approximately 16 miles from downtown Washington. And accessible to Tourmobile June 1 through September 15. It is open daily, 8:00 A.M.–5:00 P.M., April through August; 9:00 A.M–5:00 P.M. during March, September and October and 9:00 A.M. – 4:00 P.M. November–February.

For Additional Information:
The Mount Vernon Ladies' Association
Mount Vernon, VA 22121
(703) 780-2000
http://www.mountvernon.org

Mount Vernon Trail

If you like to run, hike, roller skate or bicycle, the Mount Vernon Trail offers great opportunity. It stretches for nearly 17 miles along the Potomac River on the Virginia shore between Mount Vernon and Key Bridge, (about two blocks north of the Rosslyn Metro station, although it's not well marked). The trail parallels the George Washington Memorial Parkway most of the way and traverses areas of woodland and open meadow dotted with wildflowers. Along the way you can stop and rest at the Lyndon Baines Johnson Memorial Grove, watch airplanes landing at National Airport from Gravelly Point, look at a panoramic view of Washington from the Navy and Merchant Marine Memorial, shop and eat lunch in Alexandria, observe some of the over 250 species of birds at Dyke Marsh and finally tour Mount Vernon, George Washington's home on the Potomac. It offers lovely views of the Potomac and is quite flat except for some steep slopes the last mile or so before Mt. Vernon. Some parts of the trail are too narrow for the traffic, but widening them would harm several pro-

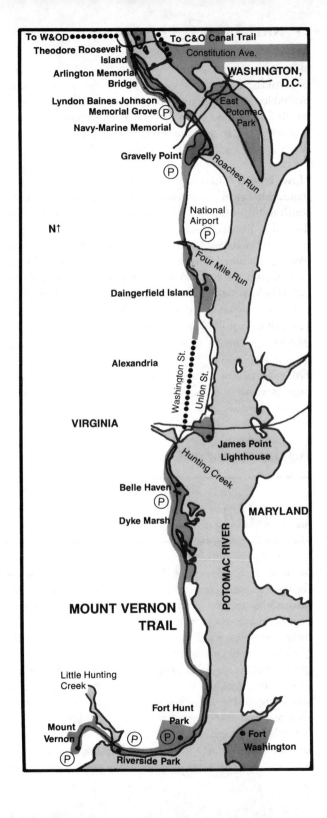

tected areas along the riverbank so cyclists must be careful. Please obey the 10 mph speed limit and be courteous to the many other users of the trail. The trail isn't shaded so it might be a good idea to bring a hat. This is a very popular trail and well worth visiting. Those wishing to avoid heavy traffic should know that peak use hours are 8:00 A.M.–11:00 A.M. and 2:00–5:00 P.M.

How To Get There: From downtown Washington, take the Roosevelt Bridge to Virginia. Follow the signs to the George Washington Memorial Parkway, take the first right into Theodore Roosevelt Island parking.

Southbound on George Washington Parkway, follow the route to National Airport, turning left just beyond the George Washington Memorial Parkway underpass. Head south to a sign that directs you to Gravelly Point, where you will find free parking. There is also free parking at Mount Vernon and at several points between. Parking may be hard to find on good weather weekends. A map is available from the office noted below.

For Additional Information:
Superintendent , George Washington Memorial Parkway
Turkey Run Park ,
McLean, VA 22101
(703) 285-2600
http://www.nps.gov/gwmp

Oatlands

Oatlands, a property of the National Historic Trust for Historic Preservation was one of antebellum Virginia's most prosperous plantations. Today, it is considered one of the most outstanding gardens of early Virginia landscape design, famed for its superior boxwood. In 1798 George Carter, a great great grandson of Virginia's famed Robert "King" Carter, inherited some 3,400 acres of land near Leesburg. In the early 1800s Carter developed the land into a successful working plantation, which he named Oatlands. Carter originally designed the four acre terraced formal garden, which includes many flowering perennials, shrubs and roses. Oatlands offers daily tours of Carter's magnificent Greek Revival mansion and surrounding gardens. The 261 acres of unspoiled Virginia countryside continues to support many of Carter's rare and unique specimen trees, such as ginkgo, European larch, and American hornbeam; an English oak on the grounds is reputed to be Virginia's oldest.

How To Get There: Take the Dulles Toll Road and Greenway to Leesburg and Route 7 to US 15 south. Proceed on US 15 south five miles to Oatlands entrance. Or, take Exit 10 from the Capital Beltway and proceed northwest on VA 7 (Leesburg Pike). Just before you reach Leesburg, turn left (south) on US 15 and proceed to Oatlands entrance. The mansion and gardens are open to the public daily, April through December 10:00 A.M.–4:30 P.M. Nominal entrance fee.

For Additional Information:
Administrator
Oatlands
Route 2, Box 352
Leesburg, VA 22075
(703) 777-3174

Pohick Bay Regional Park

On historic Mason Neck Peninsula, some 25 miles southwest of Washington in Fairfax County, is Pohick Bay Regional Park. Set among rolling hills and stream valleys covered with oak, beech and poplar, the park was once part of the plantation of George Mason, a close friend of George Washington's and father of the Bill of Rights. All of Mason Neck is a unique and sensitive area. Here the deer and beaver roam, the osprey and egret wing overhead and the bald eagle nest about the marshes. Smaller animals that live here include the gray squirrel, flying squirrel, fox, skunk, opossum, cottontail rabbit and raccoon. Most of the peninsula is planned as a wildlife refuge, with the developed recreation areas concentrated where they offer the least disturbance to the delicate balance of nature. At present, about half the 14-square-mile peninsula has been successfully preserved for the protection of wildlife. In addition to Pohick Bay, the Northern Virginia Regional Park Authority is planning a Potomac Shoreline Regional Park on the tip of Mason Neck. A substantial part of this park will be kept as a nature preserve, with no general public use permitted. Other public lands on the peninsula include Gunston Hall, the lovely colonial home of George Mason now owned by the state of Virginia, and Mason Neck National Wildlife Refuge, administered by the U.S. Fish and Wildlife Service (both described elsewhere).

Capt. John Smith, who sailed up the Potomac in 1608 to Great Falls, was the earliest European discoverer of this area, but the Indians gave the land its name. "Pohick" in Algonquin tongue means "water place." And that is what the park is today—a place of boating, swimming (a huge pool with a lifeguard is open from Memorial Day to Labor Day), fishing, camping and picnicking beside the water.

Hiking and Horseback Riding

The major foot trails for nature study in Pohick Bay Regional Park are the Blue and Yellow. They provide only limited hiking, together totaling about 3 miles, but there are some interesting things to see. The Blue Trail, beginning at the visitor center, winds through a low, wet area and an open field before leading into a dense forest. After crossing a roadway and the horse trail, it becomes the Yellow Trail. Both have scenic areas of mountain laurel and holly as well as coves filled with waterlilies. Frogs, salamanders and small harmless water snakes may be found along them. All trails return to the central section of the park. There is also a bridle trail, some 4 miles in length, within the park for the exclusive use of horseback riders. Just outside the park is a 5-mile-long bridle trail along Pohick Creek; inquire at the visitor center for details.

Camping and Picnicking

A fine, spacious camping area offers 150 family campsites in the woods, 100 with electrical outlets. Sites are rented on a first-come basis. Also available are a camp store, hot showers, restrooms, laundry facilities and a dump station. The picnic areas have tables, shelters and grills. No ground fires are permitted.

Boating

A boat-launching ramp provides access to the Potomac River. In the summer, sailboats and pedal boats are available for rent. Pohick Bay is open to boaters and offers a good view of the marsh vegetation.

How To Get There: From Exit 1 of the Capital Beltway (I-495) take US 1 south to VA 242 (Gunston Hall Road). A turn left (east) leads to all the attractions on Mason Neck peninsula. Open daily year-round, from dawn to dusk. Nominal admission fee for nonresidents.

For Additional Information:
Northern Virginia Regional Park Authority
5400 Ox Road
Fairfax Station, VA 22039-1022
(703) 352-5900
(703) 339-6104 (Camp Center)

Potomac Heritage Trail

The Potomac Heritage Trail (PHT) runs on the Virginia side of the Potomac entirely on National Park Service land from Theodore Roosevelt Island in DC to the American Legion Bridge (on I-495 of the Capital Beltway). The PHT is a unit of the National Trails System and is maintained by volunteers of the Potomac Appalachian Trail Club.

Hiking

The trail winds ten miles between the river and the steep palisades. Although most of the trail is relatively level, it has numerous short steep ascents and descents and many small stream crossings. Although it is usually possible to avoid any wading, the trail is rocky and can be muddy after rain; the trail can be awash when the Potomac is high. Most of the trail is through lowland forest of oak, poplar and beech trees. Parts of the trail are near the George Washington Memorial Parkway.

A trail pamphlet/guide is available from the GWMP (see below). This includes access information and trail descriptions. The trail can be accessed from many points along the George Washington Memorial Parkway. Major access points are **Theodore Roosevelt Island** (see DC entry), **Mount Vernon Trail** (see VA entry) North Glebe Road at Chain Bridge, **Turkey Run Park** (see entry), and Live Oak Drive, the north terminus. To reach the north end of the trail, take the Beltway (I-495) to VA 193, Georgetown Pike; head south; turn left on Balls Hill Road and left over the Beltway on Live Oak Drive to the end. Pedestrians cannot cross the Potomac on the American Legion Bridge.

A good circuit hike is to park at the Roosevelt Island Parking lot (or take the Metro to Rosslyn and the pedestrian bridge over the GWMP), go up the PHT to Glebe Road, cross Chain Bridge and go down the C&O towpath to Georgetown and cross the Key Bridge back to Roosevelt Island.

The PHT requires that dogs be leashed and prohibits bicycling.

For Additional Information:
Potomac Appalachian Trail Club
118 Park Street, SE
Vienna, VA 22180
(703) 242-0315

Superintendent
George Washington Memorial Parkway
Turkey Run Park
McLean, VA 22101
(703) 285-2600
http://www.nps.gov/gwmp

Potomac Overlook Regional Park

Amid intense development in the Washington suburbs are 100 acres of wilderness near the Potomac palisades—an urban nature sanctuary called Potomac Overlook Regional Park. The sanctuary is a haven of tranquillity, offering a retreat from the bustle of city life into cool, green forests. Nature is the star attraction here—towering tulip poplars and oaks as old as 200 years, mosses and ferns clinging tenaciously to stream banks and an old spring that supplied water for the Necostin Indians who once lived here. Wildlife, including various species of songbirds, is often visible. Among the park's other attractions are a nature center with natural and human history displays including a hive of working bees, the site of an ancient Indian village where artifacts have been uncovered by archaeologists, and a complex of gardens–herb, butterfly, rock and composting. Nature programs, usually free, are presented on weekends. Arrangements may be made by groups for special programs.

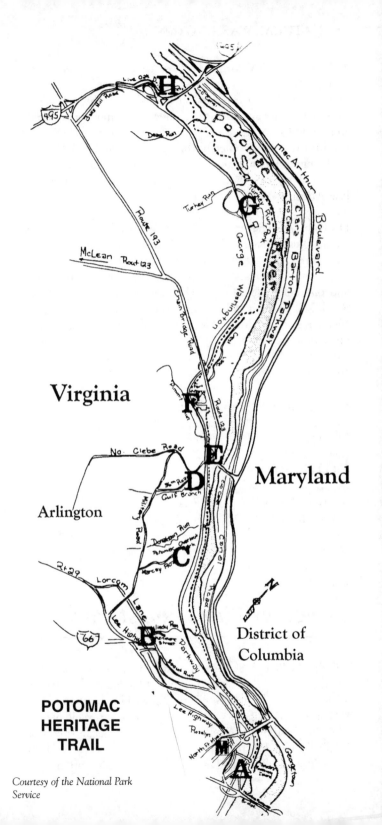

**POTOMAC
HERITAGE
TRAIL**

Courtesy of the National Park Service

Hiking and Bicycling

Although hiking is somewhat limited here, the 2.5 miles of trails in the park are perfect for family walks after work or on the weekends. Connections can be made to the streamside Donaldson Run Trail, maintained by the Recreation and Park Divisions of Arlington County, and to the Potomac Heritage Trail along the Potomac River. Bicyclists may pedal along Marcey Road, the park's main thoroughfare, but not on trails.

How To Get There: From Key Bridge, head north on George Washington Memorial Parkway. Exit west on VA 124 (Spout Run Parkway), and about one mile farther turn right (northwest) on Lorcom Lane. At Nellie Custis Drive, turn right again and continue bearing right when Nellie Custis joins Military Road. Marcey Road, which leads to the park entrance, runs off Military Road to the right. Open daily year-round, dawn to dusk. The nature center is open 10:00 A.M.–5:00 P.M. Tuesday–Saturday, 1:00–5:00 P.M. Sunday and closed Monday. No entrance fee.

For Additional Information:
Northern Virginia Regional Park Authority
5400 Ox Road
Fairfax Station, VA 22039-1022
(703) 352-5900

Potomac Overlook Regional Park
2845 N. Marcey Road
Arlington, VA 22207
(703) 528-5406

Prince William Forest Park

Prince William Forest Park, managed by the National Park Service, is located in the rolling hills of Piedmont Virginia. Little at Prince William Forest Park today will remind you of the agricultural pursuits of a century ago. It is an excellent area, however, for studying the effects of overuse of the land and what happens when nature is allowed to reclaim the stripped and depleted fields abandoned by man. It is the largest national park area in the metropolitan region and third largest in Virginia.

It all began when the first settlers came to this area in the late 17th century. Forests were cut, and the land was plowed. Lumber, furs, tobacco and grain were the marketable products of the area. Conservation was unheard of, and soon the soil lost all of its fertility. The rain carried topsoil downstream via Quantico Creek and filled Dumfries Harbor with silt. Even if the farming had continued, the day would likely have come when the farmers' products could not have been shipped, for the harbor became virtually unusable because of silt deposits.

By 1900, practically all farming operations had ceased; the land would no longer sustain it. Within twenty years' time the land began to revert to forest. In 1933, the Resettlement Administration, under the Authority of the National Industrial Recovery Act, acquired 17,000 acres of this depleted farmland and established the Chopawamsic Recreation Demonstration Area. Three years later, it was transferred to the Department of the Interior, and in 1940 Congress designated it to be made into a national park. During World War II portions of the park were used for military training by the U.S. Marine Corps (the Quantico Marine Base, described elsewhere) and the Office of Strategic Services (OSS) which trained World War II spies. Some 4,500 acres of adjoining parklands are currently under a special-use permit to the marines. Following the war, the name of the park was changed to Prince William Forest Park.

It is still possible today to tell where old home sites were by the presence of blackberry and blueberry bushes. Old fields are marked by the presence of blocks of Virginia pine trees. Pines are among the first trees to grow in a cleared area, followed by shade-tolerant hard woods such as oak and hickory. Named for the Virginia county in which it lies, the park now boasts over 80 known species of trees and shrubs among its lush forest cover. These include stands of Virginia pine, hickory, oak, beech and maple. The understory contains mountain laurel, holly, dogwood and redbud. Prince William Forest also has over 100 species of woody plants and over 100 species of herbaceous plants. Raccoon, opossum, white-tailed deer, wild turkey, ruffed grouse, red-tailed hawk, red and gray fox, bobcat, beaver, flying squirrel, chipmunk, woodchuck, gray squirrel and numerous songbirds are among the park's residents.

Since erosion has removed most of the clay, sand and gravel, the granite, schist and quartzite of the Piedmont are readily visible in many places. Also visible is pyrite, containing iron and sulfur, which was mined until 1920 near the confluence of the two branches of Quantico Creek.

Sight-Seeing

Although the roads available for driving are limited, the 7-mile loop road covers the heartland of the forest. It can be most rewarding to drive it slowly and, with frequent stops, to hike in the woodland or one of the fire roads or trails. The park is bounded on all four sides by more heavily traveled roads, along which you may enjoy taking a leisurely drive. Check with the park visitor center, located near the entrance, for a map of the area. Park rangers often schedule guided tours and nature programs. If you are visiting between November and March, you may want to look for the bald eagles that sometime congregate along the lower reaches of Quantico Creek. This area is not within the park, but it is only minutes away. From the park's main entrance on VA 619, head east to US 1, then north on US 1 to where Quantico Creek crosses the road. Turn right (east) on Possum Point Road, along the north side of the creek and look out over the water and in trees along the waterway.

Hiking, Backpacking and Bicycling

Considering its proximity to Washington, this is an unbelievably good place to hike or backpack. More than 37 miles of trails wind along streams, many so little used that visitors may, if they walk quietly, happen upon fox, beaver, white-tailed deer, even wild turkey or grouse. It is a great spot for enjoying the tranquillity of nature without intrusion. Parking areas along park roads provide convenient starting points for many hikes. Major trails are marked with color blazes so they are easy to follow.

Three self-guided nature trails have been designed to tell the story of this land. The Pine Grove Forest Trail has taped audio messages along the way that describe the plants and animals in the forest. It is paved and handicapped accessible. The Farms to Forest Trail explains how the land is being converted from farmland to natural forest. The Geology Trail guides hikers along a geological timetable of "formations" at the park. The Crossing Nature Trail tells the history of the park. Each of the trails begins and ends at a picnic area or campground. The trails are well maintained. Bicycle riding is permitted on all roads, including fire roads, throughout the park but bicyclists should be aware that there are some steep hills.

Camping

Facilities are available for almost every type of camping. Travel Trailer Village, a recreational vehicle camp operated by a concessionaire, is located just off VA 234, approximately two miles west of I-95 on the northern perimeter of the forest. It is excellent—well maintained with 75 sites, full hookups, hot showers and a coin-operated laundry, and swimming pool. Oak Ridge Campground, deep within the forest via the main entrance road, is available for family tent camping (78 sites, including 12 "walk-in" sites); no reservations accepted. Turkey Run Ridge tent campground may be used by organized groups only, and reservations are required. There are also five cabin camps available for organized groups except during winter months; each camp has cabins, a central kitchen-dining hall, washhouse, staff quarters, nature lodge and an administration building. Cabins can be rented individually by families May–October. Reservations are required.

Chopawamsi Backcountry Area is available for hiking and primitive camping (10 sites). Campers may backpack 0.2 to 1.0 mile to the campsites. No facilities are provided. Users must carry everything in and out. User permits are required and may be obtained at the visitor center during business hours. The backcountry is seldom crowded.

Picnicking

Two picnic grounds—Telegraph Road and Pine Grove, both located near the main entrance—are open year-round. Tables, fireplaces, trash receptacles, water, comfort stations and play fields are available at each. A shelter is located in Pine Grove. Groups may use Carter's Day Camp on a reservation basis.

How To Get There: From Exit 4 of the Capital Beltway (I-495), take I-95 south to Exit 150B, VA 619, and head west to the main entrance. The visitor center will provide maps of the park and advice on how to get around. Nominal entrance fee.

For Additional Information:
Superintendent
Prince William Forest Park
18100 Park Headquarters Road
Triangle, VA 22172
(703) 221-4706 (park headquarters)
(703) 221-7181 (visitor center)
http://www.nps.gov/prwi

Travel Trailer Village
16058 Dumfries Road
Dumfries, VA 22026
(703) 221-24674

Quantico Marine Corps Base

The Quantico Marine Corps Base consists of over 60,000 acres, of which 58,000 acres are under natural resources management and 3,900 acres are designated wetlands. It is open to the public for fishing, hiking, bird-watching and other related outdoor activities. A Watchable Wildlife area along the Chopawamsic Creek wetland is open to the public for bird-watching, hiking, fishing and canoeing seven days a week during daylight hours. Access to other training areas is controlled by the Range Control Office (703-784-5321) and written permission is required to enter those areas. Within Quantico, more than 600 acres of lakes and 3.5 miles of trout streams provide fishing enthusiasts with an opportunity to catch trout, large-mouth bass, catfish, blue gill and pickerel. White-tailed deer, squirrel, wild turkey and dove abound in the area. Also seen here are the eagle, barred owl, red-tailed hawk, osprey, pileated woodpecker, warbler, kingfisher and a wide variety of abundant waterfowl. Besides the base permit, fishermen must hold a Virginia state fishing license. The base is located on lands forested with Virginia pine, oak, sycamore, sassafras and dogwood. It is particularly worthwhile to visit during the spring and fall wildfowl migration. A detailed Quantico bird list is available.

How To Get There: From Exit 4 of the Capital Beltway (I-495), take I-95 south to Exit 148. Take Russel Road (or USMC Highway) east. Parking for the Wildlife Viewing area is about two miles past Route 1, on the base, on the right.

For Additional Information:
U.S. Marine Corps
Head NREA Branch
B046 Facilities Division
3040 McCawley Ave., Suite 2
Quantico, VA 22134-5053
(703) 784-5383 or
(703) 784-5810/5383 ext. 234, 235 or 240

Red Rock Wilderness Overlook Park

Overlooking the Potomac River, upstream some 33 miles from Washington, is Red Rock Wilderness Overlook Regional Park. In 1977, Mrs. Frances V. Speek donated half of the value of the property for the park to assist the Northern Virginia Regional Park Authority in its goal to preserve the Potomac River shoreline. An intersecting trail system, three miles in length, was designed to follow ridges and converge around the confluence of several small streamlets. The overlook points are situated atop high, sheer cliffs with panoramic views of the Potomac River and the blue Shenandoah foothills. A variety of wildflowers grow profusely here during spring and summer months, starting in February and ending in October.

How To Get There: From Exit 10 of the Capital Beltway, take VA 7 (Leesburg Pike) west. Just before reaching Leesburg, exit onto Bypass US 15 north and proceed to VA 773 (Edwards Ferry Road). Turn right; the park entrance is 1.5 miles down the road. Open daily, dawn to dusk, all year. No entrance fee. No restroom available.

For Additional Information:
Northern Virginia Regional Park Authority
5400 Ox Road
Fairfax Station, VA 22039-1022
Park (703) 352-5900

Riverbend Park

Up the Potomac River from Great Falls, covering some 409 acres, is lovely Riverbend Park. There are nature trails, river overlooks, shaded picnic tables beside the river and a small boat launch. Although it gets fairly crowded on summer weekends, on other days it can be a haven for those seeking solitude. The nature center offers information and insight into the natural history of the park area, the land and the people who have lived here. Trails connect the nature center, the visitor center, Great Falls Park (described elsewhere) and the more remote sections of Riverbend's wooded terrain. Two miles of the park's boundary border the flood plain of the Potomac River. Wildflowers grow profusely in spring, especially along the river floodplain. In late March and April, this is one of the authors' favorite places for spring wildflowers, particularly the thousands of Virginia bluebells and Dutchman's-breeches, also white and yellow trout lilies, trillium, squirrel corn, wild grapes and wild ramps (which bloom in summer). Also in spring, the vernal ponds alongside the river are hopping with several types of frogs—small "peepers" making a high pitched "peep peep" and larger bull frogs making a low pitched croaking. In the fall there are colorful leaves and migrating waterfowl. Occasionally, you may see white-tailed deer, wild turkey, opossum, raccoon, gray squirrel, chipmunk, snakes, frogs, salamanders and some Canada geese and ducks show up here in the fall and winter. There is also a resident hawk and owl population. Great forests of beech, oak, sycamore, sassafras, pawpaws and sweet and sour gum grow on the upland hillsides. Many special nature-oriented programs are offered for all ages at the nature center and the visitor center. Both this center and the information center are fully equipped for the handicapped.

Hiking and Horseback Riding

Hiking trails extend throughout the grounds. They are not extensive (about 7 miles in total), but they are interesting. There are two nature trails that start at the nature center. Three miles of trails along the river provide year-round access to the scenic waterway, where you can experience a kaleidoscope of colorful spring wildflowers, autumn leaves and migrating waterfowl. Unimproved horse trails are found throughout the park. The Duff N' Stuff Trail is a .25 mile loop with a paved surface designed with preschoolers in mind.

The Pawpaw Passage Trail is 1.5 miles long and traverses a variety of terrains including a hardwood forest, floodplain and part of the Potomac River shoreline. This is a favorite trail for seeing a wide variety of wildflowers, as described above. Pawpaws are delicious fruits that many people and animals like to eat, although visitors are prohibited from taking any fruit or other plant material from the park. Zebra swallowtail butterflies, identified by their large black and white stripes, lay eggs on pawpaw leaves. They can feed only on this plant. The Potomac Heritage Trail (1.75 miles long), the Upland Trail (1 mile), the Center Trail (.25 mile) and a variety of other trails provide access to the 409 acres and connect to Great Falls National Park.

Picnicking

Picnicking is permitted in tree-shaded sites with grills and picnic tables. Reservations are accepted for use of the picnic shelter. Groups should call ahead to check picnic availability.

Boating

Small unpowered or low powered boats may be launched into the Potomac for a fee from a paved ramp near the visitor center. Call ahead for details. Boat rentals were recently discontinued. **How To Get There:** From Exit 13 of the Capital Beltway (I-495), follow Georgetown Pike (VA 193) west 4.5 miles, past Great Falls Park, to Riverbend Road. Turn right 2.3 miles, then right again on Jeffery Road 1.0 mile to the visitor center. No entrance fee for county residents. To reach the Nature Center, continue on Jeffery Road .5 mile further; there is a small separate parking area at the nature center and no fee. Open daily during daylight hours, except Christmas Day. The nature center hours vary seasonally; call for details.

For Additional Information:
Riverbend Visitor Center
8700 Potomac Hills Street
Great Falls, VA 22066
(703) 759-9018

Riverbend Nature Center
8814 Jeffery Road
Great Falls, VA 22066
(703) 759-3211

Fairfax County Park Authority
12055 Government Center Parkway
Suite 927
Fairfax, VA 22035-1119
703-324-8702
http://www.co.fairfax.va.us/parks

River Farm

River Farm is a giant demonstration garden for expert gardeners as well as amateurs who would like to see the best of each species and learn which varieties are the easiest to grow in the Washington, DC area. The garden is an intriguing landscape made up of display and test gardens. These plantings make it easy to compare varieties of plants. Collections at River Farm include two rose gardens containing over 400 hybrid teas, grandifloras, floribundas and climbers, an official All-America Rose Selections (AARS) award-winning rose collection, an American Dahlia Society test garden, a display of espaliered ivy sponsored by the American Ivy Society, an American Hemerocallus (day lilies) Society display, and 12 new gardens designed to interest children. In addition, a shade garden, a demonstration fruit orchard including 100 dwarf and semi-dwarf species of fruit, ten acres of rhododendrons, azaleas, ferns and wildflowers within a woodland walk are located at this farm.

George Washington owned River Farm, also called Walnut Tree Farm. Known originally as Clifton's Neck, the property of 1,800 acres was purchased for $2,885 in 1760, when Washington was only twenty-seven years old. It became one of five farms comprising the Mount Vernon estate. Washington is said to have loved the beauty that nature lavished on his lands. At the time of his election to the presidency, Washington had to borrow money in order to attend his own inauguration in New York City. River Farm became part of the collateral required for the loan.

Today, the property is owned by the American Horticultural Society, which has its headquarters in the great old house here. It has preserved the farm much as it was when Washington was living. The great walnut trees still stand; so do two Kentucky coffee bean trees, a variety Washington himself introduced to the area. Plantings of boxwood, magnolias, wisteria and other ornamentals blend into the landscape. Standing between the River Farm house and a terrace wall near the living quarters is one of his favorite trees, a great black walnut, which has survived to the present. There are quail, woodchuck, cottontail rabbit, gray squirrel and an occasional white-tailed deer. During the fall, you may see migrating waterfowl—ducks of several species and Canada geese—on the Potomac, which seeps along one side of the farm. Great blue herons are also sometimes seen, as well as eagles.

How To Get There: Take the George Washington Memorial Parkway south through Alexandria. About 4.5 miles south of Old Town Alexandria, look for signs saying River Farm Garden Park. Attendants at Mount Vernon can also direct you to River Farm. No entrance fee. River Farm is open 8:30 A.M.–5:00 P.M., weekdays.

For Additional Information:
The American Horticultural Society
7931 East Boulevard Drive
Alexandria, VA 22308
(703) 768-5700
http://www.ahs.org

Scotts Run Nature Preserve

Scotts Run Nature Preserve encompasses a variety of different habitats including a rocky gorge, palisades along the Potomac and an upland hardwood forest. Its most distinguishing characteristic is its profusion of spring wildflowers including bloodroot, Dutchman's-breeches, round-lobed hepatica, trout lily, Virginia bluebell, sessile trillium, wild ginger, trailing arbutus, wild orchids and over 100 other species. These woodland plants are called ephemerals because the plants bloom and seed before the trees overhead have leafed. Wildflowers carpet the forest floor in the spring, and in the summer where sunlight can penetrate the canopy or along the banks of streams and rivers, where sunlight can reach the ground. Scotts Run offers some of the most beautiful views of the Potomac in the Washington area. This natural wooded parkland, consisting of 385 acres along the river, offers hiking, bird-watching and beautiful scenery. The river here, shallow and full of rapids and many small islands, is a haven for waterfowl and songbirds. Many of the huge trees along the shore date back more than 100 years. Beneath their canopy one finds an abundance of dogwood, pawpaw, mountain laurel and service berry (so called because of its use to animals as a source of food).

The nature preserve is bounded on the west by Scotts Run, a small, rock-strewn tributary of the Potomac that features a 15-foot waterfall just above its mouth. During summer months, the water is about ten degrees cooler than the Potomac. One outstanding feature of the park is a grove of eastern hemlocks that extends over a quarter of a mile in the Scotts Run valley. The park, originally called Dranesville District Park, was created in 1970 after the people of Dranesville voted to pay an additional tax to finance its preservation; it is owned and operated by the Fairfax County Park Authority.

Hiking

About three miles of trail through dense forest, with scenic views of the Potomac and secluded sites along Scotts Run, make this a good place to walk year-round.

How To Get There: From Exit 13 of the Capital Beltway (I-495), take VA 193 (Georgetown Pike) west for about one-tenth of a mile. The parking lot is on the right. Open daily year-round from daylight to dark.

For Additional Information:
Fairfax County Park Authority
12055 Government Center Parkway
Suite 927
Fairfax, VA 22035-1119
(703) 324-8700
http://www.co.fairfax.va.us/parks

Shenandoah National Park and Skyline Drive

The Shenandoah National Park (SNP) is outside our 50-mile radius, but as the area's premier national park in the region, it must be included. All residents of Washington owe it to themselves to spend some time enjoying the many wonders of the SNP. Shenandoah National Park sits astride the Blue Ridge (part of the Appalachian Mountains) between Front Royal and Waynesboro, Virginia. The Appalachian Trail runs the length of the park.

The famous Skyline Drive winds along the Blue Ridge for the entire 105-mile length of the park. At its southern end it connects with the very scenic 469-mile Blue Ridge Parkway. Skyline Drive has a reputation as the place to see the fall colors (by car). It is that, but it is also wonderful in every other season, at almost any time of day, although dawn and dusk are best for seeing animals. There are numerous trails that intersect Skyline Drive, including many short (less than 2.5 miles) self-guiding nature trails and the Appalachian Trail (See Hiking, below). Numerous overlooks offer spectacular views of the Blue Ridge, the Piedmont and the Shenandoah Valley. Waterfalls adorn many of the trails.

In 1926, Congress authorized the establishment of the Shenandoah National Park, and the Commonwealth of Virginia later purchased almost 280 square miles of land to be donated to the park. Much of what is now Shenandoah National Park was settled in the 1800s when the scarcity of prime farmland in the valleys below forced people to settle in the mountainous areas, where farming was more difficult and people had to rely more on hunting and grazing. By the early 1900s, as game became scarce and the thin mountain soil was depleted, much of the population of the area left. In 1936, President Franklin D. Roosevelt dedicated the park in an experiment to return once-populated land to its natural state. The Civilian Conservation Corp (CCC) built most of the initial recreational facilities and Skyline Drive opened in 1939. This experiment was so successful that 40 percent of the SNP is now designated as wilderness, with 95 percent of the SNP covered by forests, much of it mature hardwoods. Big Meadows, the largest open area in the park, is kept open to promote meadow wildlife.

The SNP has flora and fauna of interest in all seasons. Wildflowers are found from spring through fall. Those interested in SNP wildflowers should obtain a copy of the "Wildflower Calendar of Shenandoah National Park," which lists about 80 species and the months each is (normally) in bloom, from a park visitor center. Highlights include hepatica, bloodroot, redbud, violets, bluets, trillium, vernal iris, phlox, lousewort, anemone, wild strawberry, showy orchis, blue-eyed grass, buttercups and pink and yellow lady's-slipper in spring. Mountain laurel, columbine, penstemon, Solomon's seal, false Solomon's seal, golden Alexander and Bowman's root bloom in early summer. In late summer, you'll see Scarlet Oswego tea, wild bergamot, fireweed (magenta), fairy-candles-of-the-forest, Turk's cap lily (orange), sundrops (yellow), starry silene, bouncing bet, evening primrose, black-eyed Susan, catnip flower, sunflowers, Queen Anne's lace, impatiens, flannel mullein (yellow), joe pye weed (purple), rock sedum, bellflower, rattlesnake plantain, thistles, false foxglove and catfoot. Fall flowers include gentians (blue), harebell (blue), snakeroot, asters, goldenrod, silverrod, autumn sneezeweed (yellow), ladies' tresses, virgin's bower and witch hazel.

Animals include numerous deer (especially at dawn and dusk), raccoon, beaver, bobcat, bear, groundhogs, salamanders and snakes (most non-poisonous, but an occasional poisonous rattlesnake or copperhead). About 200 species of birds have been recorded. The most obvious are the large number of hawks and vultures that exploit the updrafts along the ridge. Barred owl, wild turkey, ruffed grouse, junco, chickadees, nuthatches, wrens, goldfinches, bluebirds, ravens, woodpeckers live in the park year-round. Many songbirds summer in the SNP, including numerous varieties of warbler, scarlet tanager, sparrows, vireos, waxwing, mockingbirds, thrushes, robins, brown creeper and more. A bird list is available from the Park Service. All plants and animals in the park are protected by law—leave them alone. Hunting is prohibited and all firearms must be disabled before entering the park. Dogs must be on leashes, at all times.

Hiking

The SNP is probably the region's favorite hiking area, with over 500 miles of trails. Many well-marked trails are accessible from Skyline Drive and from small roads on either side of the park. Although free SNP brochures show the locations of short self-guiding nature trails off Skyline Drive, serious hikers should obtain trail maps from the Potomac Appalachian Trail Club (PATC). The PATC offers guide books with circuit hikes in the

SNP and trail maps of northern, central and southern SNP (these are available at the visitor center). The PATC operates huts and cabins for hikers along the trails (contact the PATC). Hiking is without doubt the best way to see the SNP. You will be richly rewarded for your efforts with spectacular waterfalls, grand vistas, stunning wildflowers and visions of many creatures you might not see from the road. However, be aware that many of the trails involve serious steep climbs. The trails can be rough, rocky or slippery in wet weather; most trail injuries are caused by falling. Hikers must be in good physical condition, knowledgeable of the trail and weather and adequately prepared. Check with the Park Rangers about the suitability of particular trails before heading out.

The Sierra Club, PATC and other hiking clubs lead frequent hikes on SNP trails; these hikes, led by experienced volunteer outdoor enthusiasts are the best way to start hiking the park. You can car pool to the trail head, and the experienced leaders (and followers) add a great deal to the experience. (See Hiking Clubs in appendix.)

Bicycling

Bicycling is allowed on the public roads only; bikes are prohibited on all trails.

Camping

There are four family campgrounds in the SNP; hookups are not provided. There are numerous sites for backcountry camping along (but out of sight of) trails. In addition, the PATC operates primitive cabins and huts along several trails. The huts are three-sided lean-tos and are available to long-distance (three nights or more) hikers on a first-come-first-served basis; a $1.00 per night per person contribution is requested. Cabins are available only by advanced reservation through the PATC; rates for cabins run several dollars per person per night, depending on the day of the week. Backcountry campers must register with the Park Service; permits are required, but they are free.

Other Accommodations

Food service, gift shops, service stations, camper's supplies are available at various points along Skyline Drive. Most are open in summer and closed in winter. Overnight lodging is available

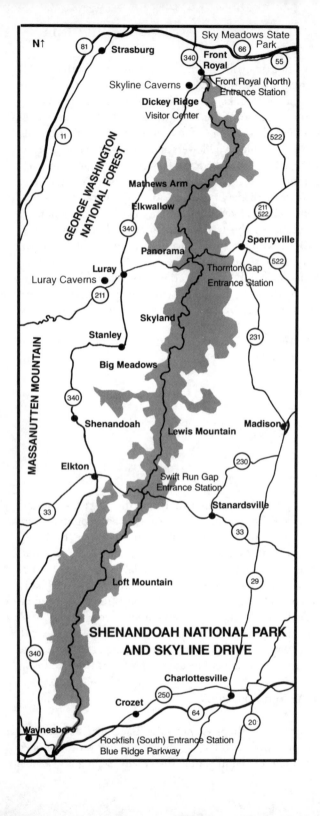

at Skyland Lodge (Mile 42) and Big Meadows (Mile 51); contact ARAMARK Virginia Sky-Line Company at 800-999-4714.

Nearby Attractions

While you're in the Shenandoah area you might want to visit Skyline Caverns, Luray Caverns, Sky Meadows Park, Blandy Farm or G. Richard Thompson Wildlife Management Area. See entries under Virginia.

How To Get There: To reach the northern entrance (mile 0), take I-66 west from Washington to Front Royal, Exit 2 or 3. Follow the numerous signs from there.

To reach the Thornton Gap entrance (mile 31.5) from Washington, take I-66 west to Route 29 south (Warrenton); at Warrenton take Route 211 West through Sperryville. The road goes up steeply as you approach Skyline Drive, which is very well marked. You can also enter Skyline Drive at Swift Run Junction (mile 65.7) at the junction of Route 33 and at Rockfish Gap (mile 105) at the junction of US 250 and I-64. Information, including a map of the park is available at all entrances. Hiking trails are accessible from many overlooks on Skyline Drive and from numerous roads on the east and west sides of the park. Admission: $5.00 per car for a seven-day permit. Annual passes are available.

For Additional Information:
Superintendent
Shenandoah National Park
3655 U.S. Hwy. 211 E.
Luray, VA 22835-9051
(540) 999-23500
http://www.nps.gov/shen

Potomac Appalachian Trail Club
Headquarters and Bookstore
Monday–Thursday 7:00 a.m.–9:00 p.m.
Thursdays and Fridays NOON–2:00 p.m.
118 Park Street, SE
Vienna, VA 22180-4609
(703) 242-0315 (store or general information tape)
(703) 242-0965 (outings tape)
http://patc.simplenet.com

ARAMARK Virginia Sky-line Company Inc. (concessions)
Box 727
Luray, VA 22835
(540) 743-5108 or 1-800-999-4714

Signal Hill Park

Signal Hill Park is both a registered Civil War historical landmark and a site of natural beauty. Some 35 miles southwest of Washington, the 110-acre Signal Hill Park is owned by the City of Manassas Park. Signal Hill is one of the best preserved hilltop fortifications in Northern Virginia. During the First Battle of Bull Run in the Civil War, Signal Hill was the highest point in the area, commanding an impressive view. At this site, Union troops of General McDowell were seen in the execution of a flanking march. The Confederate Signal Corp, using the "wigwag" flagging system, sent a message to the battlefield, "look to the left, you are turned." The first recorded use of flags in active battle secured a victory for the Confederacy. Signal Hill Park features a one-mile asphalt paved trail, pavilion with restrooms, phone, and picnic tables. Signal Hill Park is open to the public year-round from 8:00 A.M. to dusk. Manassas National Battlefield Park (described elsewhere) and the Conner House are not far away.

How To Get There: From Exit 9 of the Capital Beltway (I-495), take I-66 west to the Manassas Park exit (VA 28). Turn south and proceed approximately six miles to VA 213 (Manassas Drive). Turn left onto Manassas Drive. Go about one mile and turn right on Blooms Road, which runs through the park. The historic hill lies on the left-hand side of the road. No entrance fee.

For Additional Information:
City of Manassas Park
One Park Center Court
Manassas Park, VA 22111
(703) 631-0181 (metro)
(703) 335-8871

Skyline Caverns

Skyline Caverns is located very close to the northern (Front Royal) entrance of **Skyline Drive** and is well worth a visit if you're nearby. Skyline is one of the youngest caverns in the area and is still forming. It is a "fault and fissure" type cavern. Skyline is one of the few caves discovered by scientific deduction. Walter S. Amos examined the surface topography in the area, predicted that a cave must be in the area of the present building, started digging there and the rest is history.

Although Skyline is not nearly as big or dramatic as other caves in the region, it is kept as natural as possible, tour groups are smaller and the tour is more geologically based. One can see rare anthodites, white spikes of calcite crystal that sprout from the cave ceiling, like upside-down white chrysanthemums. It is theorized that there was (atypically) a partial vacuum in the cave that gave rise to the anthodites, but with the entry of people into the cave any vacuum that was present is now gone. This very "young" cave is also interesting as a comparison with the other, older caves in the region.

Skyline Caverns is a private business and not associated with any government-owned facility. The first tour starts at 9:00 A.M. daily; the last tour leaves at 6:30 P.M. daily June 15–Labor Day . The last tour leaves at 5:00 P.M. weekdays, March 15–June 14 and Labor Day–November 14. The last tour leaves at 4:00 P.M. weekdays, November 15–March 14. Like most caves, the temperature underground is a constant 54 degrees (F.) year-round, so bring a jacket or sweater and walking shoes. The paths are narrow at places and slightly uneven but well-illuminated; stairs and ramps must be climbed. The formations are easily damaged, even by the oils on the skin, so you should not touch any formation unless explicitly told to do so by your guide.

How To Get There: Take I-66 from Washington to Front Royal, Exit 6 or 13 and follow the signs to the northern entrance of Skyline Drive (Shenandoah National Park). Skyline Caverns is just beyond that. There are signs everywhere. Admission is $10.00 for adults and less for children, seniors, military, groups, etc.

For Additional Information:
Skyline Caverns
P.O. Box 193
Front Royal, VA 22630
(800)296-4545

Sky Meadows State Park

Sky Meadows sits alongside the Appalachian Trail; it has mountain hiking, spectacular views from the visitor center and trails (both of the Blue Ridge and from the Blue Ridge looking over the Virginia pasturelands) and history. The Mount Bleak Visitor Center is a beautiful restored two-story stone house built by Isaac Settle around 1835. Adjacent to the stone house is a log home dating back to 1798 that is believed to have been the residence of the George Washington Edmonds family and probably later served as a kitchen. Other buildings on the site include a barn and an old icehouse. Tours of the house and grounds are offered by park staff through the summer season. The tour guide explains the history of the area, how the people lived here, the features of the house, log cabin and ice house and an overview of the Sky Meadows area. Don't miss it. But if you do, you can view two videos on the history of Sky Meadows and Mount Bleak.

The Mount Bleak Visitor Center is a wonderful place to have a picnic and do a little hiking and photography. There are numerous activities at the park (in season) involving guided hikes, nature study, crafts, storytelling and history. The visitor center has restrooms, water, a telephone and soda machines. Pets must be confined or kept on a short leash. No alcoholic beverages permitted.

Hiking

Several well-marked trails can be reached from the visitor center parking lot. Maps are available at the center. The Appalachian Trail itself is a two-mile hike from the visitor center. One can combine trails to make circuit hikes from 1.5 to 4 miles in length. All the trails involve some steep sections, but offer great views in return. Hiking trails are for pedestrians only–bicycles are allowed only on regular park roads.

Horseback Riding

There are five miles of scenic bridle trails dedicated for equestrian use only. A map is available at the visitor center. The park does not rent horses at this time.

Camping

Primitive hike-in tent camp sites are available on a first-come first-served basis. There are 12 sites, each with tent pad, picnic table and fire pit; latrines and non-potable well water are available. Nominal fee.

How To Get There: Take Route 66 west from Washington to Exit 5, Route 17 north (toward Delaplane or Paris). The entrance to the park is about 7 miles on the left. The Park is open for day use from 8:00 A.M. to dusk daily. Nominal entrance fee.

For Additional Information:
Sky Meadows State Park
11012 Edmonds Land
Delaplane, VA 20144-1710
(540) 592-3556
http://www.state.va.us/~dcr/drr_home.htm

Upton Hill Regional Park

This 26-acre, heavily wooded parkland straddles the Arlington/Fairfax county line. Located in the most densely populated area of northern Virginia, Upton Hill features a large swimming pool complex and a deluxe miniature golf course and a coin-operated batting cage, in addition to its natural beauty. Visitors may picnic in a scenic setting near two large reflecting pools that feature picturesque waterfalls and a gazebo. A group picnic shelter is also available.

Though not extensive, a trail system of about one mile in length does exist. The trail ascends a moderately steep hillside sheltered by a canopy of towering poplar trees. At a spot where several streamlets converge, there is an interesting concentration of fern growth. You can appreciate the spring sun, glowing autumn trees and ripples in a pond at this small park just as well as at a larger one.

How To Get There: From Exit 8 on the Capital Beltway (I-495), head east on US 50 (Arlington Boulevard) to Wilson Boulevard (VA 613 east) near the Seven Corners Shopping Center. Continue east on Wilson to Patrick Henry Drive, which meets Wilson from the right at the Arlington/Fairfax County line. Turn right on Patrick Henry Drive to the parking area. The park is bounded by Wilson Boulevard on the north, Patrick Henry Drive on the west and Livingston Street on the east. Open daily year-round, dawn to dusk. No entrance fee.

For Additional Information:
Northern Virginia Regional Park Authority
5400 Ox Road
Fairfax Station, VA 22039-1022
(703) 352-5900
Park (703) 534-3437

W&OD Trail and Regional Park

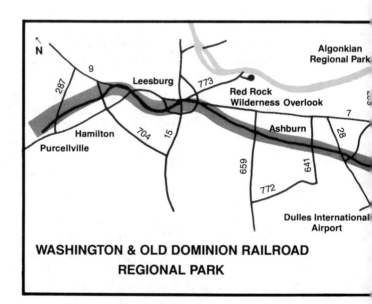

WASHINGTON & OLD DOMINION RAILROAD REGIONAL PARK

Located on the roadbed of the old Washington and Old Dominion Railroad, the W&OD Railroad Regional Park has been called the skinniest park in Virginia. This recreation facility is 45 miles long and 100 feet wide and extends from the Potomac River to the Blue Ridge Mountains. Starting from Shirlington in Arlington, it leads through Arlington, Falls Church, Vienna, Fairfax County, Reston, Herndon, Leesburg and Ashburn to Purcellville in Loudoun County.

The trail offers a long ride through nature and history. Unlike some bicycle trails in the area, this one is paved. Much of the trail is in the sun, so it's best to try it when it is still cool. The railroad opened in 1859, and you will see several old train stations and a number of Civil War sites, including a plaque at Park Street noting the first tactical use of a railroad in war. You'll pass Sunset Hills, at one time the largest farm in Virginia. The Freeman House, once used as a hospital during the Civil War and now a general store, sits on Church Street; tours are given on Sunday afternoons. Several community centers, bike shops, general stores and restaurants are located along the trail. The biker/hiker can pull off the trail for a refreshing cold drink or lunch at a nearby shop.

The wide, paved path is mainly for hikers, joggers, bicyclists and roller skaters. A parallel crushed gravel trail is designed for horseback riders, although hikers are also permitted to use it; the gravel trail runs from just west of Vienna to the trail's end in

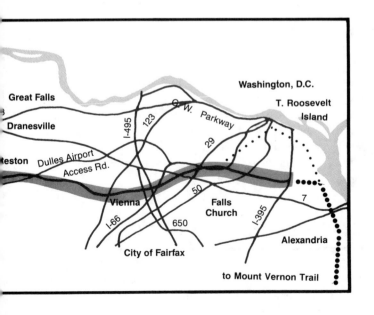

Purcellville. At the Smiths Switch Station rest area in Ashburn, trail users find refreshments, shade and information. On the east end, the paved trail joins the Mount Vernon Trail (described elsewhere) which runs north to the Theodore Roosevelt Island (see entry under DC) where there is parking and a bicycle rack. From the Mount Vernon Trail, you can cross the Potomac on the Memorial Bridge or Roosevelt Bridge to the Rock Creek Park Trail or to the C&O Canal Historical Park towpath trail. Refer to the section on Off-Road Bicycle Nature Trails.

Though some parts of the W&OD Trail pass through urban areas, other portions traverse wooded and verdant terrain. Rabbits, snakes, deer, squirrel and other animals are likely to cross the path. The W&OD is especially good for viewing summer and fall wildflowers.

How To Get There: The trail begins at I-395 Highway, near the intersection of Shirlington Road and South Four Mile Run Drive in Arlington, but it is easier to join the path from the Dunn Loring Metro station. Bike a few blocks north on Gallows Road and you'll see the trail. A 54-page trail guide on the W&OD Railroad Regional Park is for sale at all regional parks.

For Additional Information:
Northern Virginia Regional Park Authority
Attention: W&OD
5400 Ox Road
Fairfax Station, VA 22039-1022
(703) 729-0596 (p ark)

The W&OD R.R. Regional Park Trail Guide, a spiral-bound book with detailed maps denoting connecting trails, bicycle repair shops, restrooms, food stops and other hints to enjoy the W&OD is available for $4.50 (check only) by mail from the NVRPA (above) and is on sale at many of the NVRPA regional parks. This guide is highly recommended for users of the trail.

Westmoreland State Park

Along the shore of the Potomac River downstream from Washington is one of the area's finest state parks. You can canoe, hike, bird-watch or just drive around in a rural atmosphere. It is a remarkable area, considering its proximity to Washington. Lying on the northern rim of the Northern Neck Peninsula between the Potomac and Rappahannock rivers, the park is a mixed hardwood woodland cut by deep ravines that run up to cliffs over 150 feet tall along the Potomac. A marsh links the sandy beach with the cliffs. Westmoreland State Park is entirely within the coastal plain geographical region. This region is more popularly known as The Northern Neck. At Horsehead Cliffs within the park, you can study some of the fascinating geological forces that have shaped this area.

It all began about 15 million years ago when a shallow sea ran up to the fall line north and west. The climate was much warmer than it is now, similar to that of northern Florida. Sharks, whales, crocodiles and porpoises swam in the warm sea and died there. After they died, their skeletons settled into the soft sediments (sand, silt and clay) that made up the ocean floor. Fossil shells, sharks' teeth, whale bones and other remains can be seen in the cliffs today. Their removal is prohibited. When the climate began to cool, water was locked up in the great polar ice caps and the sea began to recede. The rivers rushed out to meet the falling sea level, creating deep, long valleys including the Potomac River Valley. Even now erosion is changing the shape of the park as winds and waves from the northeast and northwest wear down the soft sedimentary rocks that make up the cliffs, causing them to retreat steadily.

The birding is quite good; over a hundred different species have been sighted including a large number of diving ducks and song birds. Wild turkey nest here as do bald eagles. The forest contains oak, tulip tree, American beech and red and silver maple trees. Dogwood and mountain laurel make up the understory. There is also a beautiful assortment of wildflowers in the Big Meadows. The marsh is covered with cattails in the spring and provides a variety of freshwater marsh plants for migrating birds to feed on.

The park also has an Olympic-sized swimming pool, sandy swimming beach, boat-launching ramp, grocery store, tent and trailer campgrounds, housekeeping cabins and a visitor center that offers plant and animal exhibits. During the summer, interpreters give evening programs in the amphitheater, lead nature walks, and run children's programs.

Hiking and Bicycling

The park offers a complex of hiking trails through swamp, wetland and forest. None of the trails is challenging to the long-range hiker, but all offer a good opportunity to get acquainted with the flora and fauna of the area.

Hiking Trails

Big Meadow	red blaze	0.6 mile long
Turkey Neck	blue blaze	2.5 miles long
Beaver Dam	yellow blaze	0.6 mile long
Laurel Point	orange blaze	1.3 miles long
River Trail	white blaze	0.2 mile long
Beach Trail	yellow blaze	0.4 mile long
Rock Springs Pond	green blaze	5.0 miles long

Camping

Three camping areas are located within the park for all types of campers. Hookups are available as well as modern restrooms with hot showers. The maximum camping period is 14 days. No open fires are permitted. There is a dump station for recreational vehicles. A group camping area is also provided. Housekeeping cabins are rented on a nightly (2 night minimum) and weekly from March 1 through November 31. Cabins are equipped with modern amenities, kitchens, heat, and air conditioning. The Potomac River retreat is an upscale overnight facility for families or small groups up to 12 persons, located 30 feet from the river. Reservations are required for all facilities; call (800) 933-PARK.

Fishing and Boating

Fishing for largemouth bass, catfish and bream is permitted throughout the year. A state fishing license is required for freshwater fishing. A boat-launching ramp is provided on the Potomac River. Rental boats, including hydrobikes and paddleboats, are available. Kayak programs are offered on select Fridays and Saturdays from May through October.

How To Get There: From Exit 4 of the Capital Beltway (I-495), take I-95 south to Fredericksburg. Then take VA 3 east to VA 347; turn left (north) and follow signs. Open year-round, although most facilities are seasonal.

For Additional Information:
Manager, Westmoreland State Park
State Park Road
Route 1, Box 600 , Montross, VA 22520
(804) 493-8821
http://www.state.va.us/ndcr/parks

Wildcat Mountain Natural Area

Between the coastal plain and the Shenandoah Range, west of Washington, lies a low ridge called Wildcat Mountain. The altitude ranges from 500 feet near the bottom to 1,200 feet. Along its steep western slope is a diverse woodland that provides a rich habitat for various types of wildlife—raccoon, ruffed grouse, white-tailed deer, fox, bobcat and wild turkey. Black bears visit occasionally and 150 species of birds have been recorded. In 1960 its owners, Russell Arundel and Laurens Hamilton, gave a portion of the western slope to The Nature Conservancy, a non-profit international conservation organization. Since that time, it has been maintained as a natural area. About 760 acres, the land is blanketed by mixed stands of large oak and hickory, as well as stands of pine and younger deciduous forest. Flowering dogwood and redbud grow in fringe woodlands along with persimmon, sassafras and wild cherry.

A variety of interesting wildflowers are found here throughout the year but mainly in the spring and early summer months. Some visitors have been disappointed when looking for a lot of showy wildflowers. Wildcat is a dry woodland. It has some wonderful plants, especially for the serious botanist, but not the rich display you would find in wetter woods or more open environments; for those you might look at Riverbend Park or Scotts Run Nature Preserve—both described elsewhere. Ferns, mosses and lichens also are found in the greenstone rock outcroppings. While visitors are not specifically prohibited from walking off the trails, the managers do not want visitors climbing over the very sensitive rock communities. It takes lichens centuries to grow and visitors could hurt themselves as well as the environment by climbing on the rocks. There are wonderful ferns of many varieties growing along some of the trails.

Two poisonous snakes live here, the eastern timber rattler and the copperhead. The timber rattlesnake eats rodents, birds and small mammals. It lives in higher elevations throughout the

Piedmont but particularly likes wooded slopes where rodents are available. It is very rare in these woods. But copperheads are certainly here and visitors need to be careful. Copperheads like to eat mice, frogs, birds and insects and live on wooded hillsides and in open fields. Copperheads are said to be mild mannered and unlikely to attack without cause. Their bites are messy wounds taking weeks to heal but fatalities are rare (much rarer than fatalities from hacking, amateur attempts to treat snakebites). There are many other types of snakes in this area that are harmless and the poisonous snakes are relatively rare, but can be lethal. Watch where you put your feet while you are hiking to avoid stepping on one of these creatures.

This preserve is not geared to a lot of visitors and there are no educational programs. A network of fire roads provides hiking trails for visitors. Access to Wildcat Mountain Natural Area is by a steeply ascending trail. Visitors are required to get permission before they can visit the preserve. Maps and/or clear directions are necessary as the trails have no signs or markers and visitors are really on their own. There is a small pond surrounded by woodland. The pond draws deer, raccoon and other wild animals and provides seasonal habitat for several species of frogs. Migrating waterfowl often pause to rest here during the spring and fall months.

Old stone walls and traces of early wagon roads mark boundary lines of former fields. An old farmstead recalls the country life of another time. After the Civil War many of the homesteads in the area were abandoned. Later, in the 1930s much of Wildcat Mountain was converted into an apple orchard. However, all farming and logging on the western slope ceased in the 1940s when the owners decided to let the land go back to nature.

Hiking

The trails in the preserve are really fire roads and have no signs or markers. Visiting is by permission only. Some of the trails were part of an old system of carriage roads that once held together a community. Stone walls meandering through the woods, seemingly without pattern, once marked homesteads or small farms. One old spring house still survives from the 1800s. No fires, day use only.

How To Get There: Wildcat Mountain Natural Area is located in Fauquier County near Warrenton, west of Washington via I-66 or US 29/211. You should contact one of the sources for additional information to get permission to enter the area; you may obtain exact directions at that time.

For Additional Information:
Marvin and Peggy Mitchell , Volunteer Preserve Monitors
Wildcat Mountain
8452 England Mountain Road., Marshall, VA 20115
(540) 347-7026

The Nature Conservancy , Virginia Chapter
1233A Cedars Court, Charlottesville, VA 22903
(804) 295-6106
http://www.tnc.org

Winkler Botanical Preserve

The Winkler Botanical Preserve is a fine gem cut from rough stone. Today, its 43 acres appear like the Virginia woods, meadows, streams and ponds that existed before civilization arrived with a vengeance. Over 500 types of native plants, wildlflowers, sedges, shrubs and trees bloom here in a natural setting. Miles of unpaved trails meander through mature mixed oak forests, with mountain laurel and rhododendron understory and fern-lined floor. You hear the laugh of the pileated woodpecker and the pee-a-wee call of the eastern wood pewee. Walk though meadows of native grasses and sedges. On the ponds you see waterlilies floating with great blue and green herons stalking fish among the cattails, with hawks soaring above and painted and snapping turtles poking their noses up from below, with a mountain waterfall in the distance.

But these 43 acres are in congested metropolitan Alexandria surrounded by I-395 and numerous high rise office and apartment buildings. Twenty years ago this was an unofficial dump, a neglected place where folks disposed of junk rather than drive to the official landfill, where run-off from highways and building sites polluted the water and eroded the streams, where exotic plants and overgrowth made woods and meadows inhospitable to wildlife. It took tremendous devotion, many many man-years of staff labor, a lot of heavy equipment, and a lot of material to transform the site to its current state. Rather than a restoration, it was an act of creating a dream. That dream started when the Winkler family established a trust with the 43 acres and funds to become the Preserve. It's taken almost 20 years and, although it doesn't look it, it's still a work in progress.

The streams, ponds, 2 acre lake and waterfall that appear

natural now were built with heavy equipment, thousands of tons of stone, plastic pond liners and a lot of earth moving. The ponds were configured to slow and filter the storm run-off water. The large lake actually doubles as a disguised storm water management facility. The woods were thinned to allow the healthy trees to grow uncrowded. . The soil was improved with tons of leaf mulch and lots of tilling. Tens of thousands of native plants, grasses, sedges, cattails, ferns, and other native plants were lovingly placed and planted by hand. Native plants are hard to find, so volunteers looked for construction sites where native plants were about to be bulldozed and "rescued" them one-by-one to be transplanted here; others were grown from seed, with some species taking years to mature to the point they could be transplanted. Today it's hard to believe you're not in some distant wilderness, although you're minutes from I-395. There's much more to the story, so be sure to ask questions if you get the opportunity to take a guided tour of the preserve.

The is a wonderful place to enjoy **native wildflowers**. There are over 500 species of flowering woodland and meadow flowers in a relatively small area; a sampling follows. Flowering in early spring there is skunk cabbage, hepaticas, bloodroot, creeping phlox, bluebells, spring beauty, yellow violet, common shadblow, false marsh marigold, common spicebush, white violet, purple violet, trilliums, white bear sedge, trout lily, squirrel corn, dutchmen's breeches, wild geranium, wild larkspur, shooting star, wild blue phlox, twin leaf, bleeding heart, wild strawberry, celandine poppy, common fleabane, pink azalea, blueberry, common bluets, bearberry, rue anemone, common henbit, starry chickweed, stonecrop, wild columbine, smooth blackhaw, northern inkberry, common bayberry, grape hyacinth, sassafras, wild oats, bird's foot violet, white foamfower, wild ginger, pink lady's slipper, dwarf crested iris, green and gold, and box huckleberry.

In mid and late spring, flowering plants include Jack-in-the-pulpit, clump geranium, oxalis, black berries, spiderwart, star of bethlehem, lily of the valley, rattle snake-weed, false blue indigo, false solomons seal, yellow star grass, maple leaf viburnum, southern arrowwood, mountain laurel, rosebay rhododendron, blue eyed grass, hairy beards tongue, slender iris, blue flag iris, bullhead lily, glade mallow, white glover, crown vetch, poison ivy, american holly, common hen bit, common bed straw, sweet bells, solomon sea, eastern burning bush, indian cucumber root, southern wild raisin, red clover, lance leaf coreopsis, dull-leaf indigobush, yellow iris, pasture rose, multi flora rose, honey suckle, golden ragwort, white elderberry, ox-eyed daisy, foxglove beardtongue, water hemlock, hawkweed, cow parsnip, yellow thistle, and meadow phlox. In addition there are numerous ferns such as cinnamon, sensitive fern , christmas fern and royal fern.

Flowering trees include the alder, red maple, river birch, redbud, ironwood, red oak, black oak, scarlet oak, pin oak, dogwood, domestic apples, sassafras, white oak, chestnut oak, post oak, hawthorn, wafer tree, tulip poplar, mockernut hickory, white fringetree, black locust, and black cherry.

Bird-watching is excellent. In a short walk, with careful observation, one can see or hear deep woods, meadow, edge and pond inhabitants. These include the pileated woodpecker, nuthatch and other woodpeckers, pewee, goldfinches, scarlet tanager, robins, green heron, great blue heron, bluebird, geese, hawks and more. The island in the lake is ideal waterfowl nesting habitat. Painted and snapping turtles are visible at the lake.

Hike the two miles of trails at your leisure, taking time to take in the beauty, but please stay on the foot path; one false step can destroy these delicate plants.

There are no buildings or parking lot on the preserve now. The preserve plans to build an Adirondack lodge style education building and a parking lot by spring of 1999. A trail map will be available soon.

How To Get There: From DC, take I-395 south in Virginia to the west Seminary Road exit. At the second light, Beauregard Street, turn left; pass four lights, pass the Millbrook apartments on the left, then turn left into the next street, Roanoke Avenue (it's easy to miss); find the preserve at the end of the street. Currently the preserve is open only 7:30 A.M. to 3:00 P.M. Monday through Friday. Weekend hours and fees for some programs are expected to start in 1999. Call for current hours or to schedule a tour. No pets, bicycling, or picnicking allowed.

For Additional Information:
Winkler Botanical Preserve
5400 Roanoke Avenue
Alexandria, VA 22311
(703) 578-7888 Preserve

Director's Office
Winkler Botanical Preserve
4900 Seminary Road, Alexandria, VA 22311-9109
(703) 578-9109 Office

Wolf Trap Farm Park for the Performing Arts

The natural beauty of Wolf Trap Farm is perhaps overshadowed by the role the park has played in bringing the arts to the outdoors. But this 117-acre rolling woodland park near Vienna does offer some interesting outdoor experiences, especially when the summer theater season is over. It has a small stream, some wonderful wooded chambers and rolling meadows traversed by walking paths.

During the summer, a wide range of musical performances is presented here. You may enjoy the show from inside the Filene Center or spread your blanket beneath the stars on Wolf Trap's sloping lawn. It would be difficult to find a more beautiful setting in which to enjoy outstanding artists from around the world.

The park was created when Mrs. Jouett Shouse donated a portion of her Virginia farm and funds for the construction of the park's Filene Center to the Department of the Interior in 1966. Wolf Trap Farm Park is administered by the National Park Service while the Wolf Trap Foundation is responsible for selecting and presenting the programs. It was created as the first national park dedicated to the performing arts.

Interpretive programs, workshops, lectures and many special activities are offered throughout the summer; there is also a children's theater-in-the-woods. Tours of the Filene Center and the park may be scheduled through the Visitor Services Office at Wolf Trap; arrangements may be made in advance for handicapped parking or wheelchair accommodations. Thirty-five acres of the farm are still undisturbed woodlands that provide habitat for raccoon, opossum, red-tailed hawk, barred owl, squirrel and white-tailed deer.

How To Get There: From Exit 10 of the Capital Beltway (I-495), take Leesburg Pike (VA 7) northwest to Towlston Road, where you will see a Wolf Trap sign. Turn left on Towlston to Trap Road, then left again. Metrobus service is available from the West Falls Church Metrorail station during the performance season. The grounds are open year-round. The Filene Center is open May through September for performances. However, tours may be arranged at other times by calling the Visitor Services Department.

For Additional Information:
Interpretive Division
Wolf Trap Farm Park for the Performing Arts
1551 Trap Road ,
Vienna, VA 22182
(703) 255-1893

Woodlawn Plantation and Frank Lloyd Wright's Pope-Leighey House

Overlooking Mount Vernon and the Potomac River is Wood-lawn Plantation, once the lovely home of George Washington's foster daughter, Eleanor Parke ("Nelly") Custis Lewis. The nat-uralistic style of English gardening, introduced to this country by Washington and Thomas Jefferson, is reflected in the restored serpentine path and bowling green areas of the garden here. A collection of old-fashioned heritage roses, consisting primarily of varieties known before 1850, is a special highlight. The rose was a flower of special importance to Nelly Lewis; thus, two parterres, formal patterned beds, were included as an integral part of the garden plan when the Garden Club of Vir-ginia began the restoration of Woodlawn's gardens. More than 36 beds of roses, bordered in germander, make up the parterres.

In contrast to the elegance of the formal gardens are several nature trails, which meander over acres of woodland and through open fields. The Lorenzo Lewis Trail, named in memo-ry of the eldest son of Lawrence and Nelly Custis Lewis, was designed by the National Audubon Society. Lorenzo was inter-ested in ornithology and many of his mounted birds are dis-played. Numerous wildflowers crowd the trail during the spring, including May apples, bloodroot, jack-in-the-pulpit, trout lily, trillium, ferns, spring beauty, jewel weed, violets and maple-leafed viburnum. The variety of birds found here makes this an area of great interest to bird-watchers. Mockingbirds, blue jays, phoebes, bluebirds, titmouse, robins, woodpeckers, catbirds, brown thrasher, wood thrushes, warblers, cardinal, indigo buntings, vireos and many others are frequently seen. The trails are maintained by local troops of Boy Scouts who also conduct a wildlife program in the forest.

A second trail, the Angela Lewis trail, is a grassland that was reforested in 1989 in cooperation with the National Chapter of the Society of American Foresters and the United States Forest Service.

Located on the estate is the Pope-Leighey House, originally located in Falls Church until it was rescued from the path of highway construction in 1964. This Usonian house was designed for Loren Pope by Frank Lloyd Wright in 1939. It was designed to be a moderately priced house that incorporated many of Wright's beliefs about architecture. The house, built of cypress, brick and glass demonstrates Wright's belief that a building and its construction materials should relate to the building's natural surroundings. The landscaping is a good example of how to use wildflowers in a residential landscape. A native plant garden has been donated and installed by the Powtomack Chapter of the Virginia Native Plant Society. Native plants are becoming increasingly popular with landscape architects because they are generally easier to grow than exotic plants, are hardy for the area and require little maintenance. Woodlawn Plantation is another good area for wildflower viewing. Woodlawn Plantation and Frank Lloyd Wright's Pope-Leighey House are properties of the National Trust for Historic Preservation.

How To Get There: From Exit 1 of the Capital Beltway, follow US 1 south about 4 .5 miles. The property is located at the intersections of US 1 and VA 235 in Mt. Vernon, VA. Woodlawn is open March–December, except Christmas and Thanksgiving, 10:00 A.M.—4:00 P.M. Monday–Saturday and noon–4:00 P.M. Sundays.

For Additional Information:
Director , Woodlawn
Frank Lloyd Wright's Pope-Leighey House
P.O. Box 37 ,
Mount Vernon, VA 22121
(703) 780-4000

Public Information Officer
National Trust for Historic Preservation
1785 Massachusetts Avenue, N.W.
Washington, DC 20036
(202) 673-4000

View of the Potomac River from the Billy Goat Trail in the C&O Canal National Historical Park.   *Richard L. Berman*

Jeff Buxton

NATURAL ATTRACTIONS IN
WEST VIRGINIA

Appalachian National Scenic Trail

See the entry under Maryland for the history and overview of the Appalachian Trail. A portion of the Appalachian Trail was rerouted in 1986 to pass through Harpers Ferry, West Virginia and by Jefferson Rock. Jefferson Rock is the precise location where Thomas Jefferson is supposed to have stood and exclaimed that the view was "worth a voyage across the Atlantic." The rock itself would have long ago toppled into the village below, geologists say, except for some red sandstone supports placed under it about 1860. The Appalachian Trail now follows a footbridge across the Potomac River, where it crosses the C&O Canal National Historical Park and Towpath Trail leading either west to Cumberland, Maryland, or east along the north side of the Potomac to Washington, DC. (See the Maryland and Virginia entries on the Appalachian Trail for more details, history, maps and references.)

Harpers Ferry National Historical Park

Though Harpers Ferry is noted primarily for its history, it is located in a mountainous area of outstanding natural beauty. Two trails are particularly appealing to those seeking nature here.

Virginius Island, near the confluence of the mighty Shenandoah with the ambling Potomac, has been called the most important island in the Shenandoah, a rank it earned during the early days of settlement (1800s) in this region because of its proximity to Harpers Ferry. While its industrial importance may have diminished, it remains a very interesting place. The Virginius Island Trail, only 1.5 miles long, threads its way through history, both natural and man-made. Beginning at the railroad trestle in the Lower Town, the trail leads through land that has gone through a full cycle, from untouched nature to industrial village, then back again to near wilderness. Old water courses and bits of wall peep through the encroaching vegetation; nature is slowly reclaiming its own. It is, for that reason, an unusual study of nature re-engulfing the works of man.

A variety of trees and plants are found on the island. Mulberry trees abound and there is an especially fine stand of pawlonia trees, which bear masses of lavender flowers in the spring. The geology of the area is interesting; so is the variety of songbirds. Some 30 species nest here and, in the course of a year, perhaps 100 species might be recognized. The rabbit, raccoon, opossum, red squirrel, mole and muskrat live in the area.

There is also material available on the Maryland Heights Historical Trail. This trail divides into two sections; the longer section is 5.1 miles long and takes you past several sites of Civil War fortifications; the second section is 3.9 miles long, takes you to the Overlook Cliff and involves some fairly strenuous hiking. Three hundred feet directly below the cliff, the Shenandoah joins the Potomac, creating a spectacular view. During the Civil War, Union forces, after suffering defeat at Harpers Ferry in 1862, fortified Maryland Heights, the highest point in the area. There are other shorter trails, and the famed **Appalachian National Scenic Trail** now passes through the town.

How To Get There: From Exit 19 of the Capital Beltway (I-495), take I-270 northwest to I-70 near Frederick. Take I-70 west to US 340, then head southwest on US 340 to Harpers Ferry. The park is accessible from US 340 west of Frederick, Maryland. If you enjoy traveling by train, Amtrak offers special weekend service from Union Station in Washington, DC. Before making any trail hikes, it is best to check with the Harpers Ferry National Historical Park Information Center on Shenandoah Street in Lower Town. It is open daily, in summer, 8:00 A.M. to 6:00 P.M.; in winter, 8:00 A.M.–5:00 P.M., closed December 25th. See the Virginia locator map.

For Additional Information:
Superintendent
Harpers Ferry National Historical Park
P.O. Box 65
Harpers Ferry, WV 25425
(304) 535-6298
http://www.nps.gov/hafe/

Harpers Ferry White Water

Ever slide down a staircase? Well, there's a watery one at Harpers Ferry on the Shenandoah River, a half-mile series of small, rocky drops that long has been a favorite with canoeists, kayakers, "tubers" and white-water rafters. You can use your own craft, or you can take an organized white-water raft, canoe or tube trip with any of the several outfitters, located on US 340 between Harpers Ferry and Charles Town. The rafts offer an adventure for beginning white-water thrill-seekers on the 8-mile route of scenic riverway. The most challenging is Bull Falls, rated Class III or IV on the white-water scale of I through VI (with VI being the most difficult). The entire trip takes 4.5 hours, including a leisurely picnic lunch stop with all food and drink provided.

The Shenandoah is a lovely river to ride either on a raft or in a canoe or rubber tube. The ride includes both white-water action and some slow-water tranquillity. The waves can get up to six feet high. It is a great family experience. Riding the streams provides a refreshing way to enjoy the hot and hazy days of summer.

There are numerous outfitters running raft, canoe, kayak, ducky, and tube trips on area rivers. A few experienced companies are listed below. There are many trips, which change every year and are adjusted to seasonal conditions (varying water levels and speeds). Most includes guides, boats, safety equipment, and return transportation; many provide a simple lunch. You should book reservations in advance, and many trips run "rain or shine" with no refunds. Check with the outfitter on proper clothing to wear (and a change of clothing for after the trip), directions and restrictions.

Canoeing

All the outfitters also have rental canoes, as well as shuttle and guide service available. If you choose to take your own canoe, they will run shuttle service for you. You may also run the river in your own canoe without any services provided.

How To Get There: From Exit 19 of the Capital Beltway (I-495), take I-270 northwest to I-70 near Frederick. Take I-70 west to US 340, then head southwest on US 340 to Harpers Ferry. Call the outfitter for details. The reservation desk at Blue

Ridge Outfitters near Harpers Ferry is open year-round. Weekend hours during all months of operation and into the fall are 9:00 A.M.–5:00 P.M. Special group rates are available for ten or more. Information on raft trips is also available at the Harpers Ferry Camp Resort nearby. The River Riders take reservations 9:00 A.M.–5:00 P.M. weekdays year-round, and on weekends April–October. Call for rates and times. Departures are 8:30 A.M.–1:00 P.M. They require reservations and payment must be received seven days in advance. Call River and Trail Outfitters for reservations and a catalog at the number listed below. Classes in canoeing are also offered at several of the outfitters listed below.

For Additional Information:
Blue Ridge Outfitters
P.O. Box 750
US 340
Harpers Ferry, WV 25425
(304) 725-3444
http://www.broraft.com
broraft@intrepid.net, bioraft@aol.com

River and Trail Outfitters
604 Valley Road
Knoxville, MD 21758
(301) 695-5177
http://www.rivertrail.com

River Riders
P.O. Box 267
Knoxville, MD 21758
(301) 834-8051 (304) 535-2663 (in season)
http://www.riverriders.com/raft

Harpers Ferry Camp Resort
Route 5, Box 1300
Harpers Ferry, WV 25425
(304) 535-6895
(800) KOA-9497 (reservations)

APPENDIX

Preparations and Precautions

Some preparations will make your trip to *Natural Washington's* parks safer and more enjoyable. First of all, if you will be traveling a distance to see a park, it is always advisable to call ahead to check conditions; this is especially so if you are going to see seasonal wildlife whose timetable can vary from year to year depending on the weather. Also keep in mind that budgets are tight everywhere, and locations may reduce their hours or increase their fees without warning.

The **Golden Eagle Pass** costs $50.00 for a calendar year (doubled from $25 two years ago under pressure from Congress) and admits a person or car free to almost all national parks or fee areas nationwide. It pays for itself even if you only visit the Great Falls six times a year. The Golden Age Pass for those over 62 has the same privileges, but costs $10.00. Many individual parks also issue their own annual passes.

There are relatively few serious hazards to watch out for. The main cause of injury in parks is falling due to lack of reasonable caution. Children, especially, should be watched near cliffs and water. Another danger is crime, which is probably no worse in the parks than in our neighborhoods. Most parks close at dusk, and it's advisable to be out of the park after dark, unless you're with a group. Hunting is allowed in some parks and wildlife areas; hunting is illegal on Sundays in both Maryland and Virginia, so Sunday is the safest day for hikes in hunting season. It's a good idea to wear bright colors if there is a chance of hunters in the area.

Getting lost is usually a temporary problem, as most parks in this book are small. However, when hiking the larger parks, be sure to bring a good map and compass and plan your route ahead of time.

We suggest you dress appropriately if going out on a trail. This means boots, socks, long pants, hat and insect repellent. The Washington area is wet so trails are often bordered (or crossed, if inactive) by greenbriar (usually exotic multiflora rose, nature's barbed wire), which will bloody bare legs. Poison ivy is also widespread just off many trails; you can recognize it by its trademark three leaflets. It may have yellow-white clusters of flowers May through July and white berries in the fall. Poison ivy grows upright as a climbing vine and as a hanging vine. It is common in this area to see the "hairy" poison ivy vines up to several inches in diameter, hanging from trees—this is a tremendous temptation to children to swing on. Don't; the stalks and vines are poisonous too. If the weather's warm, you can count on mosquitoes; always bring insect repellent. In addition, Lyme disease, borne by small ticks, is entering the area—ticks can jump on your lower body from low-lying vegetation. Ticks are especially common where large animals such as deer or horses roam. If you are in tick-infested areas, check yourself. If you find any remove them by taking a piece of paper and using it to twist the body of the tick off slowly counterclockwise. Try to make sure the head of the tick comes out by doing this slowly; it can cause an infection in the wound if it is left in.

Don't drink untreated water straight from a pond or stream—bring your own water or drink from a park service drinking fountain. Almost all streams are contaminated with giardia or other organisms that will give you severe dysentery.

Contrary to popular opinion, the danger from snakebite is low. Only two species of poisonous snakes are found in the area—the timber rattlesnake and the copperhead; both are pit vipers. Copperheads are the more common in this area, and their bites are not fatal (according to the state of Maryland). Even rattlesnake bites are rarely fatal, but they are more dangerous to young children. According to the Maryland Poison Control Center, two to six persons a year receive bites from venomous snakes. If you do get bitten, see a doctor as soon as possible. The best advice is to just leave snakes alone. Simply watch where you put your hands and feet; snakes like rock piles, heavy brush and piles of debris. Remember, snakes are reticent creatures who seldom harm man and are of great value in controlling rodents.

Never feed wild animals, and be sure to pack up any food in your camp so it does not attract animals. Never touch a dead animal as rabies can be spread by the saliva of a diseased animal if it comes in contact with a cut on your hand or other part of the body. All raccoons seen during the daylight are suspect of being rabid, as they are normally nocturnal animals. Also suspect any animals that stagger or appear to be off balance when walking.

Park Ethics

"Take only photographs, leave only footsteps." Please, please don't litter; don't remove anything but trash from the parks; don't pick any flowers or plants; don't touch any animals, and don't stray from the marked trails. Remember that all wildlife in parks, is protected and many species are threatened with extinction. If you must have music, use headphones. In general try to preserve the quiet, so everyone can appreciate nature. Leave firearms at home, locked up.

Dogs must be leashed (tethered securely to the owner at all times). Dogs or other pets are not allowed on nature trails and are prohibited in sensitive wildlife areas—leave them home. (Even the most gentle dog can frighten wildlife and other visitors.)

Park legally, being careful not to block fire roads or other visitors.

We'd all like to leave the earth a better place than when we arrived. One way to do this is to pick up man-made litter when you see it and deposit it in a trash can on your way out.

Park Politics

Make no mistake about it, our natural areas, plant and animal wildlife communities are seriously threatened by development. and deteriorating water and air quality. In the last decade, "development", that is the building of roads, office buildings and homes, has proceeded at a frantic pace and will continue. Many regard our natural areas simply as "underdeveloped" land waiting for development. When a new road is proposed, politically the easy way out has been to run it through parkland. When a new sewer is needed, it's politically easiest to run it through our stream valley parks. The building of an office complex and its feeder roads destroy the natural drainage and wetlands; local politicians are all too happy to dig up a park for a new drainage basin or for "wetland mitigation". In the process, numerous woods have been chopped down, farms turned into "developments", streams "channelized", wetlands filled. When the bulldozer meets the natural area, there is little question of the winner. Even though much of this land was "private", the result is the same—loss of habitat results in loss of wildlife from the region and perhaps extinction of regional species. Animal and plant diversity is lost; a good example is the loss of songbirds in the area, with their numbers being replaced somewhat by less desirable non-native species (e.g. starlings). Many, if not most, of the natural areas we visited report loss of wildlife species within the last several years.

In addition, pollution from the area, exacerbated by the increased development, is killing the Chesapeake Bay. Just about everything liquid or soluble that goes on the ground or down a sewer in this area finds its way into the bay.

As a reader of this book, you probably value the natural areas around Washington. We feel that natural areas are a key factor in the quality of life here and without them, this area would be a much less desirable place to live or visit. Unfortunately, trees don't pay taxes, elect politicians, make campaign "contributions" or support politicians in the off-seasons, but real estate "developers" do. The biggest (legal) pay-back a local politician can make to developers who contribute to his campaign fund is to permit zoning density upgrades, waive environmental regulations or fund "infrastructure" upgrades (new roads and sewers). If we don't actively defend our natural areas and wildlife, they will continue to be eaten away by "development".

What you can do: Call and write your representatives frequently. Politicians respond to those who scream loudest and most often. Let them know you want more green space, less pollution and less development and no zoning density upgrades. Let them know that their votes on these issues determine your vote in the fall.

Hiking, Biking and Canoeing Clubs and Naturalist Organizations

Washington has numerous hiking, biking and canoeing clubs. In most clubs, experienced volunteer leaders plan trips, usually taking the trip themselves before leading a group. Club trips can take you to places you didn't know of, or places you wouldn't go on your own. Knowledgeable and observant leaders (and fellow followers) add a lot of value to a trip, pointing out features you might have missed on your own and increasing safety. Perhaps most important, club trips are a great opportunity to meet and talk with friendly people who appreciate nature and are concerned with conservation issues.

In general, clubs announce their trips through taped telephone recordings and in *The Washington Post* Friday Weekend Section, under "On the Move", in Hiking/Camping, Cycling, and Canoeing categories.

Some other clubs rent a bus and charge a fee of from $5.00–$15.00 per person to pay for the bus; for obvious reasons, more formality and advanced reservations are usually required. Sometimes membership is required. Usually the trip leader has at least some first-aid training and a first-aid kit, but the clubs can't assume liability for participants. Every club has its own rules and customs.

Club trips vary greatly in difficulty, and the ratings on the announcement tapes must be taken with caution. Some Sierra Club trips labeled "moderate" would be very stressful for anyone who doesn't hike regularly; trips labeled "fast-paced" or "strenuous" seem best suited for marathon runners or mountain goats (or better yet, some hybrid of the two). The best bet is to consult with one of the trip leaders; it benefits no one to take a trip you're not ready for.

Sierra Club, Metropolitan Washington Regional Outing Program

The Sierra Club sponsors frequent day hikes, overnight backpack trips, and occasional bicycle or canoe trips. In addition, the Sierra Club is probably the most powerful conservation lobby organization in the U.S.; the local chapter is also involved in conservation issues. Local "outings" (as the Sierra Club refers to trips) are lead by volunteers, with trips open to everyone. No reservations are needed for most trips. Pets and radios are not allowed. Trips usually go regardless of weather, subject to safety considerations. A contribution of $1.00/person to the outings program is suggested; carpoolers donate $.04/mile to driver, $.06/mile for backpack trips. Local Sierra Club outings are pretty informal and a lot of fun. A bimonthly outings calendar mailing is available for $5.00/year. Call the outings tape for current ordering information. The outings announcement tape is updated about once a week and includes local conservation activities. It is advisable to consult with the outing leader before the hike, especially if you haven't gone on Sierra Club hikes before. The Sierra Club Metropolitan Washington Regional

Outing Program (MWROP) has an excellent, usually up-to-date web page, with the current hike schedule.

(202)547-2326 (Tape of Events and Outings)
(202)547-5551 (Tape of General Information)
http://webmentor.com/mwrop/index2.html (outings)
http://www.sierraclub.org (general club information)

Potomac Appalachian Trail Club

The PATC is an organization of volunteers who maintain the Appalachian Trail and other trails in DC, Maryland, Virginia, West Virginia and Pennsylvania. These efforts are supported by contributions, membership dues, the sale of PATC maps and books, and the rental of PATC cabins. The PATC sponsors frequent day and overnight volunteer-led hikes on the Appalachian and other trails in the region. They also sponsor trail-maintenance hikes where volunteers help build and maintain trails. The PATC bookstore is one of the area's best sources for topographical maps and trail guides to the Shenandoah National Park, Appalachian Trail and other nearby trails, plus other hiking and nature-related books. For more information call the PATC tape, visit the store at the PATC headquarters in Vienna or visit their excellent web site. Or, join PATC and get their monthly newsletter.

PATC Headquarters and Bookstore
Monday–Thursday 7:00 A.M.–9:00 P.M.
Thursdays and Fridays NOON–2:00 P.M.
118 Park Street, SE
Vienna, VA 22180-0469
(703) 242-0315 (Store or General Information Tape)
(703) 242-0965 (Outings Tape)
(703) 242-0693 Headquarters main number
(703) 242-0968 fax
http://patc.simplenet.com/

Audubon Naturalist Society

The ANS is dedicated to increasing public understanding of natural history and the importance of preserving our natural resources. ANS sponsors many bird watching trips, ecology-related courses, and conservation-related lectures; some of which charge a fee. The best source of information on these, observations on local wildlife and updates on regional conservation issues is the ANS newsletter, *Audubon Naturalist News*. In addition, the ANS has a recorded message with recent bird sightings, the "Voice of the Naturalist". For more information about the ANS, and *Audubon Naturalist News* see the Maryland entry on Woodend, the ANS headquarters.

The ANS has an excellent web site; check it out. We recommend you become an ANS member to keep informed on DC area wildlife, trips, courses, and to support conservation advocacy.

Audubon Naturalist Society
8940 Jones Mill Road
Chevy Chase, MD 20815
(301) 652-9188
(301) 652-1088 Recorded *Voice of the Naturalist*.
http://www.audubonnaturalist.org/

Washington Area Bicyclists Association

WABA is a nonprofit educational organization dedicated to improving bicycling conditions in the metro area and encouraging use of bicycles for transportation and recreation. WABA is a determined lobbyist for non-polluting bicycle commuting. WABA also distributes a number of regional bicycle maps and guides, including most of those mentioned in *Natural Washington*. WABA membership includes the *Ride On!* monthly newsletter of events and cycling related news, plus discounts at selected bike stores. WABA also has an excellent web site, and e-mail listserver. If you're a serious bicyclist in the DC area, you should belong to WABA.

Washington Area Bicyclist Association
1511 K Street NW, Suite 1015
Washington, DC 20005
(202) 628-2500
(202) 628-4141 fax
info@waba.org
http://www.waba.org/

The Nature Conservancy

The Nature Conservancy is the leading non-government organization preserving critical wildlife habitat in the US. They do it the old fashioned way—they buy (or receive as gifts) the land. They own many very unique sites that preserve endangered wildlife. Only TNC members have the privilege to go on some of about 50 guided field trips to selected Conservancy preserves; some of which are inaccessible to the public. Most trips are hikes, but some are canoe or boat trips, at nominal cost. One of these trips, alone is worth the price of membership. If you're a serious conservationist and have the means, you should be a TNC member, which starts at $25.00.

The Nature Conservancy of Maryland/DC
2 Wisconsin Circle, Suite 300
Chevy Chase, MD 20815
(301) 656-8673

The Nature Conservancy-Headquarters
1815 North Lynn Street
Arlington, VA 22209
(703) 841-5300
http://www.tnc.org

Other Clubs

Appalachian Mountain Club: The Appalachian Mountain Club, founded in Boston in 1876, is one of the oldest hiking and conservation service clubs in the country. The AMC runs informal hikes, plus occasional bicycle, canoe and ski trips. There is no fee charged for the trips, but participants are encouraged to join the AMC. (See *The Washington Post* Weekend Section.)

(202) 298-1488 (recording)
http://www.idsonline.com/amcdc/amcdc.html

Canoe Cruisers Association of Washington: The CCA was established in 1956 and has over 1200 members. It sponsors classes and paddle trips (usually within a 2-hour drive of DC) for both canoes and decked boats. Dues include the monthly newsletter, *The Cruiser*. The CCA also has monthly meetings.

Canoe Cruisers Association of Greater Washington, DC, Inc.
PO Box 15747
Chevy Chase, MD 20825
(301) 656-2586 (recorded announcements)

Capital Club: Uses buses for many trips; fee charged. (See *The Washington Post* Weekend Section.)

Center Club: Uses buses for many trips; fee charged. (See *The Washington Post* Weekend Section.)

Potomac Backpackers: Potomac Backpackers is a social organization devoted to backpacking, camping, canoeing, and car camping, as well as other outdoor activities. Trips are led by volunteers to various locations, usually within a 180-mile radius of Washington; carpoolers reimburse the driver for expenses. Non-members may go on one trip before joining. Membership is $10.00 per calendar year; dues cover the monthly newsletter and special events.

P.O Box 403
Merrifield, VA 22116-0403
(703)524-1185 (Tape)

Potomac Peddlers Touring Club: Potomac Peddlers Touring Club, Inc. is the one of the largest bicycling organizations in the Washington area, sponsoring bicycle trips most weekends. There is no charge for the trips, but you are advised to consult with the leader to be sure the trip is suitable to you. If you're a bicycle tourer, you should definitely look into Potomac Peddlers.

(202) 363-8687 (tape)

Wanderbirds: The Wanderbirds use buses to the trailhead for most of their hikes. They have two hikes almost every Sunday. Membership is only $5.00 per year. Bus fare is typically abut $14, with buses leaving downtown DC at 8:00 A.M. Sunday morning. Firm reservations must be made before 11:00 A.M. Saturday. For more information about the Wanderbirds Hiking Club call or see their web page that has a listing of upcoming hikes.

(301) 460-3064 or
http://www.erols.com/hcooper/wbirds.htm

Washington Women Outdoors:(See the *Washington Post* Weekend Section.)

(301) 864-3070

Seasonal Favorites

The following are a few of our favorite places, based on pure-ly subjective criteria.

SPRING FLOWERS
Late March-April
Riverbend
Dumbarton Oaks
Ladew Topiary Gardens
Winkler Botanical Preserve

SPRING WILDLIFE
Huntley Meadows
Battle Creek Cypress Swamp

SUMMER
Kenilworth Aquatic Gardens
Appalachian National Scenic Trail

FALL BIRDS
Wildfowl Trust of North America
Black Water Refuge
Assateaque/Chincoteague

WINTER AND FOUL-WEATHER
Smithsonian Naturalist Center and Natural History Museum
National Aquarium at Baltimore
Nature Centers

ANYTIME
Off-Road Bicycle Outing
C&O Canal
National Arboretum
National Zoo
Shenandoah National Park and Luray Caverns

Off-Road Bicycle Nature Trails

Bicycling is a great way to see nature. But riding on the streets exposed to automobile traffic, noxious exhaust fumes, potholes and obnoxious commentators is not fun. Furthermore, bicycles are prohibited on almost all trails in area parks. But fortunately, the Washington area has over 200 miles of connected, mostly paved, mostly off-road bikeways, through some of the best natural areas in the metropolitan area. There are plans to greatly expand the bikeways.

The five major off-road scenic routes are the C&O Canal, Rock Creek (Rock Creek Park in DC and Rock Creek Regional Park in Montgomery County), Mount Vernon Trail W&OD, including the Custis-I-66 trail, and the Capital Crescent Trail. All are wide and asphalt paved for their entire length, except the C&O. The C&O is a wide packed earth trail; there are several places where bikes must be carried (or bounced) a short distance over obstacles (see C&O entry under Maryland).

All the trails converge where the Potomac River passes DC. The C&O ends at the Rock Creek (Beach Drive) Trail. The CCT crosses the C&O towpath and ends at Key Bridge. The Rock Creek Trail ends by Memorial Bridge, where you can cross the Potomac (at Arlington National Cemetery) to the Mount Vernon Trail, which runs along the Virginia side of the Potomac. Going on the Mount Vernon Trail to Theodore Roosevelt Island, you join the Custis-W&OD Trail toward Leesburg.

We use the bikeways to enjoy a combination of nature, exercise, and culture on our day off. We park the car near one of the bike trails, a distance from downtown and unload bicycles, bicycle about an hour on the trail to the Mall, lock the bike, eat lunch; see museums, libraries, or monuments, then bike back to the car, go home and take a nap. With these outings, we feel we have been relatively kind to environment, pocketbook, body and spirit. We have eliminated the traffic, parking and parking-ticket hassle of visiting the Mall. Bike commuters use these trails too, thus greatly reducing Washington's traffic and air pollution burden.

For maps and general bicycling information, the Washington Area Bicyclists Association is the place for "one stop shopping". See the WABA entry under Hiking and Biking Clubs.

Metro DC Area Bike Trails

Trail	Outer End	DC End	Miles
Anacostia Tributary Trail System	a)Greenbelt b)Wheaton Regoinal Park via Sligo Crk & Q Takoma Park c)Oakview, MD	Colmar Manor, PG County, MD south of Hyattsville	a) 3 b) 17 c) 7
Arlington Loop	W&OD Trail at Shirlington	National Airport -M.V. Trail	6
C&O Canal Towpath	Harpers Ferry, WV or Cumberland, MD	Georgetown (Bet. K & M at 29th), at Rock Creek) Rock Creek Trail	184
Capital Crescent Trail	Bethesda, at Bethesda Ave. Silver Spring downtown (future)	Key Bridge, Georgetown at K Street	11
Metropolitan Branch Trail (*construction started 1998)	Silver Spring via Catholic University	Union Station	9*
Mount Vernon	Mount Vernon, VA	T. Roosevelt Island-Custis-W&OD Trail	18.5
Rock Creek	Lake Needwood Rock Creek Regional Park, MD	The Mall Georgetown to C&O Memorial Bridge to Mount Vernon Trail	21.5
W&OD and Custis Trail	Purcellville, VA	T. Roosevelt Island Mount Vernon Trail	45

Other Area Bikeways

Trail	Start	Finish	Miles
Baltimore & Annapolis Trail Park	Annapolis, MD	Glen Burnie, MD	14+

For More Information

Trail	Source
Alexandria Loop	City of Alexandria
Arlington Loop. Excellent map available with a total of 36 miles of off-road biking trails	Planning and Engineering Div. Arlington County Dept. of Public Works One Courthouse Plaza, Ste 717 2000 Claredon Blvd., Arlington, VA 22201
Capital Crescent Trail and Metropolitan Branch.	See CCT entry under DC
C&O Canal Towpath	See C&O entry Maryland
Magruder Branch Map available "Trails in Montgomery County"	Upper Montgomery County Dept. of Parks, M-NCPPC 9500 Burnet Drive, Silver Spring, MD 20901 (301) 495-2535
Mount Vernon	See Mount Vernon entry, Virginia
Rock Creek	See Rock Creek entries under Maryland and DC
W&OD	See W&OD entry, Virginia

SOURCES OF INFORMATION

Books

Potomac Appalachian Trail Club Publications:
    Appalachian Trail Guide —Maryland and Northern Virginia.;
        available with detailed topographical maps of the AT
        (1995).
    Circuit Hikes in Shenandoah National Park (1996).
    *Circuit Hikes in Virginia, West Virginia, Maryland, and
        Pennsylvania* (1994).
    Hikes in the Washington Region:
        Part A: Montgomery and Frederick Counties in Maryland
            (1992).
        *Part B: Arlington, Fairfax, Loudoun, and Prince William
            Counties in Virginia* (1993).
        *Part C: District of Columbia, Prince George's, Charles,
            and Calvert Counties in Maryland* (1998).

Adventuring in the Chesapeake Bay Area. Bowen, John. San Francisco: Sierra Club Books, 1990.

The Audubon Society Field Guide to the Natural Places of the Mid-Atlantic States. Lawrence, Susannah, ed. New York: Pantheon Books, 1984.

The Audubon Society Field Guide to North American Reptiles and Amphibians. Behler, John L. and King, F.Wayne. New York: Alfred A. Knopf, 1997.

The Audubon Society Nature Guides: Eastern Forests. Sutton, Ann. New York: Alfred A. Knopf, Inc. 1985.

Bay Country: Reflections on the Chesapeake. Horton, Tom. Baltimore: The Johns Hopkins University Press, 1989.

Beauty and Bounty: One-Day Nature Trips In and Around Washington, DC Smith, Jane Ockershausen. McLean, Virginia: EPM Publications, Inc, 1983.

A Beginners Guide to Wildflowers of the C&O Towpath. Martin, Edwin M. Washington, DC: Smithsonian Institution Press, 1984.

City of Trees: The Complete Field Guide to the Trees of Washington, DC Choukas-Bradley, Melanie, and Alexander, Polly. Baltimore: The Johns Hopkins University Press, 1987.

Country Adventures in Maryland, Virginia and West Virginia. Mooney, Elizabeth C. Arlington, Virginia: The Washington Book Trading Company, 1984.

Country Walks Near Washington. Fisher, Alan. Boston: Appalachian Mountain Club, 1996.

Family Bicycling.in the Washington-Baltimore Area. Pescatore, John. McLean, Virginia: EPM Publications, 1993.

Finding Birds in the National Capital Area (A Smithsonian Nature Guide). Wilds, Claudia. Washington, DC: Smithsonian Institution Press, 1992.

The New Maryland One-Day Trip Book. Ockershausen, Jane. McLean, Virginia: EPM Publications, Inc, 1998.

The Peterson Field Guide Series: A Field Guide to the Birds East of the Rockies. Peterson, Roger Tory. Boston: Houghton Mifflin Company, 1998.

The Peterson Field Guide Series: A Field Guide to the Insects of America North of Mexico. Borror, Donald J. and White, Richard E. Boston: Houghton Mifflin Company, 1998.

The Peterson Field Guide Series: A Field Guide to Wildflowers of Northeastern and North-central North America. Peterson, Roger Tory and McKenny, Margaret. Boston: Houghton Mifflin Company, 1975.

The Potomac River and the C&O Canal (five colorful strip maps, Georgetown to Opequon Creek); published by the Interstate Commission on the Potomac River Basin.

A Sierra Club Naturalist's Guide: The Piedmont. Godfrey, Micheal A. San Francisco: Sierra Club Books, 1980.

Trail Guide: W&OD R.R. Regional Park, published by the Northern Virginia Regional Park Authority (1996).

The New Virginia One-Day Trip Book. Ockershausen, Jane. McLean, Virginia: EPM Publications, Inc, 1996.

The New Washington One-Day Trip Book. Ockershausen, Jane. McLean, Virginia: EPM Publications, Inc, 1992.

184 Miles of Adventure: Hikers Guide to the C&O Canal, published by the Baltimore Area Council—Boy Scouts of America.

Maps

ADC's Book Maps
Washington, DC
Northern Virginia
Montgomery County

American Automobile Association:
Charles County, MD
Montgomery County, MD
National Capital and Nearby Areas
Northern Virginia—Beltway and Vicinity
Northern Virginia—Southwestern Fairfax and Prince William Counties
Prince George's County, MD
Washington, DC Street and Visitor's Guide

Maryland -National Capital Park and Planning Commission
Trails in Montgomery County Parks

Potomac Appalachian Trail Club Appalachian Trail Maps:
#5-6 Maryland
#7   Northern Virginia Harpers Ferry—Snickes Gap
#8   Northern Virginia Snickers Gap—Front Royal
#9   Shenandoah National Park, Northern
#10   Shenandoah National Park, Central
#11   Shenandoah National Park, Southern
D   Trails in the Potomac Gorge Area, Va/Md. and the Cabin John Trail, Md. (Includes the Potomac Gorge from the American Legion Bridge past Great Falls, with Great Falls, Scotts Run, and Riverbend Parks, plus the Billy Goat Trail and the River Trail)

Maryland, Maryland Department of Transportation

The Potomac River and the C&O Canal (five colorful strip maps, Georgetown to Opequon Creek), Interstate Commission on the Potomac River Basin

Virginia, Virginia Department of Transportation

ACKNOWLEDGMENTS

The authors wish to express their gratitude to the many people whose research and assistance helped make this revised edition possible.

In the District of Columbia: Joanne Murphy, Washington National Cathedral Grounds; Andrew Coulson, Capitol Hill Trees; John A. Dugger, Capital Crescent Trail; Mary Ann N. Jarvis, National Arboretum; Walter McDowney, Lady Bird Johnson Park & T. Roosevelt Island; Christine A. Flanagan, U.S. Botanic Garden; Carol Owens, Hillwood Museum & Gardens; Dwight L. Madison, Kym M. Elder, Kenilworth Aquatic Gardens and Lara Papi, National Aquarium.

In Maryland: Corinne Parks, Leakin and Gwynns Falls Parks; Patricia Fankhauser, Potomac Appalachian Trail Club; Marie Brooks, Watkins Regional Park; Jill Seipe, Baltimore Zoo; Ben Smart, Sugarloaf Mountain; Jim McMahon, Black Hill Regional Park; Elizabeth Scheifer, The Wildfowl Trust of North America, Inc.; Peyton Taylor, Gunpowder Falls State Park; Dorothy Kengla, Seneca Creek State Park; Stephen McCoy, Wye Oak, Martinak and Tuckahoe State Parks; Maggi Briggs, Blackwater NWR; Greg Lewis, Patuxent River Park; Amy Painter, Accokeek Foundation; Jessica Brown, National Aquarium in Baltimore; Jane Huff, Woodend; Debbi Dodson, Oxford; Larry Points, Assateague Island National Seashore; Chuck Bowler, Cunningham Falls State Park; Mary Ellen Dore, Merkle Wildlife Santuary; Colleen A Wilcoxon, Little Bennett Regional Park; James Harris, Seth Demonstration Forest; Ngozi Dibia, Brookside Nature Center; April Havens, Calvert Cliffs State Park; Barbara Boland, Sandy Point State Park; Marjorie L. Johnson, WSSC (Patuxent River State Park); C. Douglas Alves Jr., Calvert Marine Museum; Robert Cantin, Cedarville State Forest; Rachel E. Mobley, Mt. Briar Wetlands Preserve; Donna Terrone, William Paca Garden; Mark Haddon, Smithsonian Environmental Reseach Center; Al Preston, Gathland State Park; Dwight Williams, Battle Creek Cypress Swamp & Flag Ponds Nature Park; Liz Briscoe, Loise F. Cosca Regional Park; Roger Steintl, Catoctin Mountain Park; W. Daniel Estevez, Myrtle Grove WMA; Charles B. Thomas, Lilypons Water Gardens; Fred Cunningham, Greenbelt Park; Bob Powell, Rock Creek Regional Park; Bill Nopper, Cabin John Regional Park; Karen

Babcock, Ladew Topiary Gardens; Kerrie Nichols, Wheaton Regional Park, Brookside Gardens and McCrillis Gardens; Walter Brown, Patapsco Valley State Park; David F. Webster, Sugarloaf Mountain; Gwen Fariss Newman, Maryland Science Center; Dave Davis, Wye Island NRMA; Ron Norris, McKee Beshers, Hugg-Thomas & Gwynnbrook WIldlife Management Areas; Martin C. Kaehny, Eastern Neck NWR; Rod Sauter, C&O Canal NHP near Great Falls & the Billy Goat Trail; Robin Melton, Smallwood State Park; John Kucharski, U.S.D.A. Agriculture Research Service; Lydia Wood, St. Clement's Island Museum; Tiffany Cox, Cylburn Arboretum; Sara Lustbader, Brookside Nature Center; Anne Miller, Carroll County Farm Museum; Patricial Nagel, Patuxent Research Refuge and Wildlife Research Center; Whitney Hahn, Catoctin Wildlife Preserve and Zoo; Patty Walsh, Maryland and District of Columbia Chapter of the Nature Conservancy; Donald Myers, Helen A. Tawes Garden; Loren W. Lustig, Piney Run Park; Dorothy Kengla, Seneca Creek State Park; George Wilmot, Nanjemoy Marsh Santuary; and Amy Henry, Tawes Garden.

In Virginia: Jodie Smolik, Winkler Botanical Preserve; Walter McDowney, George Washington Memorial Parkway; Chris Strand, Green Spring Gardens Park; Sally McDonough, Mount Vernon; Merni Fitzgerald, Farifax County Park Authority; Carol Ann Cohen, Northern Virginia Regional Park Authority; Tim Farmer, Blandy Experimental Farm; Len E. (Buddy) Little, Riverbend Park; G. Zell, Long Branch Nature Center; Robert Wilson, Chincoteague National Wildlife Refuge; R.T. Stamps, Quantico; Rosemarie Dexter, G.R.Thompson WMA; Charles E. Smith, Ellanor C. Lawrence Park. Yvonne Shultz, Mason Neck Wildlife Refuge & State Park; Diane Hughes, Morven Park; Gretchen Brodtman, Claude Moore Colonial Farm; Kathy Budnie, Sky Meadows State Park; Karl J. Hakala, Wolf Trap Farm Park; Denise Chauvette, Gulf Branch Nature Center; Cornelia G. Spain, Luray Caverns; John Zawatsky, Caledon Natural Area; Brendon C. Hanafin, Leesylvania State Park; Lonnie Hill, Skyline Caverns; David Boyce, Oatlands; Carolyn Gamble, Huntley Meadows Park; Catherine Morretta, Signal Hill Park; Joanne Amberson and Karen Michaud, Shenandoah National Park; Micheal McDonnell, Hidden Oaks Nature Center; Russ Whitlock, Prince WIlliam Forest Park; Joseph T. Keiger, Fraser Preserve; Marvin Mitchell, Wildcat Mountain Natural Area; Sara King, Westmoreland State Park and Sally McDonough, Mount Vernon.

In West Virginia: Marsha Starkey, Harpers Ferry National Historical Park; Brian King, Appalachian National Scenic Trail.

INDEX

LOOK TO THESE EPM TITLES FOR MORE TRAVEL ADVENTURES IN THE MID-ATLANTIC

The New Virginia One-Day Trip Book   **$14.95**
Jane Ockershausen, author of ten One-Day Trip books for the Mid-Atlantic area, admits to being surprised by the wealth of things to see and do in the Old Dominion. From the Appalachian Trail along Virginia's western mountains to the barrier islands of the Atlantic coast, a staggering 375 places are covered—every one personally visited and researched by her.

The New Maryland One-Day Trip Book   **$14.95**
From boiling rapids and rugged trails high in the western mountains to frontier forts, horse country, Baltimore's urban treasures, the Chesapeake Bay and the plantations and reserves of the Eastern Shore, Maryland offers more than you can imagine!

The New West Virginia One-Day Trip Book   **$14.95**
Popular folk artist Colleen Anderson writes about 150 affordable day adventures in the magic mountain state: historic mansions, craft centers, caverns, art museums, Civil War battlefields, state parks, even a palace of gold and a miniature Swiss village. Includes very accessible info on fishing, skiing and white water rafting. Maps/photos/charts.

One-Day Trips Through History   **$10.95; undergoing revision**
Describes more than 200 historic sites within 50 miles of the nation's capital where our forebears lived, dramatic events occurred and America's roots took hold. Sites are arranged chronologically starting with pre-history.

The South Carolina One-Day Trip Book   **$16.95**
You'll find a love of history, horticulture, humor and horses throughout the state's ten regions. Many roads remain unpaved and signs unchanged in deference to horses and their riders. Also, there's a town that boasts an intersection of Easy and Whiskey Streets.

Family Bicycling in the Washington-Baltimore Area   **$10.95**
John Pescatore, a cyclist, parent and writer, details 35 of the best and safest family bike routes in D.C. , Maryland and Northern Virginia. Spiral-bound and sized to fit neatly in a pack. Includes maps, directions and resource information.

Washington, D.C. Museums   **$14.95**
Some 65 museums and historic homes are featured in Betty Ross's informative narrative. She includes biographies and historical backgrounds, in-depth reports on collections, anecdotes and information on hours, shops, restaurants, libraries, public transportation and facilities for the handicapped.

The Kennedy Center $10.95

In this "Insider's Guide to Washington's Liveliest Memorial," volunteer Barbara Morris takes you through its grand hallways—all the way up to the roof—imparting fascinating details about the past and future of America's center for the performing arts.

Undercover Washington $9.95

A tour guide to the sites where famous spies lived, worked and loved. More than 70 museums, bars, bookstores, libraries, hotels and graveyards are described. Whether you visit on foot, in a car or by armchair, you'll be amazed by the information and entertainment uncovered.

Trips & Treats: Kid-Tested Fun In & Around Baltimore
reduced to $4.98

More than 40 ideas for family excursions in the Baltimore and Washington area. Includes well-known and not-so-well-known museums, parks, zoos, aquariums and historical sites.

Capital Horse Country   reduced to $7.50

A rider's and spectator's guide to races, hunts, shows and many other colorful equine traditions of Virginia, Maryland and Washington.

Order Blank

EPM is an imprint of Howell Press, Inc. Please make your check payable to Howell Press, Inc. and mail with your order to:

Howell Press, Inc./EPM Publications
1713-2D Allied Lane
Charlottesville, VA 22903

Or, call toll free 1-800-868-4512

Qty	Item	Price	Total

Subtotal	_____
For delivery in VA, add 4.5% sales tax	_____
Shipping/handling: add $3.50 for one item, $.50 for each add'l	_____
TOTAL	_____

Name _____

Street Address _____

City _____ State _____ Zip _____

Remember to include names, addresses and enclosure cards for gift purchases. Please note that prices are subject to change. Thank you.

ABOUT THE AUTHORS

Richard L. Berman, veteran amateur naturalist, photographer and hiker, has an undergraduate degree in biology from the University of Pennsylvania and a master's degree in business administration from George Washington University. He has pursued additional graduate studies in biophysics and computer science. He has lived in the Washington area for about 20 years doing consulting on data networks and electronic commerce for a multinational corporation. He is currently taking some time off from the day job to explore and enjoy life and to pursue other fields of interest.

Deborah McBride is a nature lover, photographer and hiker. She has a master's degree in journalism from Ohio State University and a master's degree in landscape architecture from the University of California at Berkeley. Currently, she works as a freelance newspaper columnist and park planning researcher in Berkeley, California.

D.C. PUBLIC LIBRARY

8 1172 04408 5629

CPK

32 charges
2015 last circ

JUN 0 1 2000

BAKER & TAYLOR